A NOT TOO GREATLY CHANGED EDEN

A NOT TOO GREATLY CHANGED EDEN

THE STORY OF THE PHILOSOPHERS' CAMP IN THE ADIRONDACKS

To Lee,

James Schlett

JAMES SCHLETT

CORNELL UNIVERSITY PRESS
Ithaca and London

This publication has been aided by a generous
subvention from Furthermore, a program of the
J. M. Kaplan Fund.

Furthermore:
a program of the J. M. Kaplan Fund

First published 2015 by Cornell University Press

Printed in the United States of America

Library of Congress Cataloging-in-Publication Data

Schlett, James, author.
    A not too greatly changed Eden : the story of the
Philosophers' Camp in the Adirondacks / James Schlett.
        pages cm
    Includes bibliographical references and index.
    ISBN 978-0-8014-5352-6 (cloth : alk. paper)
  1. United States—Intellectual life—19th century.
2. Adirondack Mountains (N.Y.)—History—19th century.
3. Emerson, Ralph Waldo, 1803–1882.   4. Stillman, William
James, 1828–1901.   I. Title.
    E166.S325 2015
    973.46—dc23   2014049164

Cornell University Press strives to use environmentally
responsible suppliers and materials to the fullest extent
possible in the publishing of its books. Such materials
include vegetable-based, low-VOC inks and acid-free
papers that are recycled, totally chlorine-free, or partly
composed of nonwood fibers. For further information,
visit our website at www.cornellpress.cornell.edu.

Cloth printing   10 9 8 7 6 5 4 3 2 1

For my parents, John and Pat Schlett

❧ CONTENTS

✒ ILLUSTRATIONS

Figures

✤ PREFACE

The holidays were fruitful, but must end;
One August evening had a cooler breath;
Into each mind intruding duties crept;
Under the cinders burned the fires of home;
Nay, letters found us in our paradise;
So in the gladness of the new event
We struck our camp, and left the happy hills.
The fortunate star that rose on us sank not;
The prodigal sunshine rested on the land,
The rivers gamboled onward to the sea,
And Nature, the inscrutable and mute,
Permitted on her infinite repose
Almost a smile to steal to cheer her sons,
As if one riddle of the Sphinx were guessed.

—Emerson, "The Adirondacs"

In 2008, I found myself working as a business reporter for the *Daily Gazette* in Schenectady, New York. I pitched to my editors the idea of writing a story about the 150th anniversary of Ralph Waldo Emerson's Adirondack camping trip, which I knew of solely through his poem. My editors approved the story, and I soon learned that the common name for this outing was the "Philosophers' Camp" and that its organizer was William James Stillman. Coincidentally, it turned out that Stillman was a painter and a journalist who not only was born in Schenectady but also graduated from Union College in the city. I also discovered that Follensby Pond, where Emerson and his friends camped, was the largest single-party, privately owned body of water in the Northeast. More important, given my need to visit the site, I found out that its ninety-four-year-old owner, John McCormick Jr., was not keen on letting the general public tour his woodland paradise. I heard numerous stories of other journalists, scientists, and canoeists who had been rebuffed in their efforts to visit the site of the Philosophers' Camp. Getting the access I needed to write the story, it seemed to me, would be a daunting task.

From the newsroom, I called McCormick (who lived in Vermont at the time) on the day after Memorial Day and introduced myself as a reporter from Stillman's hometown interested in writing about the anniversary of the

Philosophers' Camp. To my surprise, he was quite cheerful and welcoming. We talked some about Stillman and much about Thoreau, whom he had studied at Princeton University in the 1930s. Despite this cordial introduction, I still thought I'd be lucky if I could obtain permission to view Follensby from a distance. But at the very least, I had an invitation to pay a visit to the property.

McCormick had the lake's caretaker open the gate to Follensby Park for a photographer and me and, as luck would have it, give us a rare tour of the site of the Philosophers' Camp. The story that resulted from this adventure ran in the *Gazette* on June 22, 2008, under the headline "Return to the Philosophers' Camp." While doing research for this article, I was struck by how strongly the tale resounded with environmental conservationists. The mere mention of the Philosophers' Camp would strike a chord of interest and, often, longing. Equally interesting was that despite its place in numerous Adirondack history books and tales, little was known about the encampment beyond what was conveyed by Emerson's 1867 poem and an essay that Stillman had written on the topic that appeared in the *Century Magazine* in 1893 ("The Philosopher's Camp. Emerson, Agassiz, and Lowell in the Adirondacks"). I was further intrigued by the fact that a young painter from Schenectady had managed to lure the age's leading intellectuals into the wilderness and then, in later years, present this story so that it became an inspirational and unifying source for conservationists.

As inspiring as the tale of the Philosophers' Camp has been to many, to me Stillman's account of this venture in the *Century Magazine* seemed flat. Indeed, the story that has come down through generations, drawing often on Stillman's published words, is oddly uncomplicated, as though the task of bringing a large group of refined and famous intellectuals to the wilderness for an extended period was as easy as organizing a dinner party. Perhaps that was how Stillman remembered it, or how he wanted it to be remembered, when he, at the age of sixty-five and thirty-five years after the fact, first published his account of the camp. The common story also struck me as insular. This is another shortcoming that can be traced back to Stillman. In describing his time at Follensby in "The Philosopher's Camp," he said, "The outside world was but a dream" (p. 604). Consequently, the world outside the Adirondacks (with the exception, perhaps, of Boston), has barely existed at all in the modern-day narrative of the camp. Stillman's account of the Philosophers' Camp, I concluded, did not add up. Its participants were not simple men, and they did not live in simple times. I realized there was a bigger, more complex story to tell—a story that contains vistas onto landscapes of American life that existed before, during, and after the Civil War. There was a book to be written, and I threw myself into the research.

Several scholars have played integral roles in advancing the story of the Philosophers' Camp and keeping it alive in the Adirondack chronicle. Chief among these are Alfred L. Donaldson in the 1920s, Paul Jamieson in the 1950s, and Philip Terrie in the 1980s and 1990s. It was their works that further familiarized me with and stoked my interest in the Philosophers' Camp in particular and Adirondack history in general. With the help of their writings, by the time I visited the site of the Philosophers' Camp in 2008, I was in search of a deeper understanding of this gathering of great men. It was then that I came across Eva Everson's 1958 essay "William J. Stillman: Emerson's 'Gallant Artist,'" which pointed me to one place where I could attain that more complete and accurate account: Stillman's letters to Charles Eliot Norton held at Harvard University's Houghton Library. That archive proved to be critical in the writing of this book.

Indeed, from beginning to end, primary sources were crucial to filling many of the holes in the narrative of the Philosophers' Camp. In all, more than one hundred original manuscripts housed by several institutions are cited in this book. Amid this wealth of information, however, Stillman's personal and published writings have proven the most plentiful source on the camp. With that in mind, it is important for readers to know that Stillman wrote letters as if he were painting a landscape. He was a visual writer. He was often effusive. So wherever possible I have checked Stillman's account against other reports in order to see if his assertions were warranted and if his descriptions were accurate. He is a master guide to the Adirondack landscape and a key voice in the culture of the period, but both writer and reader need to maintain a healthy skepticism. I have striven to do just that as I have gathered together this more complete account of the Philosophers' Camp.

When it comes to storytelling, of course, Stillman's colorful prose is a great resource. I am indebted to his artistry in writing, which has allowed me to vividly present in these pages the world in which he lived. There are sections of this book in which I have combined details from Stillman's letters or essays with some warranted speculation to set a scene. My method generally involved changing Stillman's first-person account to a third-person narrative and incorporating facts from third-party sources or my personal knowledge of places about which Stillman wrote. (The introduction to this book, which recounts Stillman's return to Follensby Pond, provides a good example of this method.) I have striven to keep this narrative true to the facts—providing either in the text or in the endnotes explanations for my employment of warranted speculation. To the greatest extent possible, I have stated what observations originated with Stillman, and readers should read words such as "likely" and phrases such as "may have" as cues for warranted speculation.

I am deeply thankful to all the institutions that allowed me to review their original manuscripts cited in this book. Among these are the Special Collections and Archives department of Union College's Schaffer Library, Harvard's Houghton Library, Concord Free Public Library's William Munroe Special Collections, Cornell University Library's Division of Rare and Manuscript Collections, Winterthur Library, New York Public Library's Manuscripts and Archives Division, New York State Archives, and the Massachusetts Historical Society. For their exemplary service in furthering my research efforts, I must extend special thanks to Leslie P. Wilson, Ellen Fladger, Tracy Potter, Bryon Andreasen, and James D. Folts. Kudos to Stacey Stump, too. Thanks are also due to Jeffrey Winter for his help with copyediting and to Michael McGandy for further assistance with editing, in addition to his constructive criticism and his abundance of ideas on how to broaden the scope of my narrative. I am indebted to Philip G. Terrie and an anonymous reader for Cornell University Press for their feedback on my manuscript. The anonymous reader, for example, encouraged me to explore late nineteenth-century trends outside the Adirondacks, such as those in Boston, and Stillman's role in mythmaking. Terrie was especially helpful in tempering my claims as to the historical significance of the Philosophers' Camp and in clarifying several aspects of Adirondack history. I must also thank Michael Hirsch, whose humor and hospitality during my many trips to Harvard made researching this subject so memorable and enjoyable. Last, I thank my wife, Jennifer Schlett. Without you and your love, support, and patience, *Eden* would surely have been lost.

A NOT TOO GREATLY CHANGED EDEN

Introduction

Amid the Ruins

> We cannot part with our friends. We cannot let our
> angels go. We do not see that they only go out that
> archangels may come in. We are idolaters of the old. . . .
> We do not believe there is any force in to-day to rival
> or recreate that beautiful yesterday. We linger in the
> ruins of the old tent where once we had bread and
> shelter and organs, nor believe that the spirit can feed,
> cover, and nerve us again. We cannot again find aught
> so dear, so sweet, so graceful. But we sit and weep in
> vain. . . . We cannot stay amid the ruins.
>
> —Emerson, "Compensation"

During the summer of 1884, a fifty-six-year-old William James Stillman, recently returned from Europe, ventured deep into New York's northern wilderness to revisit what he remembered to be "the grove where wit and wisdom held tournament a generation before." Upon arriving at the southeastern corner of a massive secluded lake named Follensby Pond, he made a devastating discovery. Standing in a half reforested clearing in the woods, Stillman barely knew where he was. Around him grew tangled thickets of raspberry bushes, lady's willow, birch saplings, and tall grass. Had it not been for the massive landmark boulder he found amid the unruly undergrowth and a choked-up spring, he would not have believed that this was the site of the famous Philosophers' Camp in the Adirondacks.[1]

It was to the shore of Follensby that Stillman twenty-six years earlier had led nineteenth-century America's preeminent intellectuals for several days of camping that brought—and continues to bring—national attention to the Adirondacks. This was the spot where men such as the Swiss scientist and Harvard College professor Jean Louis Rodolphe Agassiz, the transcendental philosopher Ralph Waldo Emerson, the Republican lawyer and judge Ebenezer Rockwood Hoar, and the Cambridge poet James Russell Lowell surprised the nation by living like "Sacs and Sioux" and conducting "symposia" around the campfire. And it was here that two of the great

1

traditions of what was then a young nation met: the frontier, represented by the Adirondack wilderness, and New England intellectualism, represented by the great men of Boston and Cambridge who aspired to turn their cities into the "Athens of America." But at Follensby during that summer of 1884, there were, as Stillman later said, only "ashes and ruin."[2]

Looking westward, Stillman surveyed the extent of Follensby Pond and its shores. To call the woods surrounding the lake a forest would have been an insult to nature. Where once white pines had towered over the water, there were either thickets of undergrowth or scorched patches of earth. With their roots charred, some trees that had once lined the shore of the lake had toppled into it. When Stillman had last visited Follensby, a virgin forest surrounded it. But in the quarter century since that time it had been defiled by "careless tourists" and a "vulgar new forest was on its way."[3]

Not a trace of destruction escaped Stillman's observation. His were eyes that saw with a hawk's precision and in earlier years had earned him the reputation of the "American Pre-Raphaelite" for his attention to detail in painting. As a war correspondent for the *Times* of London and a former diplomat assigned to the war-torn Mediterranean island of Crete, Stillman was familiar with scenes of destruction. But the ruins he knew were in Europe, where he had spent most of the past quarter century living, not in his homeland, not in the Adirondacks, not in this wilderness he had so closely associated with paradise. He could not help but notice the absence of the huge maple trees that had once populated this former campground dubbed Camp Maple by Lowell and his companions. Dense underbrush tugged at Stillman's legs as he walked across the former campsite. Years later, when he wrote about his return to the Philosophers' Camp, as the guides called it, he recalled traversing this wasteland where memory could not be reconciled with reality. He was reminded of the lines from Thomas Moore's poem "The Light of Other Days," which told of someone who "feel[s] like one who treads alone / Some banquet-hall deserted."[4]

Ten "scholars," including Stillman, camped at this site in August of 1858. Each man, excluding Stillman, had his own guide. Among the most prominent members of the camp were Agassiz, Emerson, Lowell, and Hoar. Less prominent members of the party included the Boston lawyer and socialite Horatio Woodman, Lowell's brother-in-law Estes Howe, the talented and witty writer John Holmes, the Harvard naturalist Jeffries Wyman, and Amos Binney, who went on to serve as the U.S. Army's chief paymaster during the Civil War. By 1884, half of the party had died, with the ranks of the deceased including Agassiz, Emerson, Wyman, Woodman, and Binney.

Stillman scanned the area around him, but none of his "sacred" memories "could be quickened by this ruin." By Camp Maple's landmark boulder, he would recall, these New England intellectuals had established a firing range, where, to the surprise of all, even Agassiz and Emerson picked up their rifles and tried to hit the mark with varying success. A few steps away from the firing range there had been a makeshift laboratory on a tree stump on which Agassiz and Wyman dissected the deer shot or trout caught by members of the party or their guides. Agassiz, the influential creationist who almost single-handedly delayed by years the adoption of Darwinism in mainstream American science, had weighed the brain of a trout. It is possible he had used the findings from this experiment to demonstrate God's hand in the origin of species. The camp had also featured the bark-covered lean-tos built by Stillman and guides in which the intellectuals had slept comfortably. An American flag had "waved in sublime ostentation" over one lean-to. There had been a kennel for the hunting dogs, a butchery, and a covered kitchen. And beside a huge tree had stood a dinner table around which the scholars had dined on venison and had drunk ale from hunters' pans and a "sup of wine." At the table they had recounted the day's adventures of hunting or rowing and engaged in unforgettable conversations filled with insights and laughter. It was a joyful ruckus then rarely heard in the wilderness. Even "the owls came in the trees overhead to wonder," Stillman recalled.[5]

News that New England's intellectual elite were vacationing in the isolated, uncultured realms of New York's northern wilderness had spread quickly through the region and beyond during the summer of 1858. Even before, but mostly after, the scholars returned to their homes in Boston, Cambridge, or Concord, the Philosophers' Camp made national headlines. Their gathering in the wilderness was immediately recognized as a noteworthy event. A *New York Evening Post* correspondent who visited the scholars in the wilderness proclaimed, "No such coterie of minds is assembled at one hearthside from the land of the chivalry to where 'the fisher baits his angle and the hunter twangs his bow' on the larchen banks of the Temiscouta." A few months later, after the scholars had organized a formal club, a reporter for the *New York Times,* like the *Evening Post* correspondent, highlighted the unusual makeup of this "congregation of philosophers, *savans,* authors, artists, and ordinary human beings who every summer proceed to the wilds of the Adirondack on a few weeks' visit to Nature."[6]

Inspired by the Adirondack woods as well as the pleasures of their intimate intellectual companionship, most of the campers vowed to return in 1859 and for years after to enjoy one another's rustic society. Their short-lived

"Adirondack Club" attempted to acquire land there, and an inaugural meeting in the woods was held in August 1859, but no other noteworthy meetings of Stillman and this cohort of Bostonians occurred in the forests of New York. Yet, even as the Adirondack Club passed into memory, the wider popularity of these early gatherings in the wilderness was giving rise to other treks and other camps in the Adirondacks.[7]

Over the following two and a half decades, as some Americans flocked to the Adirondacks to escape crowded and corrupt cities and to rediscover themselves in what they considered to be primitive experiences, the fame of the camp grew and its inspiration proved significant. Follensby became a retreat for Americans in search of the classical or romantic Adirondack experiences that Emerson had captured in his 1867 poem "The Adirondacs" and that Stillman had portrayed in his 1858 painting *Morning at Camp Maple: Adirondack Woods*. Guidebooks published in the post–Civil War years showed tourists the way to Follensby, and the lake quickly became a victim of its own renown.[8]

To Stillman, Follensby's destruction was unfortunate but also inevitable, and he acknowledged his own role in its decline. "It was well that the charm once broken, the desecration, it should be complete," he wrote in 1893. (The charm of the Adirondacks, however, did not lose its appeal for all of New England's intellectuals; in the 1870s, for example, a group of Harvard men that included William James established in the Adirondacks' Keene Valley the "Putnam Camp," which is sometimes also referred to as the Philosophers' Camp.) The damage evident on Follensby's shores during the summer of 1884 not only reflected the great change the Adirondacks underwent in the latter half of the nineteenth century but also symbolized other great changes afoot in American life during that period. Even as tourism and industrial booms changed New York's northern wilderness, the surviving great men who partook in the Philosophers' Camp witnessed their enthusiasms in the sciences (i.e., creationism), the arts (i.e., landscape painting), politics (i.e., Lincoln's Republicanism), and philosophy (i.e., transcendentalism) become outmoded through the rise of Darwinism and the disillusionment that followed the Civil War. When Stillman returned to Follensby in 1884, the lake and forest had changed radically and so too had American society, culture, and politics. The Philosophers' Camp had, it appeared, been truly lost.[9]

What remained was the story. Rare is the book or essay on Adirondack history that does not devote at least a paragraph or a page to the Philosophers' Camp. These accounts tend to treat it as an interesting anecdote or a relic of the early years of camping and exploration in the Adirondacks. In a way, of course, the Philosophers' Camp is a minor event in Adirondack history and, more broadly, the nation's conservation movement. The gathering was brief and the Adirondack Club was short-lived. Yet the motivations that brought about the encampment of August 1858 were emblematic of American culture even as the United States was on the cusp of great change and disruption. The conditions that brought this cohort of men together in such a remote locale were to be shattered by war, social and economic upheaval, illness, and death. Thus the differences marked by Stillman between his very first Adirondack painting expedition at Upper Saranac Lake in 1854 and his sad return to Follensby in 1884 serve as an index of stupendous change.

The story of the Philosophers' Camp—the physical site and the men involved—does more than describe an age in a moment. Spanning the period from 1854 to 1901, it also provides a means for measuring the evolution of America. And it was an evolution that Emerson seemed to anticipate when, in his 1841 essay "Compensation," he wrote, "Such is the natural history of calamity. The changes which break up at short intervals the prosperity of men are advertisements of a nature whose law is growth." This law calls for "compensation for the inequities of condition," which in its simplest form amounts to making "the distinction of More and Less."[10] In the 1850s, for example, American science had too much divinity; American letters, too much moralism; American art, too many romantic landscapes; and the American wilderness, too little civilization. The Philosophers' Camp of 1858 stood at the point when More shifted to Less, and Less to More, and the world in which Agassiz, Emerson, and Lowell were major actors began to come apart.

Nine years after Stillman returned to Follensby, the "compensations of calamity" were not lost on him. He in many ways became one of Emerson's "idolaters of the old" who "linger in the ruins of the old tent where once we had bread and shelter and organs" and who "walk ever with reverted eyes, like those monsters who look backwards." Indeed, in 1893, when Stillman broke a long public silence about the Philosophers' Camp, he did so in order to mourn what had been lost. Stillman's essay, "The Philosophers' Camp. Emerson, Agassiz, and Lowell in the Adirondacks," was published in the *Century Magazine* and provided an important addition to what was already a popular Adirondack story. In addition to invoking the memory of what a critic then called the "lights of another time, before the war," Stillman detailed his tragic discovery of the ruins at Follensby in 1884. He also fondly recalled that summer of 1858, when the great changes that would soon fall upon him and his friends were held at bay, allowing the men to enjoy an intellectual society and unsullied wilderness that few would ever experience again. Stillman wrote of that summer of 1858, "We seemed to have got back into a not too greatly changed Eden, whose imperious ties to the outer world were hidden for the day in the waters and woods that lay between us and it."[11]

In this book I look back on that legendary yet short-lived encampment near the shores of Follensby Pond. A remarkable event replete with a cast of famous characters, the Philosophers' Camp and the society reflected in the creation of the Adirondack Club are fascinating in their own right. The camp also, as I note just above, offers an interesting and telling perspective on the shift in American culture toward an industrial and consumer-oriented society, one that was pushing westward and penetrating wilderness all across the United States. Finally, I consider the story of the camp as a durable part of Adirondack lore. The history of the Philosophers' Camp will always have gaps, and many of the sources we have are partial. However, on these pages I mean to take fully into history an event that has to date remained in the category of legend.

Stillman is the key protagonist in this history: its narrator, its artist, and its guide. He was involved in all the key events, managed to penetrate Boston's most elite literary circle, and led its most prominent members out of their highly cultured, urban environment and into the uncultured wilderness. However, the biography of this Schenectady, New York, native remains unknown to many. This is unfortunate because Stillman is important and interesting in his own right. He possessed a power of personality and artistic talents that made him stand out and allowed him to take charge of the expedition to Follensby Pond. Yet, as we meet him here, Stillman is a compelling but flawed character. He is burdened by debts, depression, doubts, grand ideas, and a talent that falls just short of letting him bring these ideas into actuality. His intellect and talent with words, paintbrush, and camera drew the members of the Philosophers' Camp and Adirondack Club into his company, while his anxiousness or moodiness and passionate fits tended to push them away. No matter the reaction, Stillman was memorable and in his day a recognized man of talent about whom many people had strong opinions.

Stillman was the first pupil of Frederic E. Church, the leader of the Hudson River School's second generation, and he cofounded the nation's first art journal, the *Crayon*. His art received the praise of painters on both sides of the Atlantic, including Asher Durand and Dante Gabriel Rossetti. Despite never being very interested in domestic politics, he had an affinity for international affairs. Stillman served as a secret agent for the leader of the Hungarian revolution, Lajos "Louis" Kossuth, as well as a credentialed diplomat in Rome and Crete. His photography of the Acropolis and other ruins continues to be exhibited in museums across the country. As William Dean Howells said in 1901, Stillman's variegated experiences were reminiscent of those that belonged to an "old America," in which "the versatile and adventurous type . . . was the national type."[12]

His larger life as artist, writer, and diplomat will be explored in this book. But it is Stillman's social, economic, and, most important, aesthetic motivations—which come to light through his biography—for founding the camp that are critical. It is precisely these factors that made the gathering influential and are often lost on contemporary readers of Adirondack history. The serene landscapes painted by artists such as Stillman, Church, and Durand reflected the age. Idealism soared, and American artists began coming out from under the shadow of the European establishment and its academic classicism. These new artists distinguished themselves by focusing on the pristine and rugged landscapes of New York's Hudson Valley, New Hampshire's White Mountains, and other wild regions. But that is not to say that American art had completely sloughed off its European influences. Like the influential cohort of European artists influenced by the British art critic John Ruskin—including the Pre-Raphaelite Brotherhood, which included Rossetti and John E. Millais—the Americans were part of an aesthetic insurgency that aimed not only to revise painterly techniques and highlight new artistic subjects but also to open a new inquiry into the very relationship of humanity to nature.[13] The camp at Follensby was of a piece with these reforms in aesthetics and philosophy, and it was part of the break from the academic, urban, and pastoral.

Given the connection between nature and art, it is not surprising that artists like Stillman were also among the early waves of explorers in the Adirondack region. In 1837, the landscape painter Charles C. Ingham joined the nation's leading geologist, Ebenezer Emmons, on the New York Natural History Survey and produced a landmark painting, *The Great Adirondack Pass, Painted on the Spot, 1837*. (A lithograph of this work was included in Emmons's 1838 report, and the painting was displayed at the National Academy of Design the following year.) The artist had to be a camper and to trek through the wilderness on what was understood by some to be a spiritual journey as much as a practical undertaking. As these journeys became more common, some naturalists, explorers, and artists who went to the wilderness in search of experiences of sublimity and awe realized that the vast and untrammeled landscapes that drew them were undergoing significant change. The country's wild lands were vanishing at the hands of lumbermen and being penetrated by railroads. The steady degradation of forests, streams, and mountains came as industry and tourism opened up the wilderness.

As early as 1836, Thomas Cole, the father of the Hudson River School, bemoaned that "the ravages of the ax are daily increasing—the most notable scenes are made desolate." And in his 1837 sketching for *View of Schroon Mountain, Essex County, New York, After a Storm* (1838), he drew a stump and a felled tree. Yet these unsightly reminders of civilization were omitted from the final painting. In the years to come, other artists, Stillman in particular, would omit similar details to perpetuate the myth that the Adirondack region, even in the 1850s, was "an almost undisturbed primeval forest" visited only by a few "landscape-painters and sportsmen." By omission in art and exhortation in writing, Cole tried to encourage Americans to embrace their beautiful country. "We are still in Eden," he said; "the wall that shuts us out of the garden is our own ignorance. . . . May we turn from the ordinary pursuits of life to the pure enjoyment of rural nature; which is in the soul like a fountain of cool waters to the way-worn traveler."[14]

Other intellectuals, such as Emerson, Lowell, and Stillman, shared Cole's attitude toward nature, and the aesthetic sensibilities that define American romanticism moved in the same tracks as transcendentalism. In the same year that Cole made these statements in the *American Monthly Magazine*, Emerson, in his groundbreaking essay "Nature," likened the woods to the "plantations of God" where man "return[s] to reason and faith." Like Cole, Emerson linked man's psychological and spiritual well-being to the sanctity of and harmony with nature. "The health of eye seems to demand a horizon. We are never tired so long as we can see far enough," he said.[15] It was principally artists such as Stillman, Cole, Church, and Durand who had taught Americans what could be found in nature. And those aesthetic lessons in turn helped to underline what was wholly lost when, after the Civil War, the wilderness turned less wild as the lone canoeists paddling along the Adirondacks' lakes and rivers became largely outnumbered by the swarms of tourists who were brought to the region's luxury camps via train lines.

Among the artists who followed Cole's and Ingham's lead into the Adirondacks was Sanford R. Gifford, a landscape painter with a gift for capturing the effects of light on canvas. His professional career as an artist began in New York City in 1847—one year before Stillman moved there to study under Cole's prized pupil, Church.[16] Gifford's early landscapes in the mid-1840s were mostly of scenes around his hometown not far from New York's Catskill Mountains. Once he set up his studio in New York City, he moved on to painting scenes in the southern Adirondacks and New Hampshire's White Mountains. He later visited the central Adirondacks' Saranac Lakes region. It was around this time that Gifford painted *Morning in the Adirondacks* (1854), which featured a lakeside cabin in the middle distance and a towering mountain in the background. Sometime after that Saranac painting expedition he returned to New York and encountered Stillman. It is not clear when or where Gifford and Stillman first met, though their acquaintance is not surprising given their residence in New York and their fondness for Ruskin. It was Gifford who encouraged Stillman to seek out the pristine landscapes around Upper Saranac Lake, which the latter visited in 1854. Late in life, Stillman said Gifford had provided him with "the clue to the labyrinth" of the Adirondacks' lakes region.[17]

It is with that chance meeting and moment of inspiration that the story of the Philosophers' Camp begins. The camp was born in a confluence of philosophical ideas, aesthetic sensibilities, and naturalist longings. At the point of their confluence stood Stillman, who both took in and gave expression to each of these trends of thought and practice. Newspaper accounts of the Philosophers' Camp recognized it as a signal event and a curious meeting of urban intellectualism and wild nature. As time passed and Stillman's reputation faded, the story of the Philosophers' Camp became more a nostalgic tale of the old rustic Adirondacks and less one of art, philosophy, and nature study. It turned into a campfire yarn and not an intellectual history.

It is only appropriate that the story of the Philosophers' Camp evolved as the region itself changed. The celebratory tale of the region's primitive and pristine character in the mid-nineteenth century gave way to a tragic and nostalgic account in the late nineteenth and early twentieth centuries as the region suffered from deforestation and degradation. And in its latest evolution, it has become a story of hope in the late twentieth and early twenty-first centuries as environmental conservationists have worked to return the Adirondacks to something approximating the wild character that the scholars had enjoyed at Follensby in 1858.

This book follows the development and evolution of the Philosophers' Camp and its narrative in three parts. The first part, which includes chapters 1 through 7, covers the origins of the camp from 1854 to 1857. The second part, chapters 8 through 11, describes the convening of the Philosophers' Camp at Follensby and its successor, the Adirondack Club, at Ampersand from 1858 to 1859. The third part, chapters 12 through 15, considers the evolution of the stories of these camps and the dramatic changes that befell their participants and the Adirondacks between 1860 and 1901. The conclusion examines twentieth- and twenty-first-century conservation efforts regarding Follensby and Ampersand and shows how the stories of the Philosophers' Camp and Adirondack Club influenced them. Across the chapters readers will find the legend returned to history and an Adirondack myth converted into a tale of human ideals, actions, and failings.

✖ PART I

Nature and Society

❧ CHAPTER 1

Path to the Adirondacks

It was as though the boat was caught in a storm. It rocked back and forth and came closer to capsizing with every movement. Toward the stern of the rowboat sat William James Stillman, a young painter nervously holding a steering paddle. There he was, a mile into his trip on Lower Saranac Lake, on the verge of falling into the deep and cold water. The thought that he was a poor swimmer haunted him, and he was acutely aware of the fact that he would likely not make it to shore should the boat capsize.[1]

It was not a passing storm in the Adirondacks that so unsettled Stillman that summer day. Instead, it was the drunk farmer toward the boat's bow. The farmer, Mr. Johnson, had broken into song while rowing and was heavily beating time on the gunwale of the boat, making it rock. Stillman, who for the past two weeks had been lodging at the farmer's cabin on Upper Saranac Lake, implored him to stop shaking the boat. But old man Johnson chided Stillman and only sang louder and rocked the boat more violently.[2]

A few days earlier, Johnson had asked his lodger to pick him up at a settlement near Lower Saranac Lake on a predetermined day. Like many of the backwoodsmen Stillman had encountered in the Adirondacks, Johnson had a penchant for hard drinking. He frequently ventured to wilderness settlements such as Saranac Lake, where he drank until he either ran out of money or could not borrow any for booze. After rowing the boat alone sixteen miles from Upper Saranac, Stillman had found Johnson at a landing on

Lower Saranac Lake. Johnson was drunk and, as he put it, was "all on fire" inside him. He begged so piteously for a half pint of rum "to ease up on" that Stillman bought him one—a purchase the painter would soon regret.[3]

It did not take long for Johnson's antics on the lake to drive Stillman to action. The painter lifted his oar out of the water, raised it over Johnson's head, and sternly warned he would knock the farmer off the boat if he kept up with his rowdy behavior. The threat worked, and Johnson sulked quietly in the boat. He kept behind him the bottle of rum, which Stillman unsuccessfully attempted to nab whenever the old man took a swig from it. Eventually the painter managed to swipe the bottle from his host and toss it aside as they hauled their boat along a "carry" to Middle Saranac Lake. After rowing three miles across this lake, they came to another carry. Since Johnson was too drunk to shoulder the boat, Stillman left him at the landing, carried the boat by himself to Upper Saranac Lake, and then went back to retrieved his host.[4]

For the rest of the trip along the Upper Saranac, Johnson caused no trouble, but that night he disappeared from the cabin, and his wife feared he had attempted suicide. Frantically, Stillman searched the house, barn, loft, and stable for Johnson. The painter finally found him passed out in a wood yard. Stillman helped the wife drag Johnson to the cabin and put him to bed. The next morning a repentant Johnson vowed never to drink again and even bet Stillman his best oxen to $100 that he would keep his word. The bet was put in writing, and the farmer abstained from drinking for at least the duration of Stillman's stay in the wilderness.[5]

The roots of Stillman's journey into the Adirondack wilderness can be traced to his years growing up in Schenectady, New York. He was twenty-six years old during that summer of 1854 when he embarked on his first painting expedition in the northern Adirondacks and lodged at the Johnson cabin. It was not his first visit to the region, as he had gone on a fishing excursion to the northern edge of the Adirondacks years earlier with a fellow student at Union College in his hometown of Schenectady. He was over six feet tall, with a slender build. His hair was long and brown, his forehead broad. His eyes were wide. Stillman sometimes sported a beard but at other times was clean-shaven, and he had a well-shaped mouth on which, it was said, a smile was something to be remembered.[6]

When he was young, Stillman's art training had been erratic, often coming after chance encounters. A British portrait painter who had moved to Schenectady to teach photography at Union College taught him the basic rules of painting in watercolor and perspective in return for room and board.

FIGURE 1. Samuel W. Rowse (1822–1901), *William James Stillman* (1828–1901), mid-1850s. When Lowell saw this portrait of Stillman in his late twenties, he said, "You have nothing to do for the rest of your life but to try to look like it." From *The Autobiography of a Journalist,* vol. 1 (Boston: Houghton Mifflin, 1901).

A local shoemaker, who had learned all he knew about painting by attending the annual American Academy exhibits in New York City, advised Stillman on the use of oils. The boy loved roaming the countryside and making sketches along the Mohawk River. For a short period he received his formal schooling in New York City, where his brother Thomas lived on Seventh Street, near the East River, at a time when the city's northern limit was Fourteenth Street. When Stillman was fourteen years old, his parents sent him to DeRuyter, New York, a village more than thirty miles south of Syracuse. Stillman's fifth-oldest brother, Jacob, ran the DeRuyter Academy. Stillman attended this school, but financial problems forced it to close, and the boy was sent home. Stillman had "enjoyed intensely this life on the edge of a large natural forest," and he left it with "great regret."[7]

Stillman's parents opposed his desire to pursue a "technical education in the arts," forcing him to put off his formal art training for a few years. This lapse in his art education occurred during what he later said was "those years when facility of hand is most completely acquired and enthusiasm is strongest against difficulties—the years when, if ever, the artist is made." He continued his college preparation at a lyceum in Schenectady, where one of his schoolmates was Chester A. Arthur, the future twenty-first president of the United States. They both became members of Union's class of 1848. Stillman did not find his classes at Union very intellectually stimulating until his senior year, when he came under the influence of Dr. Eliphalet Nott, who had been named the college's first president in 1804. The waffling undergraduate fell under the spell of Nott, a Presbyterian clergyman known for his commitment to poor students.[8]

After graduating from Union in 1848, Stillman began his pursuit of a career as a landscape painter. He moved to New York City. It was probably around the time he graduated that Nott told his esteemed pupil that, should he ever need it, the college president would be willing to use his influence for Stillman's benefit. Initially Stillman's plan had been to serve as the pupil of the renowned Thomas Cole in Catskill, New York, during the winter after graduation. Stillman's gravitation toward Cole, with whom he had corresponded while in college, is not surprising. Not only was Cole's studio only approximately fifty miles south of Schenectady, but he was, in Stillman's assessment, "the leading painter of landscape in America" and "unrivaled in certain poetic and imaginative gifts."[9]

Cole had emigrated from England to America in 1818, initially working in Philadelphia as an illustrator and a year later relocating to Steubenville, Ohio. He started painting landscapes after moving to Pittsburgh in 1823, and he soon after returned to Philadelphia to study America's early landscape painters. In 1825, he moved to New York City and made his first sketching expedition in New York's wild Hudson Valley and Catskill regions. Cole's arrival in New York marked the beginning of a cultural movement, dubbed the "Hudson River School," that would last forty-five years. According to Elizabeth Mankin Kornhauser, curator in the American Wing at the Metropolitan Museum of Art in New York, this movement revealed the "changing relationship between humans and their environment, from dominance by nature's forces to a reversal of roles as the landscape was gradually integrated into human life by the century's end." In 1825, the very year Cole came to the city, Asher Durand, Samuel F. B. Morse, Charles C. Ingham, and several other artists cofounded the New-York Drawing Association. A year later, the association enlarged its ranks and became the National Academy of Design, which Cole cofounded. With its annual exhibitions in New York and its long list of associates, the academy was the nation's most influential art organization for almost a half century.[10]

In 1834, Cole had established his studio in Catskill. There, starting in 1844, he mentored Frederic E. Church, the eighteen-year-old son of a Hartford, Connecticut, businessman, jeweler, and silversmith. At the age of forty-seven, Cole died on February 11, 1848, from pleurisy, just as Stillman was getting ready to graduate from Union and begin his apprenticeship. Cole's untimely death prompted Stillman to apply for an apprenticeship to Cole's only artistic rival, Durand, then the president of the National Academy of Design. Durand, too engrossed in his work and not confident in his skills as a teacher, declined the application. Stillman then applied to Church, Cole's star pupil, who had just set up his studio at the Arts Union Building in New York City in the fall of 1848. He was only two years older than Stillman when the Union graduate entered the Arts Union Building studio in the winter of 1848–49.[11]

According to Cole, Church had the "finest eye for drawing in the world." It was in this eye, however, that Stillman later found the artist's greatest flaw. Church's zealous attention to detail "blinded him to every other aspect of our relations with nature," Stillman said. Church's art, while stunning, seemed like mimicry to Stillman. The apprentice claimed to have learned "nothing that was worth remembering" during his winter under Church's tutelage. It is important to remember, however, that Stillman made this harsh assessment of Church late in life. Stillman's detail-centric style of painting during his early adulthood suggests that the pupil readily embraced the teachings of the master. Stillman's apprenticeship in Church's studio was not entirely fruitless because he was introduced to several other prominent American artists and writers, beginning a long career of encounters with great men. For example, he met the poet Edgar Allan Poe and William Page, one of the era's best portrait painters and an intimate friend of the Cambridge poet James Russell Lowell. More important, Stillman found a copy of John Ruskin's influential book on the philosophy of art, *Modern Painters.*[12]

The first volume of *Modern Painters,* which praised the British painter Joseph W. M. Turner and landscape painting, had been published in England in 1843. It was followed in 1846 by a second volume, which had stronger religious overtones, especially regarding the divinity in nature. Ruskin's words read like scripture to Stillman. Stillman spent the summer of 1849 in upstate New York, painting scenes of the Mohawk Valley and obtaining "the first clear ideas of what lay before me in artist life [sic]." That fall, Stillman sold his first painting to the Art Union of New York. The work was of a view from his window in Schenectady across gardens and a churchyard with a church spire in the distance. It fetched Stillman thirty dollars and convinced him to go abroad to view the works of British painters, particularly Turner. He sailed for London in late December. He was almost desperate to receive formal art training, and he bounced around studios in the city looking for a master's guidance Although he had many artistic encounters—including with Turner and the minor landscape painter James B. Pyne—Stillman could not afford formal lessons from "competent masters." Pyne's monthly charge for his pupils was one hundred pounds, and Stillman had planned to make his fifty pounds last six months. For a few weeks he studied under Charles Davidson, a watercolorist whose "excessive precision" seemed to Stillman the "antithesis" of Pyne. As with Church, Stillman again found himself receiving formal lessons from an artist who steered him toward an objective method of painting.[13]

At the gallery of Turner's special agent in London, Stillman met Ruskin, who surprisingly bore none of the "fire, enthusiasm and dogmatism of his book." Instead, the young painter's idol, then about thirty years old, was a refined man with the behavior of a gentleman despite his dogmatic opinions. Later, at Ruskin's house, the two talked as much about art as about religion (Ruskin was a Calvinist, and Stillman had been raised in a Seventh-Day Baptist household). Not content with what London's art scene had to offer, Stillman next made a ten-day trip to Paris, where he "saw with great profit the work of the landscape painters and of [Eugene] Delacroix." Stillman believed "the greatest of the French landscape painters" was Théodore Rousseau, one of the leaders of the French Barbizon School, whose members painted landscapes far less wild than those of the Hudson River School artists.[14]

After completing his Parisian trip, Stillman returned to London, where he finally but briefly met Turner. A more influential encounter Stillman had in that city came during the spring of 1850. It was then that the Royal Academy exhibited the works of the Pre-Raphaelite Brotherhood, the group founded two years earlier by rebellious artists such as William H. Hunt, Dante Gabriel Rossetti, and John E. Millais. The Pre-Raphaelites, especially Hunt, had also fallen under Ruskin's spell. One of Millais's paintings at the exhibition, *Christ in the House of His Parents,* or *The Carpenter's Shop* (Stillman referred to it as *Christ in the Carpenter's Shop*), strongly influenced Stillman. The painting's depiction of Christ, the Virgin Mary, John the Baptist, Joseph, and St. Anne, however, appalled British critics. With a sharp degree of realism, Millais placed the group in a simple carpenter's shop. Christ, showing a wound on his hand, stands meekly while a distraught Mary kneels beside him. Charles Dickens famously described the child Christ at the center of the painting as "a hideous, wry necked, blubbering, red-haired boy in a night gown" and the Virgin was "so horrible in her ugliness." The work caused so much controversy that Queen Victoria ordered it removed from the exhibition so she could view Millais's painting privately.[15]

Figure 2. Sir John Everett Millais (1829–96), *Christ in the House of His Parents* (*The Carpenter's Shop*), 1849–50. Oil paint on canvas, 864 × 1397 mm. Stillman said Millais's *Christ in the House of His Parents,* which he had viewed at the London's Royal Academy exhibition in 1850, "impressed me very strongly." (In his autobiography he referred to the painting as *Christ in the Carpenter's Shop.*) From an organizational standpoint, Stillman's *Morning at Camp Maple: Adirondack Woods* resembles Millais's painting. Stillman, like Millais, divided his painting's characters into two groups at opposite ends of the canvas, with the focal point resting on the perplexed individual (Emerson or a young Christ) standing between them in the center. ©Tate, London 2014.

Stillman left the Old World for New York with a "fermentation of art ideas" in his mind. He spent the remainder of 1850 and much of the next year painting nature out of doors. His fledgling career as a painter looked promising as he made his first appearance at a National Academy of Design exhibition in April 1851 with a painting titled *Sunset*. However, just as he was establishing himself as a painter, Stillman became less focused on his artistic aspirations. In December 1851, the Hungarian patriot and statesman Lajos "Louis" Kossuth, the leader of the failed Hungarian revolution of 1848, came to America to raise funds for arms for another uprising against the Hapsburg monarchy. Kossuth's mission struck a chord with Stillman. At the time, Stillman was "eager for adventure and ignorant of danger," prompting him to offer his services to Kossuth. While Stillman waited to be called to the Hungarian cause, he showed five works at the National Academy's 1852 exhibition, including ones titled *The Mountain Brook* and *Study of Distance, City of Schenectady*.[16] Despite Stillman's involvement in this exhibition, his work for Kossuth would amount to the first of many campaigns that would detract from the aspiring artist's efforts to make a career out of painting.

Stillman had not completely abandoned his artistic aspirations, however. In some ways his service for Kossuth was a means to an end rather than an end in itself because it brought him back into Europe's artistic sphere of influence and allowed him to reconnect with Ruskin. For instance, after touring the United States, Kossuth returned to London, and Stillman joined him there. Taking advantage of this stay in London, the painter reconnected with Ruskin by January 1853. Initially, Stillman was charged with providing Kossuth with intelligence on the procurement of arms and materials of war. As the Hungarian cause for independence teetered on failure, Stillman was later sent on a secret mission to Pesth to recover Hungary's crown jewels, which Kossuth had hidden and feared could fall into Austrian hands. However, this mission proved to be less a matter of international espionage than three months of folly. Stillman returned to London and reported to Kossuth on his failed secret mission. With this distraction behind him, he refocused on his painting career and traveled to Paris to continue his studies of art. He enrolled in a workshop taught by Adolphe Yvon, a French historical painter best known for his paintings of the Napoleonic Wars. Stillman remained in Paris through spring. The Hungarian revolution for which he had been waiting never erupted.[17]

Stillman returned briefly to England, and in early June 1853 he boarded the steamer *Humboldt*, which was bound for New York. Also aboard the *Humboldt* was William Cullen Bryant, who for the past twenty-eight years had served as the principal editor of the *New York Evening Post*. Bryant, who was also one of the nation's leading poets and the former president of the American Art Union, had just wrapped up a six-month tour of Europe and the Near East. Bryant had traveled mostly with the painter Charles Leupp and Asher Durand's son, John Durand, who also met Stillman on the *Humboldt.* Sympathies for Kossuth and interests in art likely forged a bond between Stillman and Bryant during their transatlantic voyage. Bryant saw much more of Stillman after the steamer docked on June 22. The artist later became the *Evening Post's* part-time fine arts editor.[18]

After he returned to the United States, Stillman's painting career regained its momentum as he focused on refining his craft and sought new landscapes to capture on canvas. He went on a walking tour of the Connecticut and Housatonic valleys. However, the rural landscapes in America then did not impress him as strongly as those in England had. Nevertheless, at his uncle's farm in Rensselaer County, New York, he painted *The Forest Spring,* a highly detailed presentation of a beech branching over a spring. The clear spring's surface was said to have reflected objects "like a mirror," and the moss, flowers, grass, and leaves were "painted with wonderful delicacy and accuracy." By early 1854, Stillman was working at Bryant's *Evening Post.* In mid-March, for example, he reported on the National Academy of Design's 1854 exhibition in New York. *The Forest Spring* was featured at this exhibition. Asher Durand remarked that its stones "seemed to be, not painting, but the real thing."[19]

The critics were quick to identify Stillman's British influences, and it was not long before he was called the "American Pre-Raphaelite." A critic for *Putnam's Monthly* called it "a marvelous piece of greenery, in which every object is represented with a degree of accuracy and beauty which we hardly imagined to be compatible with such a breadth of effect and apparent freedom of touch." The critic had heard this work was "a pre-Raphaelite picture." However, he questioned whether any Pre-Raphaelite artists, who usually painted religious or mythological works, had "attempted any thing in this style."[20]

By the summer of 1854, Stillman had combed New England and the Mohawk Valley for picturesque subjects to paint, but it was mostly all in vain. Then, in July, he embarked on a walking tour of Massachusetts and Vermont. From Bellows Falls, Vermont, Stillman wrote to a brother that he had hiked up Mount Holyoke in central Massachusetts and had traveled north through Deerfield, Massachusetts, to Brattleboro, Vermont. He had planned to walk to Burlington and then cross Lake Champlain on July 27. A trip across the lake could have taken Stillman to Port Kent in New York, five miles east of Keeseville, the gateway to the Adirondacks. It is likely that at this time, at the recommendation of Sanford Gifford, Stillman headed into the "desert" of northern New York to find his desired subject. He found this prized land-scape near the Johnson family cabin, where he stayed for the season, paying two dollars per week for board and lodging.[21]

For three months, Stillman painted a scene of Upper Saranac Lake viewed from within the woods near its shore. His *Study on Upper Saranac Lake* (1854) became his best-known early work. Art, however, was not all Stillman sought

FIGURE 3.   William James Stillman (1828–1901), *Study on Upper Saranac Lake,* 1854. Oil on canvas, 30-1/2 × 25-1/2 in. Stillman produced this work during his first Adirondack painting expedition in 1854. By the time he showed it at the National Academy of Design's 1855 exhibition, he had earned a reputation as the American Pre-Raphaelite for his attention to detail. Photograph © 2015 Museum of Fine Arts, Boston. Gift of Dr. J. Sydney Stillman.

in the wilderness. When he was not painting, he was either fishing, boating, or hiking in the woods. He also craved experiences that would bring
him into harmony with nature. He was filled with spiritual longings and
reasoned that all that was necessary to achieve this "self-purification" was to
"get down to myself, simple and alone" and to "shut out all the world," he
later told a friend. Stillman actually was far from being unique in wanting to
escape the burdens of civilization and to find refuge in a solitude furnished
by the wilderness. In the Adirondacks, he encountered a like-minded hunter
who had built a cabin deep in the woods and strove to avoid human contact. He was a rugged character, with an intellectualism that kept in check
the crude influences that life in the wilderness could unleash on men. This
hunter, possibly named Simons, intrigued Stillman; he was the first man the
painter had ever met who had managed to live at length in solitude without
having his "healthy intellect" deteriorate from lack of social contact.[22]

Far away from the wilderness, in Boston, the publishing firm of Ticknor &
Fields that summer published a book that demonstrated the effects of solitude
on a healthy intellect probably far more eloquently than Stillman's reclusive
Adirondack hunter ever could. On August 9, the firm published two thousand copies of Henry David Thoreau's *Walden*. Stillman had been attending
Union when Thoreau had resided at Walden Pond in Concord, Massachusetts, from July 4, 1845 to September 6, 1847. As Thoreau explained in his
book, he, like Stillman, "went to the woods . . . to live deliberately, to front
only the essential facts of life."[23] In either rural Concord or the wilderness
of northern New York, Thoreau and Stillman sought to know themselves on
simpler terms and consequently transcend themselves.

However, in 1854, the prospect of secluding oneself from society and
living primitively for the sake of finding oneself was a radical concept. One
critic said *Walden* contained "many shrewd and sensible suggestions, with a
fair share of nonsense." Another said Thoreau's "selfish philosophy darkly
tinge[s] the pages of 'Walden.'" Even Thoreau's close Concord friend and
mentor Ralph Waldo Emerson did not see the value in becoming a hermit
in the wilderness. Such reclusive men matched the solitude they found with
the solitude they brought—"desart with desart."[24]

Emerson considered it better, or at least more pleasant, "to go to the
woods in good company, & with heyday, & bonbons, & comfort, & gentlemen & ladies, & also with the legs of horses." In fact, he had been invited by
Emily M. Drury of Canandaigua, New York, to join such a party in the "the
woods" in the spring of 1853, but he declined the invitation. He later told
Drury that he respected the gentlemen who participated in this adventure

and claimed that he "could very gladly have been of the party." However, he acknowledged that "woods and waters are stronger than men," and it would not take long for them to quickly "melt down" his personality and reveal his antisocial side. As he explained, "I am bad company for more than one, & do not often or believe I ever go to walk with more."[25]

At the time of *Walden*'s publication, Thoreau was living with his parents, sister, and aunt at their Main Street home in Concord. He continued to take regular walks around Walden and pay close attention to the minutiae of the changing seasons. However, often he found his studies of the natural phenomena around the pond disrupted by worries about national issues, particularly those pertaining to slavery. In 1850, Congress had passed the Fugitive Slave Law, which required the federal government to assist in the recovery of runaway slaves anywhere in the country. To New Englanders such as Thoreau, the law, which was part of the Compromise of 1850, encroached on their moral conscience. In a July 4, 1854, address to an abolitionist crowd in Framingham, Massachusetts, Thoreau complained about how the slavery question spoiled his walks. He told the crowd that the serenity he used to find during his walks to "one of our ponds" had been spoiled by the "remembrance of my country." He declared, "My thoughts are murder to the State, and involuntarily go plotting against her."[26]

As Thoreau's comments demonstrate, his pond and its surrounding countryside could not at times provide an adequate buffer against the pressing questions of the times. The undisturbed serenity intellectuals such as Thoreau longed for was instead reflected in lakes farther removed from civilization and in a forest far wilder than that of Walden's. In 1854, Stillman found himself at one such place at Upper Saranac Lake. It would not be long before he brought some of Thoreau's contemporaries to other serene waters in the Adirondacks. It was also during the spring and summer of that year that some of those men—particularly Emerson, Ebenezer Rockwood Hoar, and Thomas Wentworth Higginson—became more deeply involved in the slavery debate, especially after a fugitive slave named Anthony Burns was captured by a U.S. marshal in Boston.

❧ CHAPTER 2

Turning Points

On July 3, 1954, Judge Ebenezer Rockwood Hoar sat at his bench in Boston's municipal courthouse. Just five weeks earlier, a mob composed of members of the Boston Vigilance Committee had besieged that formidable, three-story stone building in an attempt to liberate an approximately twenty-three-year-old runaway slave, Anthony Burns, who had been captured in May and held in a jail cell inside. The rioters had taken a battering ram and axes to one of the building's entrances. Two made it inside, one of whom was Thomas Wentworth Higginson, a radical thirty-year-old Unitarian minister from Worcester, Massachusetts, but they were quickly ejected by an overwhelming number of guards. The rescue attempt failed, and a Massachusetts judge, Edward C. Loring, later approved Burns's rendition. Burns was escorted out of Boston on June 2.[1]

Hoar was thirty-eight years old, and on that hot summer day he was preparing to begin the July term of criminal court. During his charge to the grand jury, he explained to the jurors their duties and the nature and obligations of their oaths. He then discussed various laws, such as those pertaining to lotteries and stock fraud. Noting how it was probable that the grand jury would hear cases related to the "riotous proceedings" that had recently occurred in the county and city, Hoar at length discussed riot law. He focused on the issue of whether the civil authority of the commonwealth had legally employed the military to suppress the Anthony Burns courthouse riot. During that riot, Boston Mayor Jerome V. C. Smith had ordered out two companies of artillery, with one being stationed at the courthouse and the other at City Hall. The U.S. marshal, too, had dispatched two companies of Marines, one from Fort Warren and the other from the Charlestown Navy Yard. The judge's commentary on this topic would end up reflecting his political views, which over the past several years had been evolving.[2]

Hoar had graduated from Harvard College in 1835 and from Harvard's law school in 1839. Starting in 1840, he quickly rose through the ranks of the Massachusetts Whig Party. But his allegiance to the party ended when the Whig National Convention nominated Zachary Taylor, a Mexican War general and Louisiana slaveholder, as its candidate for the 1848 presidential election. Hoar emerged as an ardent supporter of the Free Soiler campaign, and he played a leading role in a June 1848 convention in Worcester where delegates were chosen for the national Free Soil convention in Buffalo in August. There delegates nominated former president Martin Van Buren as the presidential candidate for the Free Soil Party, which consisted of northern "Barnburner" Democrats and "Conscience" Whigs. In 1849, Hoar left his law practice based in Concord after being appointed to the court of common pleas by Governor George N. Briggs.[3]

Hoar was a tall, broad-fronted man with light brown hair and wired-rimmed spectacles. He was said to have a "columnar erectness" and he "never allowed his head to stoop." Well read, he had stored in memory an abundant supply of poems, psalms, and historical anecdotes from which he could pull to make a point. He was known to have "more than New England wit and wisdom" and a "stern, uncompromising New England conscience." Hoar put all these traits on display as he addressed the grand jury of nineteen men. According to the Boston press, the renditions of fugitive slaves had turned the municipal courthouse into the "Bastille of Slavocracy." Sitting at his bench, Hoar likely could feel the tug of the Fugitive Slave Law's chains as much as he could feel the summer heat. He was put in the awkward position of having to recognize a law that represented the type of tyranny his grandfather, two great-grandfathers, and three great-uncles had fought against at North Bridge in his hometown of Concord when the Revolutionary War broke out on April 19, 1775.[4] Adding insult to injury, six days after the riot, on May 30, President Franklin Pierce had signed into law the Kansas-Nebraska Act, which allowed people in Kansas and Nebraska to decide whether they wanted their territories to enter the Union as free or slave states. The act, sponsored by Illinois senator Stephen Douglas, negated the terms of the Missouri Compromise of 1850, which had barred slavery from territories north of the Mason-Dixon Line.

Figure 4. Frank Hector Tompkins (1847–1922), *Ebenezer Rockwood Hoar* (1816–95), 1887. Oil on canvas, 44 × 34-1/16 in. Hoar was a Concord lawyer who in 1849 was appointed to the court of common pleas in Boston, and he returned to private practice in 1855. He was a rising star in the fledgling Republican Party, running for Massachusetts attorney general as the party's candidate that year. He later served as the U.S. attorney general for the Grant administration and as a member of the House of Representatives. Hoar purchased Stillman's 1858 painting of the Philosophers' Camp and bequeathed it to the Concord Free Public Library in 1895. Harvard Art Museums/Fogg Museum, Harvard University Portrait Collection, Gift by subscription to Harvard College, 1888, H191. Photo: Imaging Department © President and Fellows of Harvard College.

While addressing the grand jury, Hoar held out the hope to the grand jury that the Fugitive Slave Law would one day be deemed unconstitutional, and he claimed the rationale used to support its constitutionality, "so far as our Supreme Court is concerned," was "placed on the ground of authority, and not of right." He went on to chip away at the manner in which Boston's mayor had used the military to assist in suppressing the mob. Citing the commonwealth's laws relating to calling out militias, Hoar left little doubt that the mayor had overstepped his legal bounds in using military forces to suppress the riot. Although a statute empowered the mayor to employ all ordinary and peaceable measures to enforce his civil authority and to have a military force ready to respond to an exigency, the judge noted a shortcoming in the law: It did not empower the mayor to wield that force. Hoar did not let the grand jury forget the consequences of this infraction. He said in his concluding remarks: "But when the law is disregarded by its own guardians and supporters, it is 'wounded in the house of its friends,' and all the sentiments of reverence for law in the public mind are weakened."[5] As the grand jury retired to investigate a case, Hoar probably felt at least a little satisfaction in knowing he had eloquently articulated a loophole that could limit the government's ability to use the military to enforce the Fugitive Slave Law.

Hoar's charge to the grand jury was printed in full the next day in the *Boston Daily Atlas* and later made headlines in newspapers across the country, including the *New York Daily Times* and *Fayetteville Observer* in North Carolina. The day after the judge delivered the charge—Independence Day—several other prominent New Englanders made similar bold statements against their government. On that day, in Concord, Emerson draped the gate around his home in black to protest the oppressive law. In Framingham, William Lloyd Garrison organized an antislavery convention. At the event, Garrison burned a copy of the Fugitive Slave Law, then Judge Loring's charge and decision in the Burns case, and then the U.S. Constitution.[6] Amid the cheering crowd of three thousand people in Framingham stood Thoreau, the event's keynote speaker. There he delivered his speech, "Slavery in Massachusetts," in which he complained about how recent events had spoiled his walks around a pond, presumably Walden.

Hoar left his bench at the Bastille of Slavocracy a year later to return to private practice. He became an early supporter of abolitionists' efforts to fight the expansion of slavery. In April 1854, Massachusetts had chartered the New England Emigrant Aid Company, which sent antislavery settlers to the western territories. The first settlers in Kansas from New England founded the city of Lawrence in August of that year, later followed by Topeka, Humbolt, Osawatomie, Claflin, Manhattan, and others. By August 1855, Hoar contributed $125 for rifles for those Kansas settlers. That year, he ran for Massachusetts attorney general on the new Republican platform. He later expressed a desire to rid the Union of what he called "those twin relics of barbarism, polygamy and slavery."[7] He was a rising star in the fledgling Republican Party.

The mounting tensions between North and South—and the endeavors of men such as Hoar and Garrison to help tilt the political scale toward the former—were not pressing concerns to Stillman, who remained engrossed with the subject of art. It did not take long for him to abandon his pursuit of painting as a full-time career. By November 1854, he was fully engaged in a new project: a journal solely devoted to covering the arts in America. His abrupt career change from painter to journalist was driven more out of necessity than passion. For most of his young adult life, Stillman had leaned on his brother Thomas for financial support. Since the 1830s, Thomas had been involved with a revolutionary steamship engine manufacturing enterprise in lower Manhattan later known as the Novelty Works. He initially served as the superintendent of this enterprise founded by Union College's president, Eliphalet Nott, but in 1838 Thomas became one of its co-owners. He also had helped establish the first line of coastal steamships that primarily ferried passengers and freight between New York and Charleston, South Carolina, thus affording him the title of the "father of coastwise navigation in this country."[8]

It was Thomas who had largely bankrolled Stillman's European adventures and his artistic pursuits. By the fall of 1854, Stillman had been "driven to a kind of despair." Although he painted consistently and his work received good reviews, he failed to attract a major purchaser other than Thomas. He could "barely have realized a starving income," so when the opportunity arose to establish an art journal called the *Crayon,* he seized it, assuming that it was "better than earning nothing."[9] For this enterprise, he partnered with John Durand, whom he had met two years earlier during his transatlantic journey home aboard the *Humboldt.* Crucial to the success of their venture, Durand and Stillman knew, was the support of not only New Yorkers but Bostonians as well. The task of soliciting such support fell upon Stillman, who around early November began this mission to penetrate the preeminent literary circles of Boston. He started with an unannounced visit to the home of Cambridge's famed rambunctious satirical and romantic poet, James Russell Lowell.

At the time Stillman showed up at Elmwood, the Lowell family estate in Cambridge, Lowell was an established poet who had not published a book of verse in several years. He was thirty-five years old, with dark, serious eyes and wavy auburn hair. He usually sported a reddish beard. He had graduated from Harvard College in 1838, and after a brief stint in law he devoted himself to a literary career. In 1843 he founded a short-lived literary journal called the *Pioneer,* and in the mid-1840s he served as a regular contributor to the *National Anti-Slavery Standard.* He made his mark on American letters in 1847 and 1848 with the publication of four volumes of poetry. Among these volumes was *A Fable for Critics* and *The Biglow Papers,* his two-most acclaimed poetical works.[10]

The Biglow Papers was a political satire in which Lowell attacked the Mexican War and slavery. *Fable* was a satire in which Lowell lampooned America's literati. He coyly criticized the editor of the *Dial,* Margaret Fuller, as being self-centered and Theodore Parker for preaching misguided beliefs. Such witty attacks were Lowell's specialty, and few were spared from his affronts. He managed to insult Emerson in his Harvard class poem (Lowell was elected poet of the class of 1838)—an affront the philosopher forgave—and he crossed Hoar by writing an ode about his fiancée, Caroline Brooks.[11]

Lowell had married Maria White in 1844. Over the next few years, Maria gave birth to two daughters: Blanche in 1845 and Mabel in 1847. However, tragedy struck the Lowell family when Blanche died at fifteen months and Maria died on October 27, 1853. When Stillman visited the poet a year after Maria's death, Lowell was despondent and inclined to grieve in solitude. The poet tried to keep busy by preparing for a series of lectures he was scheduled to present at the Lowell Institute beginning in January 1855. His closest friends from the period when his life with Maria had begun were far from Boston and could not cheer him up. Chief among these were William Page, the portrait painter whom Stillman had met while studying in Church's studio, and Charles F. Briggs, the editor of *Putnam's Monthly* in New York. Page painted portraits of Lowell and his wife that remained hanging in Elmwood long after the poet's death.[12]

Stillman may have come to Lowell with a letter of introduction from either Page or Briggs. Page years earlier had introduced Stillman to Lowell's poetry, which Page frequently read out loud in his New York studio. Stillman listened to these poems until his "blood ran quick" and his enthusiasms made him see "what was never to be seen again, even in dreams." Regardless of who, if anyone, had provided the introductory letter, Lowell likely saw in Stillman a glimmer of Page's idealism and romanticism that had so appealed to the poet. Stillman and Lowell knew of each other through the painter's work at the *Evening Post.* When Stillman presented himself to Lowell, the painter was engrossed with the idea of the *Crayon,* which seemed to him to

FIGURE 5. Unidentified artist, *James Russell Lowell* (1819–91), circa 1855–65. Lowell was a Cambridge poet who served as the first editor of the *Atlantic Monthly*. He succeeded Henry Wadsworth Longfellow as Harvard's modern languages professor and also served as a United States ambassador to Spain and England. Courtesy Library of Congress.

be "evangelical." He wanted to "preach and labor for the revival of art." In Lowell, the young journalist found a receptive audience.[13]

As a matter of business, Stillman solicited from Lowell a poem for the first edition of the *Crayon*. Lowell had earlier shown Stillman a passage from a poem about an August afternoon on Appledore, the craggy island that is one of the Isles of Shoals off Portsmouth, New Hampshire. Stillman secured Lowell's pledge to furnish the *Crayon* with the poem, later titled "My Appledore Gallery," though the poet refused payment for the piece. An intimate friendship quickly followed this new business relationship. Each man seemed to provide the other with the energy that had been missing from his own life. For weeks before visiting Cambridge, Stillman had been "in a most lifeless state" and "utterly indifferent to existence," but in Lowell he found a "spiritual energy" that "re-energized" the painter. Lowell felt the same: Stillman's visit left the poet feeling fifteen years younger. Stillman entered into Lowell's loneliness "like an incarnate aspiration," the poet said.[14]

Stillman's entry into Lowell's life could not have been better timed. He filled a void at Elmwood that had been left there by the death of Maria—loneliness, a lull in work, and a lapse in fame. It is not clear how long Stillman stayed at Elmwood during this initial visit. Either during this visit or subsequent ones, Lowell introduced Stillman to some of his friends, including Charles Eliot Norton and Richard H. Dana, a Boston lawyer who had famously written the travel memoir *Two Years Before the Mast* (1840). Dana had also represented fugitive slaves such as Thomas Sims and Anthony Burns. At a later visit, Lowell also introduced Stillman to Emerson, the poet John Greenleaf Whittier, the banker Samuel Gray Ward, Massachusetts senator Charles Sumner, the literary critic Edwin Percy Whipple, the Harvard scientist Louis Agassiz, and Thomas G. Appleton, the brother-in-law of Henry Wadsworth Longfellow, the Cambridge poet and Harvard's foreign languages professor. Probably during a subsequent visit, Lowell also took the journalist on a tour of his favorite spots around Cambridge, including Beaver Brook and the Waverley Oaks. During Stillman's initial visit to Elmwood, his conversations with Lowell grew increasingly intimate, and the poet revealed the depth of his grief. Lowell read to Stillman poems such as "The Wind Harp" and "Ode to Happiness," which revealed the poet's anguish over the loss of his wife.[15]

By mid-November Stillman returned to New York. Despite their intimate conversations, he worried he had given Lowell the unfavorable impression that he was "wasting" his life by dividing his passions among several ideals. The painter later tried to assure Lowell that he had no choice but to explore all the arts. "I must live and be all—picture, statue, poem, song," Stillman proclaimed. He also tried to convince Lowell that, despite being nine years the poet's junior, the painter was not too young to "feel the bitterness manhood sometimes brings." Not even a month into their friendship, Stillman began revealing his own depression to Lowell. "Do you know, my friend, though I hope to God you do not, that there is a colder, darker, drearier thing than Death?" In a disturbing confession, Stillman claimed he had learned to "bless Death," though not his own. In a misguided attempt at empathy, Stillman assured Lowell that his heart "has fathomed the glacier ice as deeply as yours," and this mutual experience would strengthen their friendship.[16]

Stillman's depression cast a long shadow over his young adulthood. He increasingly suffered from an anxiety that was worsened by failing health. He frequently found himself so fatigued that he was not able to hold a job or perform even household chores. Some of this anxiety stemmed from his inability to hone his skills on one passion, one art. He became torn between writing and painting, as neither art alone could afford him financial security or success. In the mid-1850s, Stillman strongly embraced his Christian faith as he trudged through this dark night of the soul. It is important to understand the psychological factors behind Stillman's behavior because they significantly affected his relationships with the men in many of the eminent social circles he entered. Stillman may have suffered from a generalized anxiety disorder, which, according to the *Diagnostic and Statistical Manual of Mental Disorders,* is marked by uncontrollable and excessive, though not always continual, anxiety or worry for at least six months. Through much of his late twenties and early thirties, Stillman reported symptoms associated with this condition, such as restlessness, being easily fatigued, sleeplessness, and irritability. He also exhibited the depressive symptoms that commonly accompany a generalized anxiety disorder diagnosis. Additionally, either the anxiety or physical symptoms caused Stillman what could be categorized as "clinically significant distress or impairment in social, occupational, or other important areas of functioning." This diagnosis would fall in line with that of a doctor who said Stillman suffered from "exhaustion of the brain." Stillman often used the fast-acting and potentially lethal sedative chloral hydrate for his sleeplessness. To counter his fatigue, he also at times used stimulants, though it is not clear what kind.[17]

Unshaken by his worries over Lowell's impression of him, Stillman turned his attention to another prominent Boston area writer: Ralph Waldo Emerson. Since the 1836 publication of "Nature," in which he had expounded transcendental philosophy's core principles of harmony with nature and self-reliance, Emerson had slowly seen his reputation as a great American writer rise. He was fifty-one years old in late 1854 and living in Concord.

Figure 6. Unknown artist, *Ralph Waldo Emerson* (1803–82), date unknown. Emerson was a former Unitarian minister whose essays and lectures on nature, religion, social reform, and art defined the transcendentalist movement in the mid-1800s. Despite writing extensively about nature, Emerson had never experienced the Adirondack wilderness prior to his August 1858 camping trip. Courtesy Library of Congress.

Twenty-two years had passed since he had resigned as a Unitarian minister for the Second Church of Boston, though his preaching skills served him well on America's lecture circuit. However, Emerson's lectures and addresses, most of which were printed as collections of essays, were harshly reviewed by many contemporary critics. His views had been attacked as anti-Christian and promoting self-worship. In sum, they were dangerous. For example, Emerson's "Divinity School Address" at Harvard Divinity School in 1838 resulted in his banishment from the college for almost thirty years. As one reviewer for the *Boston Daily Advertiser* said of this address, Emerson exhibited "extraordinary brilliance of language" and "beauty of imagery," but he also preached "a doctrine which leads man to worship his own nature and himself." Over the next two decades, such criticisms dogged Emerson's published works, such as *Essays* (1841) and *Essays: Second Series* (1844). Even though his *Representative Men* (1850) received more critical acclaim than its predecessors because it was his "most objective" and was ripe with a "freshness of expressions," he was still viewed as a dangerous intellectual.[18]

Regardless of the controversy surrounding him, Emerson remained an influential literary figure in eastern Massachusetts, the region that served as the base of the transcendental movement. Stillman likely knew that Emerson's support was crucial to the *Crayon*'s success in Boston. On November 20, Stillman sent to Emerson the prospectus for the *Crayon* and asked for his "co-operation if possible." The objective of the journal, Stillman explained, was "to enforce the claims of beauty and of Art as its gospel upon the world."[19]

🐦 CHAPTER 3

The *Crayon*

Stillman was filled with rage and sadness and a dash of joy too. He was at an evening party in New York. A group of writers and artists had been called together to view a painting by the German American painter Emmanuel G. Leutze, possibly his *Washington at Monmouth*.[1]

By mid-October 1854, this recently completed painting by Leutze, who was best known for his massive work of 1851, *Washington Crossing the Delaware,* had been temporarily placed at the National Academy of Design. *Washington at Monmouth* depicted the pivotal event of the Battle of Monmouth, when General George Washington rode on horseback to the front line to find his army in retreat after attacking British troops as they marched from Philadelphia to Sandy Hook, New Jersey. All around Stillman, he heard men clamoring over Leutze's latest work. Durand and Bryant sang its praise. Stillman stood amid the crowd, confounded. To him, it seemed a "miserable apology for an idea." Looking around he saw "miserable artists" preying on "unsuspecting tradesmen." Even though the celebrities of New York's art and literary circles surrounded him, Stillman felt as though he was in the "midst of an assembly of dead souls."[2]

Stillman considered the spectacle a tragedy because "poor Art" was being thrown by unworthy sellers into a market for unworthy buyers. "When will her slavery end," he asked Lowell in a letter later. While disappointed with the party, Stillman delighted in the belief that he knew how to free Art from such bondage. He left the party before dinner was served, and he prided himself in knowing that *he* was an artist who "would rather starve than betray my God." He walked home, ate a few dried dates, drank a glass of Mosette wine, and wrote to Lowell about the showing. Probably referring to his own and John Durand's efforts to launch the *Crayon,* Stillman added that a firm had "declined our proposition and we have concluded to publish it ourselves." The two publishers later raised $5,000 for the launch of the journal, half of which was secured by Stillman's brother Thomas.[3]

Stillman was eager to share his liberating aesthetic ideas with the world through the *Crayon,* even though, as the dinner party illustrates, he was in the minority in holding such views. He found some allies in New York, however, particularly among the so-called Brooklyn School. This group subscribed to the Pre-Raphaelite's principles and had been founded after Stillman's return from England. The group regularly met at the home of Henry K. Brown, a Brooklyn sculptor and avid Adirondack fisherman. Stillman, along with the Pre-Raphaelites, was an ardent believer in what Ruskin called "truth to nature." As Ruskin said of the latter group, its "one principle" was "that of uncompromising truth in all that it does." The Pre-Raphaelites painted directly from nature and produced elaborately detailed works, "selecting nothing, rejecting nothing," in Ruskin's words. The *Crayon* noted how they were excessively detail-oriented but their aim was not mere mimicry or realism. The journal acknowledged that this "unfaltering devotion to truth" created on the canvas a certain "hardness and rigidity of . . . forms" that was "temporarily repulsive in all its forms." But anything less would capture the "partial truth and partial grace" common to the "namby pamby" works of the English artists against whom the Pre-Raphaelites rebelled. And if some painters such as Ruskin approached their art with a scientific eye, it was because they regarded themselves as scientists. In the mid-nineteenth century, as noted by Paul Sawyer, Ruskinians saw the sciences and arts as being unified, though other romantics tended to see the two as divided. Believing that life was a "mystical and unanalyzable force," Ruskin saw the arts as being crucial to scientific inquiry. By employing an objectivism marked by "virtues like watchfulness and sympathy," as Sawyer noted, artists were uniquely positioned to accurately describe and categorize nature and its energies.[4]

This belief that art should provide an uncompromising, almost scientific portrayal of nature was not a foreign concept to Americans when Stillman began championing it in the *Crayon* in 1855. In fact, according to John I. H. Baur, the former director of the Whitney Museum of American Art, American artists had embraced realism long before the founding of the Pre-Raphaelite Brotherhood in 1848. Such realism can even be traced back to painters such as the portraitist John S. Copley in the late eighteenth century. Further, years before Ruskin wrote the first volume of *Modern Painters,* transcendentalists had already recognized that clearly perceiving nature was a gateway to virtue. "The moral law lies at the centre of nature and radiates to the circumference," Emerson wrote in "Nature." "All things with which we deal, preach to us." As J. David Greenstone has noted, it was through this virtue embodied in nature that the transcendentalists obtained their characteristic moral certainty through which they were able to discern justice and truth "as if by an 'involuntary perception' whose substance (though not its particular expression) is therefore beyond error." And from this moral certainty, Emerson established a basis for moral community and the imperative for individual action, otherwise referred to as "self-reliance."[5]

Ruskin did exert a significant amount of influence over the Hudson River School's second generation. For example, his comment that water was "the best emblem of unwearied, unconquerable power" likely prompted Church to paint *Niagara, 1857,* one of his most important paintings. Many artists, however, took Ruskin's "truth to nature" too literally, at least initially. Stillman's friend and fellow Ruskinian Sanford Gifford had been perplexed by Ruskin's high praise for Turner, whose paintings had seemed "careless and slovenly." It was only after Gifford met Ruskin in 1851 that he understood the value of Turner's impressionism. As Ruskin explained, Turner "treated his subject as a poet, and not as a topographer; . . . he painted *the impression* the scene made upon his mind, rather than literal scenes." After this meeting, Gifford came to understand this lesson better than many of his contemporaries. Stillman, meanwhile, had not yet reached this understanding, probably because all his formal training as an artist in New York, London, and Paris had taught him otherwise—hence *Putnam's* criticism a year earlier that *The Forest Spring* was too realistic. And when the National Academy of Design's 1855 exhibition began March 12, Stillman showed another highly detailed work, *Study on Upper Saranac Lake,* which he had painted the previous summer.[6]

Stillman and Durand established an office at 237 Broadway, off Park Place. In its first month alone, the *Crayon's* circulation was above 1,200. The first issue of the weekly art journal was issued on January 3, 1855. Not surprisingly, the *Crayon* launched a blistering attack on Leutze's *Washington at Monmouth* in its second issue, dated January 10, 1855. The art of landscape painting was a recurrent theme in the initial issues. One of the journal's most important early features was Asher Durand's "Letters on Landscape Painting," a series of nine letters on the ideals and techniques of painting landscapes. "The Landscape Elements in American Poetry"

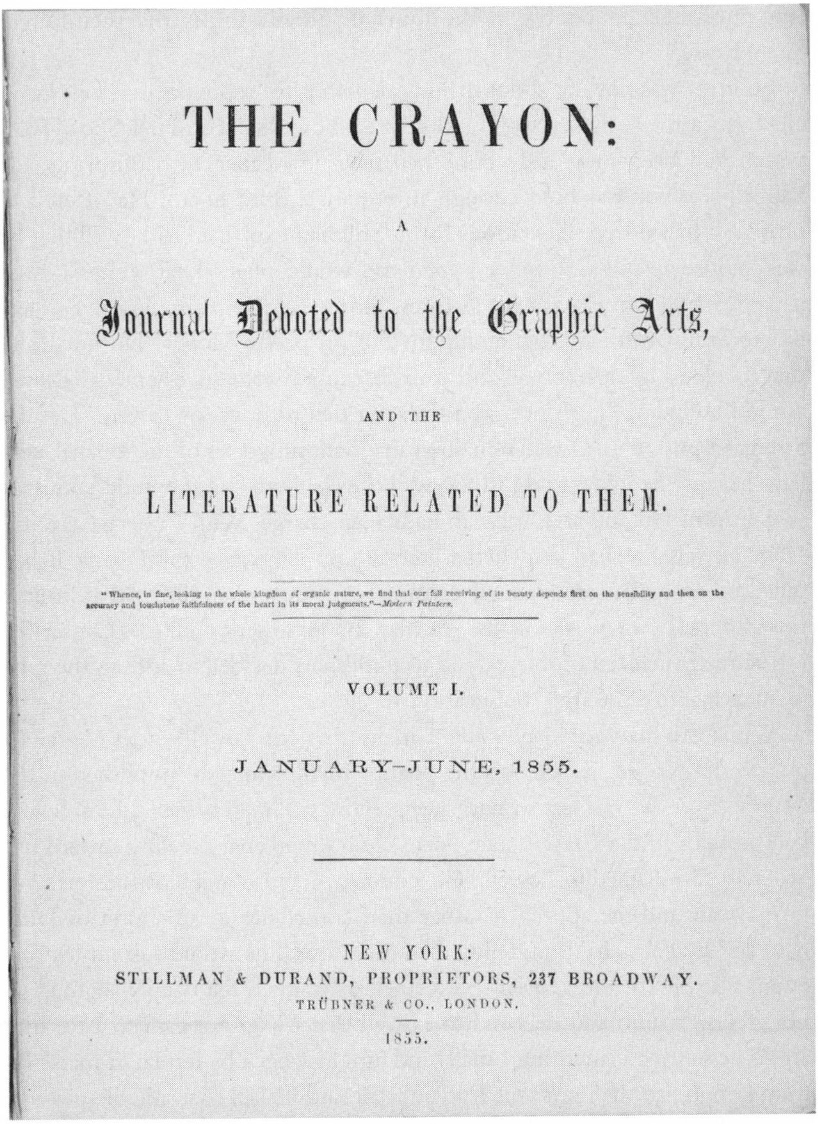

THE CRAYON:

A

Journal Devoted to the Graphic Arts,

AND THE

LITERATURE RELATED TO THEM.

" Whence, in fine, looking to the whole kingdom of organic nature, we find that our full receiving of its beauty depends first on the sensibility and then on the accuracy and touchstone faithfulness of the heart in its moral judgments."—*Modern Painters.*

VOLUME I.

JANUARY–JUNE, 1855.

NEW YORK:
STILLMAN & DURAND, PROPRIETORS, 237 BROADWAY.
TRÜBNER & CO., LONDON.

1855.

FIGURE 7. The *Crayon*, volume 1, 1855. This pioneering art journal, which made its debut on January 3, 1855, was Stillman's key to Boston's leading literary circle, the Saturday Club. His late-1854 efforts to recruit contributors for the *Crayon* brought him into contact with two of the best-known members of the Philosophers' Camp: Lowell and Emerson. Courtesy of Special Collections, Schaffer Library, Union College.

was another landscape-centric series that began in the first issue and was written by Stillman but penned under the pseudonym of G. M. James. Established poets, such as Lowell, Bryant, and Alfred Street, along with several minor poets, also submitted poems that painted landscapes. Stillman, too, published his poetry in the journal initially under the pseudonym W. Sylvester.[7]

Stillman was not shy about making demands for more poems from Lowell. Even after he had revised and printed Lowell's "The First Snow-Fall," which had been previously published in a newspaper with misprints, the admiring editor was bold enough to request a third poem. He offered to provide a half dozen illustrations for it. Stillman explained to Lowell that he was "not so absurd as to order a poem as I would a hat." That winter, Lowell was "fearfully busy" with his lectures, and he frequently apologized in letters to Stillman for not being attentive to his needy editor. "Do not think that I feel less interest in you and yours because I write such scrawls," Lowell assured Stillman. "I am not used to being tied to hours or driven." Despite Stillman's pushiness, Lowell remained an ardent supporter of the journal, perhaps because he understood all too well the challenges of the undertaking of which John Durand and Stillman had taken charge. With Robert Carter in 1843, Lowell, too, had launched a literary journal, named the *Pioneer.* It had failed because of inadequate advertising revenues and an illness that limited Lowell's ability to work on the journal. By summer's end, the *Crayon* fell into similar financial problems, and its publishers decided to address them by turning it into a monthly publication.[8]

While Stillman could be patient in waiting for Lowell's next contribution to the *Crayon,* which was the poem "Invita Minerva" published in the May 30 issue, he was less so with Longfellow. Stillman believed Longfellow had no faith in the *Crayon.* The poet held a "mercenary feeling toward us," Stillman complained to Lowell. The editor believed Longfellow preferred to take a wait-and-see approach rather than contribute to an "inferior journal." But by February Longfellow had told Lowell he would submit his first poem suitable for the *Crayon.* Nevertheless, Stillman felt deeply slighted by Longfellow's snub and declared to Lowell that "I do not care to have him and if he sends me anything I shall send him his check by return of mail." By May, Longfellow had not sent a poem, claiming he lacked a suitable piece to submit. Lowell pressed Longfellow to contribute some verse, not necessarily a long poem, so that "his *name* would be of service to the *Crayon.*"[9] Regardless of cause, Longfellow preferred to keep Stillman at an arm's length.

In addition to using the *Crayon* to advance Lowell's career, Ruskinian principles, and the Pre-Raphaelite movement, Stillman also used it to sound a call to the wild. Starting in mid-March 1855, the *Crayon* took its readers into the Adirondack wilderness. Over the next three months, the journal printed thirteen chapters of a serially published book titled *The Wilderness and Its Waters* by Stillman, under his pseudonym W. Sylvester, and Henry

Brown. Brown was the sculptor at whose home the Brooklyn School met. Stillman, Brown, and a third person had likely embarked on this Adirondack adventure sometime during Stillman's stay at the Johnson cabin on Upper Saranac Lake. Although an editorial note stated that *The Wilderness and Its Waters* was the "joint labor" of "H. K. Brown" and "Mr. Sylvester," Stillman was clearly the author of these travel essays. When introducing the members of the three-person Adirondack party, the author identified himself, saying, "I, the third, was simply and only an Artist."[10]

The *Crayon* serially published this book just as Adirondack travelogues were becoming widely popular. Joel T. Headley, a biographer who had written about Napoleon Bonaparte and George Washington, years earlier had also written the prototypical Adirondack travel book, *The Adirondack, or Life in the Woods*. First published in 1849, the book went through multiple editions over the following three decades. The book had even stoked Stillman's interest in seeing Raquette Lake, which he visited later in 1855. Stillman later that year mentioned in the *Crayon* that he had encountered a man named Mitchell, who was "made famous by Headley." This individual was Mitchell Sabattis of Long Lake, who, as Headley explained in his travel book, was his "old faithful Indian guide."[11] It is possible that Stillman wrote *The Wilderness and Its Waters* in an attempt to emulate Headley's classic travelogue.

The Wilderness and Its Waters followed a September adventure in the Adirondacks and began with a boating excursion across Lower Saranac Lake. Sylvester and Brown had previously camped together in "the woods." They were joined by Brown's former pupil, identified only as "W." Sylvester said he had been to the woods before, "yet from the clamor of city life the change was great." After stopping to fish, the trio worked their way to Upper Saranac Lake, where they came to a shoreline cabin. There they were served a supper of venison, potatoes, corn, and wheat bread by "Mother J." This woman was likely the wife of Mr. Johnson, the alcoholic farmer. She is likely the same "Mother Johnson" who opened a renowned hostelry on Raquette Falls around 1860. She was a former lumber camp cook. Her husband's name was Philander.[12]

Following their stay at the Johnson cabin, the trio ventured into the forest with two guides named Bill and Moodie, the latter likely a member of the famed Moody clan of Adirondack guides. From these guides and others Stillman hired during subsequent summers, he learned how to navigate the central Adirondacks' woods and waters, and where they took him would prove to be significant to his future journeys in the region—either while alone or with friends. The guides took the small party down Upper Saranac Lake, toward the Raquette River, to the Indian Carry. Second-growth pine

FIGURE 8.   Joseph R. Bien, map of Franklin County, 1895. Color map. The story of the Philosophers' Camp and Adirondack Club is primarily set in the southern portion of Franklin County, particularly in Township Twenty-Six, which contains Follensby Pond, and Township Twenty-Seven, which contains Ampersand Pond. This map features the mislabeled "Agassiz Bay" (actually Osprey Bay) at Follensby Pond that Stillman mentioned in his August 1893 *Century Magazine* essay on the Philosophers' Camp. Map from *Atlas of the State of New York* (Julius Bien, 1895). From the Lionel Pincus & Princess Firyal Map Division, New York Public Library.

trees grew along the carry, because, Moodie informed Sylvester, an Indian village had been located there. Sylvester surmised that the path they traveled had "existed for centuries," and "we could not help thinking of the race who had passed away from treading it." The village along the Indian Carry was believed to have been occupied during the summer months by Indian hunting bands. After completing the carry late in the afternoon, the party established a camp at a little pond near Stony Creek Ponds.[13]

After embarking on various fishing and boating excursions, the party visited the cabin of a hunter named Mike. There they also encountered a hermit named Simons, a native of New Hampshire who bore a strong resemblance to a reclusive intellectual whom Stillman late in life described as having "attempted the solution of the problem which so interested me—the effect of solitude on the healthy intellect." Bill assumed Simons was "love cracked, or something." From Mike's cabin, the party went hunting with some dogs, which were used to drive a deer into a lake. The student became the "hero of the hunt" by shooting a buck and a "noble fat doe." Toward the end of their journey, Sylvester claimed he had "no desire to leave the wilderness," but he wished he had brought some dried fruit to break the monotony of a diet of fish, dry bread, and fowl. Eventually the party decided to head home "stopping on the way to fish as much as we pleased."[14]

According to Sylvester, the purpose of this trip to "the outer edge of civilization" was to find a reprieve from city life. They sought to "enjoy the solitude without the intrusion of uncongenialities" and "to breathe in, unmingled, the spirit of silence and loneliness that reigned around, unreminded of the world we had left by anything *belonging* to it." It was with *The Wilderness and Its Waters* that Stillman began refining the writing style that he would repeatedly employ in his Adirondack prose. Particularly, he began experimenting with the themes and terminology (e.g., "primeval forest," "Lethean") that would play into his later writings on the Philosophers' Camp. He may have borrowed the phrase the "forest primeval" from the opening line of Longfellow's "Evangeline: A Tale of Acadie." With the 1855 travel series he also painted the Adirondacks as a dream world. In future years, this dream world would evolve into a "Paradise" or "Eden." Unfortunately, *The Wilderness and Its Waters* identified few specific places by name. The lake on which the story begins, for example, is identifiable by Sylvester's clue: "The Lake, the lower one of a chain of three, by the further link of which we should stop that night, narrowed to a 'river,' as hunters call it—the connection between the lakes." Commenting to the editors of the *Crayon* on the travel series, Asher Durand said he had trouble obtaining directions "to these desirable localities."[15]

❦ CHAPTER 4

"Adieu to the World"

In Cambridge, Lowell's lectures had been so well received that they earned him an offer from Harvard to serve as the college's professor of modern languages, a position from which Longfellow planned to retire. After completing the Lowell Institute series, Lowell spent much of March and April on a lecture tour in western New York and Illinois. Shortly after he returned from the lecture circuit, which he loathed, the poet reconnected with Stillman. In mid-May, the poet assured his editor he had read all the back issues of the *Crayon* and that he liked what he read in it. "I am proud to have made such a friend," Lowell told Stillman.[1] By this time, the journal had published the first eight chapters of *The Wilderness and Its Waters,* which might have piqued Lowell's interest in the Adirondacks.

Needing to refine his understanding of foreign languages for his post at Harvard, particularly German and Spanish, Lowell planned to study abroad for a year. He was scheduled to set sail for Europe in June. On May 10 he invited Stillman to Elmwood "as soon as we have a leaf or two" and volunteered to help his editor while "on the other side" of the Atlantic. Lowell was to sail to Europe alone. He would leave Mabel in the care of Frances Dunlap, a governess from a once-wealthy family in Portland, Maine. While Lowell was away, Dunlap was to care for Mabel at the Cambridge home of Estes and Lois Howe. Lois was the oldest of Maria's three sisters, and Estes Howe was a native of Northampton in central Massachusetts. After graduating from

Harvard Medical School in 1835, he had practiced medicine in Cincinnati and Pomeroy, Ohio. When his first wife died in 1843, he returned to Cambridge and married Lois in 1848.[2]

The relationship between Lowell and Howe went back years. In the 1840s, the two men, along with Robert Carter and John Holmes (the witty and ever-affable younger brother of Cambridge's other beloved poet, Oliver Wendell Holmes) had founded the Whist Club. The members of the club regularly met on Friday nights at each other's homes. On the night before Lowell left Boston, many Whist Club members, along with other prominent intellectuals, gave Lowell a farewell dinner at the Revere House in Boston. Among those in attendance were Emerson, Longfellow, Norton, John Holmes and his brother, Tom Appleton, and Agassiz, the eminent Harvard scientist. Stillman subsequently organized another farewell dinner for Lowell in New York. At this dinner, along with Stillman and Lowell, were Massachusetts senator Charles Sumner, the journalist and *Crayon* contributor Bayard Taylor, either the junior or senior Durand, and Bryant.[3]

Although the dinner mended the rift between Lowell and Bryant, which the former had opened by insulting the latter in *A Fable,* it also opened one between Stillman and Lowell. Shortly after Lowell sailed away on June 4, Stillman wrote to him profusely apologizing for "noticing you as a correspondent of the Crayon." It is not clear whether Stillman had just assumed Lowell would furnish the journal with writings from abroad or whether he had prematurely made a public announcement saying as much. Such an assumption would not be entirely unjustified given that Lowell a month earlier had offered his assistance while abroad. However, it is possible that Lowell had made this offer not at first realizing how busy he would be with his own studies. Rather than go back on a promise, he may have become defensive toward Stillman when pressed for a pledge to provide foreign correspondence. Stillman apologetically explained that his work for the journal had skewed his thinking. The journal had become "much a thing of the soul," he said, and "I think only how I shall serve it."[4] Lowell, while abroad, appears to have adopted a strategy of avoidance toward his editor. About four long months passed before Stillman heard again, or at least anything noteworthy, from Lowell, and during that time the artist felt abandoned by the poet. Bitterness now tainted their friendship.

In Lowell's absence, a scorned and anxious Stillman turned to the same person who had consoled Lowell after the death of his wife: Charles Eliot Norton. Norton was only seven months older than Stillman. By the spring of 1855, he was a twenty-seven-year-old rising intellectual star. The lucrative mercantile-importation business that had been run by his grandfather,

Samuel Eliot, enabled Norton, a member of Harvard's class of 1846, to devote himself to cultural and social pursuits. By 1853, he had launched his literary career by publishing his first two books: *Five Christmas Hymns,* of which he was an anonymous editor, and *Considerations on Some Recent Social Theories,* which he wrote. However, Norton was embraced by his contemporaries, such as Lowell and Ruskin, as much for his heart as for his mind. According to the British historian Frederic Harrison, Norton's "genius" rested in his ability to combine temperaments that were "at once critical and yet appreciative" and "incise and enthusiastic."[5]

Stillman, too, quickly fell under the influence of Norton's deep sympathies. Faith was one subject that initially strengthened their bonds. Growing up in Schenectady, Stillman had received what he called a "Puritan education," and he had attended a Seventh-Day Baptist church. As work for the *Crayon* became more physically trying and its success more uncertain, Stillman leaned more heavily on his faith and believed God was guiding him to success. He was tempted to abandon the *Crayon,* but he remained convinced that art was "a holy thing" and that he was a competent artist divinely charged to teach "not only by works [but] by words."[6]

A fiery sunset flashed across the New York City skyline. It was two days before Independence Day 1855. Stillman sat on his housetop and gazed on the beautiful scene. (He was likely atop his brother Thomas's home on Seventh Street.) More and more, a desire arose within him to paint such a sunset. The desire made him feel like an artist, and it was a feeling that depressed him as much as it pleased him, because he was now a journalist and not an artist. When he went back inside, he wrote to Norton and declared he should never have traded his unsuccessful career as a painter for a literary occupation. Instead, he should have been "hastening onto establish a new school of Art." Stillman surmised that he had lacked faith and "faltered like the wanderers in the wilderness when the promised land was about to be opened." Just two months earlier, the National Academy had named him an associate. However, he did not show any works at the academy's next exhibition in spring 1856—marking his first failure to exhibit in the annual event in two years.[7]

To Stillman, it increasingly looked as though the *Crayon* would fail by the end of 1855. The decision of Durand and Stillman to fund the journal primarily through subscription revenues proved to be disastrous. Publishers had convinced the two to print their advertisements free of charge, and without revenues from those ads the journal became unprofitable. Even if the *Crayon* could outlive the year, Stillman looked forward to "leav[ing] it when it is strong enough" or when he could find someone else to whom he could hand over his share in it. The *Crayon* was not all that was failing, however. Stillman's health was also growing worse. By summer, he felt "wretched" and weak, though it is not clear whether these were symptoms of overwork, anxiety, or both.[8]

Burned-out, Stillman began his summer vacation in early July. He first retreated to Plainfield, New Jersey, where some of his family, including his brother Charles, a doctor, lived. Next, Stillman made a short visit to Norton at his Newport home. Through this visit Norton left an even greater impression on Stillman, and it sealed what was to become a lifelong friendship. The warm hospitality he found in Norton's home enlivened Stillman. Meanwhile, the aspiration and agony Norton found in Stillman similarly moved the ever-sympathetic Norton. "I have never known anyone more earnest and faithful in his desire and search for spiritual improvement," Norton later told Lowell. "His [Stillman's] character is one of very marked individuality. It is too intense, too self-introverted to be happy, and the circumstances of his life have been so sad as to make it one long suffering."[9]

Before returning to Plainfield, Stillman gave Norton a painting of the wilderness that had received the praise of Asher Durand. In mid-August, Stillman planned to join Durand in New Hampshire and visit "artistically unexplored sections" in the northern part of the state, probably around North Conway. Stillman asked Norton to join him on this trip, but the adventurous artist canceled the journey four days after this invitation went out when he became ill. "I feel . . . just fit to lie down and die," Stillman told Norton. However, the painter hoped to be well enough by mid-September to take Norton to the place where the gifted wilderness picture had been painted, probably in the Adirondacks.[10]

The prospect of going to the Adirondacks with Norton excited Stillman. There he hoped Norton would see him in his own "kingdom," where he was "myself supreme." However, Norton's constitution was even frailer than Stillman's. For unknown reasons, his health constantly teetered between strength and weakness. In July, he had physically collapsed while in Cambridge and retreated to his Newport home. Aware of Norton's frail health, Stillman promised the journey would not be overly strenuous, with the hardest part being a day's stage ride through a picturesque wilderness. Once they were in the Saranacs, the longest walk they would take would be no more than a mile and a half. Stillman swore he would care for Norton "as if you were my own child." Stillman also held out the hope that Norton could benefit from the wilderness's therapeutic effects. All it would take would be two days in the Adirondacks to be cured of any "troubles and annoyances" and be left with the "most delectable state of serenity," the painter claimed.[11]

Stillman was also looking to purchase property in the Adirondacks. On August 31 he told Norton he expected within a week to be in possession of the title to the land on which he planned to build a cabin, though it is not clear whether this acquisition was ever finalized. The cabin would be large enough to house eight to twelve guests. There they could "be a part from all the world else."[12] The mention of this land acquisition represents the earliest disclosure of Stillman's plan to organize large camping parties in the Adirondacks. However, two more years would pass before he finally led a group of his Boston-area friends to the Adirondacks, and almost five years would pass before his dream of building a cabin in the wilderness was realized.

Norton declined Stillman's invitation to go camping in the Adirondacks, probably on account of his illness. Instead of venturing into the wilderness, in October he sailed for Europe with his mother and two sisters. While Norton's cancellation disappointed Stillman, it did not upset the artist nearly as much as Lowell's continued silence. Looking back on his interactions with Lowell, Stillman increasingly became self-conscious. He felt as though he had "bored" and "annoyed" Lowell and "intruded myself on him." He asked Norton, "What was I to him?" Stillman believed he had held Lowell in too high regard, but he could not see himself as an equal to the poet, partly because he was not "a [N]ew England man." Indeed, a sense of shame pervaded Stillman's memory of his relationship with Lowell, and the painter vowed to Norton that "it is all gone though and I will never seek to renew my acquaintance with him [Lowell]." However, Stillman's embarrassment was not limited to Lowell. He even confessed to being too ashamed of his poor home in Plainfield to invite Norton to New Jersey to talk and eat peaches. As always, Norton sympathized with Stillman. In September, Norton encouraged Lowell to reach out to the disheartened artist. "He needs inspiriting, and I know nothing which would do him more good than to receive a letter from you," Norton wrote to Lowell. "I hope you have already written him; if not pray write to him soon."[13]

As Stillman's comments about Lowell show, the artist remained keenly aware of his humble roots in Schenectady, even as he became more accepted in Boston's wealthy intellectual class. Unlike most of the men to whom Lowell introduced Stillman, the painter had graduated from Union College, not the more prestigious Harvard. Longfellow's reluctance to contribute to the *Crayon,* coupled with Lowell's long silence, further piqued this sense of inferiority. It was futile, Stillman thought, to try to rise above his socioeconomic status. This belief, coupled with low self-esteem, flagging career prospects, illness, and an ever-growing debt load, severely limited Stillman's ability to take advantage of the impressive social network he had established through the *Crayon*. He was not a social climber, and by acting as the antithesis of an arriviste, he was not viewed as a threat to the men in the literary circle into which he was then entering.

On September 24, Stillman boarded a barge at a wharf in New York. The sun was just starting to set, and the hint of an autumn chill was in the air. A steamer swung the barge into the Hudson River and towed it through a maze of sloops and schooners. The artist's Adirondack vacation was under way. Although Norton could not join Stillman on this trip, he did not travel alone. Joining him on this journey was a man identified only as "R." They quietly floated past the moonlit Palisades, and by the next day the barge docked at Newburgh, where they stayed for a day.[14]

From Newburgh, Stillman sent to the *Crayon* a letter detailing the first stage of his journey to New York's northern wilderness, and the journal printed this "editorial correspondence" in its October 3 issue. Over the course of two months, through December 5, the journal published several of Stillman's letters. In these letters, Stillman further detailed how he became intimately acquainted with the lakes and rivers around Follensby Pond. In these letters he did not withhold the names of the places he visited, whereas they remained unidentified in his serially published book. Unlike *The Wilderness and Its Waters* series, these letters were not published under his pseudonym W. Sylvester. They show Stillman's early encounters with men such as the Lower Saranac Lake hotelier William F. Martin and his younger brother Stephen C. Martin, who both became important players in the story of the Philosophers' Camp. In many regards, this series serves as a prequel to that event in 1858. Incorporating the theme of escapism that he worked into *The Wilderness and Its Waters,* Stillman ended his second letter from Saranac Lake by saying that the next day they would row up the lakes and bid "adieu to the world for some week or ten days."[15]

At this time, Stillman ventured deep into a swath of wilderness in the heart of the Adirondacks. The Raquette River runs through the region to Long Lake, which is actually a widened river. More than fifty lakes and ponds are found in the region, including sizable bodies of water such as Big Tupper Lake, Upper Saranac Lake, Long Lake, and Follensby Pond. To the east lies a more rugged section of wilderness that includes Mount Alford, Ampersand Mountain, Mount Seward, and Mount Seymour. Disappointment greeted Stillman when he arrived at Martin's Hotel (also referred to as Martin's Landing) on Lower Saranac Lake. The guide he wanted to hire was out on another job, so Stillman and R. decided to wait for him. Not wanting to keep his guests sitting around, the hotel's owner, William Martin, asked the pair to join him on a hunting trip in which dogs were used to drive deer into the lake. Martin about four years earlier had built his hotel near the northeastern shore of the lake, about a mile from the center of the Village of Saranac Lake. The L-shaped building became the region's first hotel that catered specifically to affluent sportsmen and tourists, making it a hub for the central Adirondacks guide industry. Martin was said to be "one of the few men in the world who seemed to 'know how to keep a hotel.'" His hotel, which doubled as the headquarters of the Long Lake guides network, featured accommodations for families and sporting parties. He kept his tables "abundantly provided with necessities" and "luxuries of diet." There were trout and venison "ad libitum."[16]

Martin was born in 1823, just south of the New York-Canadian border in Westville, Franklin County. From there the Martin family had relocated to a farm sixteen miles south in Bangor, but Martin and his two younger brothers later moved to the Adirondacks. In 1836, the Adirondacks entered what the guide and writer Charles Brumley has called the region's "golden years," which ran to 1865. It was during this period that the Adirondack guiding tradition began. Brumley has traced the roots of this tradition to three guides, all of whom had been born in 1816. They included Orson "Old Man" Phelps, Bill Nye, and Alvah Dunning. Like most Adirondack males, they likely began guiding as teenagers sometime in the 1830s. They primarily took sportsmen on hunting and fishing trips, using guide boats to take them to remote locations where game and fish were plentiful. These early guides were loosely associated and tended to not to solicit customers from places outside their geographic region, such as Blue Mountain Lake, Saranac Lake, or Long Lake. It was in the 1840s that the demand for guides significantly increased, in part as a result of the publicity the Adirondacks had received in the *Spirit of the Times,* a New York City sporting newspaper.[17]

Lower Saranac Lake was defined by deep bays and rocky points and surrounding pristine forests. When Stillman arrived there in late September 1855, the first autumn tints were showing. Contrasting the foliage's golden greens and bright yellows was the green of towering pine trees that dotted the landscape. Offsetting the beautiful autumn colors, however, was the lake's "disfigurement." For at least the past six years, lumbermen had been cutting down many of the lake's oldest pines. Those that remained standing left a marked impression on Stillman. They appeared to him the "high-minded remnant of a lofty race supplanted by an ignoble breed, upon whom he looks down in sorrow and in pride." Most of the lake's islands had been burned over, along with large mainland tracts. Dead, blackened trees haunted the shoreline. William Martin blamed the carnage on "careless hunters."[18]

On October 1, Stillman and R. left Martin's in two boats paddled by two guides. R.'s guide was an approximately twenty-five-year-old quiet and deferential man with a light mustache and beard. His name was Straw, though he also went by Bill. Stillman took with him Stephen C. Martin, an athletic outdoorsman who was six months the artist's senior. He was tall like Stillman, standing about six feet, with curly hair, blue eyes, and a dimple "half hidden in the edge of his beard." His reputation for being able to whip or throw any man in Franklin and St. Lawrence counties did not detract from his overall good nature and likability. Stillman claimed he and "Steve" were "old acquaintances" who got along together "capitally." Stephen Martin lived in a cabin along the mile-long Indian Carry, where the party would later rest for a night.[19]

Just as the hired men had done the previous summer, Straw and Martin, through the execution of their guide duties, equipped Stillman with a more intimate knowledge of the region that would later enable him to serve as an Adirondack guide to others. The party rowed and carried their way across the Saranac lakes, stopping at the hotel run by Virgil C. Bartlett. Bartlett had established his Sportsmen's Home (commonly known as Bartlett's) in the tract separating Middle Saranac Lake from Upper Saranac Lake. They trekked down the Indian Carry to Stony Creek Ponds. They followed Stony Creek three miles to the dark, deep, and fast-moving Raquette River. Stillman noted seeing some "noble old pines" standing near the river's entrance, but a few miles farther downstream areas of cut woods and a few cabins appeared. Stillman and his companion followed the river in the rain to Raquette Pond. After an unpleasant overnight stay at a Raquette Pond shanty, a sick and tired R. returned to Martin's with Straw, leaving Stillman to roam the wilderness with Stephen Martin. The pair then rowed to Big Tupper Lake, which greatly impressed the painter. He deemed the mountain lying on the lake's eastern side "the most picturesque peak in this vicinity." Stillman was equally impressed by Bog River Falls, which falls fifteen feet over a granite ledge at Big Tupper Lake. The two visited Mr. Jenkins's complex of cabins a half-mile into the woods from the falls.[20]

Jenkins's complex consisted of a main cabin, a buttery, a lodging house, a barn, a boat shop, and a blacksmith shop. With the weather still inclement, Stillman took out a sketch pad and drew the mountain peaks viewed from Jenkins's complex at the head of a deep bay. Prior to embarking for Raquette Lake, while surveying an island with Jenkins, Stillman reluctantly shot and killed a massive buck as it swam across a lake. Despite being an excellent marksman and experienced outdoorsman, up until this point, he had yet to acquire a taste for hunting. This deer was the first he had ever killed. His sympathies ran strong for animals, and while the killing left him feeling uneasy, the sight of its trophy antlers filled him with a pride that quelled his misgivings.[21]

It was a long journey to Raquette Lake, and the lake seemed unimpressive to Stillman. "This lake is monotonous and uninteresting in its general appearance compared with the others," he told the *Crayon*'s readers. After a brief tour of the lake, Stillman and his guide headed back to Bartlett's. There they picked up a "Raquette man," who bore a strong resemblance to Stillman's Upper Saranac Lake host from the previous summer, Mr. Johnson. Unknown to Stillman and Martin when they picked up the man, he was already drunk. When they reached the falls by the carry and attempted to get out of the boat, the man "began to feel reckless and merry." He sang, beat time with his feet, and begged for more whiskey. Despite the man's drunken antics on the boat, which had Stillman wanting to knock him atop the head with an oar, they arrived late at night at Martin's Hotel. Stillman called this last leg of the trip with the drunk passenger "exciting in the extreme, and a more fearful ride than I ever before took." Years later Stillman claimed he had encountered Johnson during the summer following the summer he lodged at his Upper Saranac Lake cabin in 1854. Johnson was "drunk as ever," and when Stillman asked him about the bet they had made the previous year that Johnson would never drink again, the man "jeered and cheered and joked with drunken cunning."[22]

On October 14, three days after returning to Martin's, Stillman headed back to New York. That same day, Lowell wrote to the artist from Dresden, breaking his long silence, perhaps under Norton's influence. Lowell assured him that he had not forgotten the artist and explained that he had failed to write sooner because he lacked anything to contribute to the *Crayon*. Even though Stillman had sworn to Norton that he would never rekindle his relationship with Lowell, the artist had sent a few letters to him after they parted in June. Only Lowell, seemingly oblivious to the rift that had arisen between himself and Stillman, asked "why so short? One would think you were writing across Broadway instead of the Atlantic." Lowell promised to submit to the *Crayon* an account of his visit to Retzsch. By mid-December Stillman had not received it, and he told the poet not to bother writing the piece. Nevertheless, the man who would soon enable Stillman to take Boston's luminaries to the Adirondacks was back in his life. "Write me, when you are not over-worked," Lowell said.[23]

✿ CHAPTER 5

The Artist Reborn

A snowy afternoon afforded Stillman the opportunity to break from his work. It was October 23, 1856. He was in North Conway, New Hampshire, then a popular destination for America's landscape painters, such as Asher Durand, John Kensett, and Daniel Huntington.[1] Unable to paint, Stillman that day picked up his pen and wrote letters to his brother, John Durand, Norton, and Lowell. He updated them on what seemed to him to be his new life. During the spring, overwork for the *Crayon* had taken its toll on Stillman's mental and physical health. But he felt much stronger standing in the White Mountains' autumn air. He was an artist again.

Prior to returning to his painting career, Stillman had taken steps to permanently leave the *Crayon*. The July 1856 issue of the monthly journal announced Stillman's resignation due to continued ill health. His resignation note was dated June 1. Earlier in March, he had complained about being "weighed down with all kinds of anxieties," and being "reduced to a state where vigorous action . . . was only to be induced by stimulants." John Durand assured *Crayon* readers that he planned "no change of purpose" for the publication. However, Stillman held some doubts about Durand's competencies as editor and publisher. Stillman informed his former partner that some articles were being laughed at, and Durand was deluding himself in believing Norton, Lowell, Huntington, and others would ally themselves with "such rubbish."[2]

With the *Crayon* behind him, Stillman traded his pen for a brush, and after a nearly two-year hiatus returned to painting full-time. For six weeks he worked on a painting of a brook scene. Before going to North Conway, Stillman had spent three weeks camping in the Adirondacks. However, he deemed the White Mountains more important to his return to painting, and so he spent over three months there. In his last dispatch to the *Crayon* from Martin's Hotel the previous autumn, Stillman had noted that the Adirondacks, except for their "grand monotony and impressiveness," paled in comparison with the White Mountains' "Alpine sublimity." Instead of finding scenes worth painting in the Adirondack Mountains, he said the artist could turn to them for the silence and dreaminess of the wilderness that produced a "lulling, harmonizing effect on the mind."[3]

The *Crayon* was not Stillman's only loss in 1856. At some time that year, Stillman had pursued a romantic relationship with a fellow Ruskinian and reader of the *Crayon*. Her name is not known. This affair amounted to a "skirmish with Cupid" and Stillman's "first real passion" but nothing more. The mother of the woman Stillman admired had objected to the relationship, and it ended there. Before separating from this unnamed woman, Stillman had promised to paint her a picture of a pine—a tree that had "a most mystic influence" on him. To Stillman, the pine was a symbol. It rose majestically over its forest kingdom, despite being "uncourtly and uncouth." Feeling just as unrefined and awkward as the pine, Stillman admired the tree's ability to overcome its shortcomings. The painting was perhaps the most personal picture he had produced up to that point. It had been "painted in love and for love," but he finished it after the relationship ended. Not willing to give the painting to the woman who had broken his heart, Stillman instead offered it to Lowell.[4]

One of Stillman's brothers had visited him in New Hampshire. A newlywed couple, Amos Binney and Nancy Talbot Clark, also encountered Stillman in the White Mountains that autumn. Clark was from Sharon, Massachusetts, and in 1852 she became the first woman to graduate from Western Reserve College's Cleveland Medical College. (She was also the second woman to ever receive a medical degree from an accredited, coeducational medical school.) She had met Binney aboard a steamer while traveling to Paris, and a romance blossomed between them. Binney was the son of Dr. Amos Binney, a prominent Boston businessman who had received his medical degree from Harvard in 1826, though he never practiced medicine. The junior Binney had entered Harvard in 1847, but a year later he studied abroad with a professor. He married his first wife in November 1851, but she died of consumption less than three years later. Binney married Clark on July 6,

1856, in Boston. It was Clark's second marriage too, as her first husband, a Boston apothecary, had left her a widow.[5]

When the Binneys came to North Conway in late autumn, Binney was twenty-six years old and his wife was thirty. In Clark, Stillman found a confidante who could sympathize with his heartbreak over the relationship forbidden by his lover's mother. Clark's "tact and knowledge of human nature," Stillman said late in life, "befriended me profoundly." Before leaving New Hampshire, Binney commissioned Stillman to paint two pictures. He also invited Stillman to produce these works while staying at his home near Boston. The commissions meant Stillman was to come to Boston at a pivotal time in the city's literary history. Lowell was back in Cambridge, and in the autumn he began teaching at Harvard. More important, a new social circle consisting of Lowell and his eminent friends started taking a more definitive shape in Boston. However, Lowell returned to Cambridge even graver and sadder than he left. Not wanting to return to Elmwood, with its memories of a happier life with his late wife, he moved in with the Howe family. Estes and Lois Howe had housed Lowell's daughter, Mabel, and her governess, Francis Dunlap, while the professor was in Europe.[6]

Stillman in late September learned of Lowell's return to Cambridge. He immediately wrote to Lowell and said he expected to see him during the winter while he was working in Boston, presumably on Binney's commissions. By mid-October, Stillman still had heard little from Lowell, suggesting that either the rift in their friendship had not mended or the new professor was too busy or depressed to write. Stillman wrote to Lowell to assure him that he was no longer the clingy young artist who had bidden him farewell sixteen months earlier in New York. He again apologized for the "rubbish" he had sent during that period. "You won't know me when you see me— any more than I shall you," the painter said. Stillman informed Lowell of his return to painting and promised to "glorify Cambridge" in a year or two when his skills were more developed.[7]

It is not clear when Stillman arrived at the Binney household. A letter by Stillman to Lowell places the artist in New York on February 28, and he likely stayed with the Binneys not long after April 26. Sometime that winter Stillman called on Lowell, though their reunion was not a joyful one. Lowell, overwhelmed by his lectures, had been anything but "jolly and companionable," so much so that he felt compelled to apologize to Stillman weeks later. As consolation, the professor promised to be better company for the artist's next visit in spring. However, toward the end of April, Stillman was eager to leave Boston. In an April 26 letter to a brother, probably Thomas, Stillman directed him to send a telegram to Binney saying, "Tell Wm to come home immediately." Stillman did not explain why such a telegraph was necessary. The fact that Stillman needed to recruit his brother to create a ruse so he could return to New York City suggests his stay with the Binneys was not entirely pleasant. At the least, Stillman later claimed to have completed Binney's commissions. It is also possible that he wanted to return to New York to prepare for the National Academy's 1857 exhibition, which began on May 18.[8]

Stillman returned to New York, where he met his brother. He also made his largest showing at the National Academy's annual exhibition, where six of his works were on display. Two of these paintings were of Kearsarge Brook in North Conway, and one or two more were likely inspired by the Adirondacks. They included *View on Tupper Lake, Adirondack Wilds,* and *Night-Fall in the Wilderness.* Another painting from his New Hampshire expedition was *Mount Chocorua* (1856), which was of a summit southwest of North Conway. This painting was not displayed in the 1857 exhibition. Still on the prowl for new landscapes, Stillman embarked on a painting expedition in South Manchester, Connecticut, shortly after the exhibition began. He was more than $3,000 in debt, and his health was again failing him, though it had improved since he left New York. He complained to a brother of being "unfit for work or hard thinking of any kind" and suffering from digestive problems and anxiety. With Stillman's future uncertain, stress appears to have exacerbated his anxiety disorder. He planned to retreat to the Adirondacks by late June.[9]

By the middle of the spring of 1857, Lowell became far more sociable. On May 28, he journeyed to Boston with some Cambridge friends, including Longfellow; Benjamin Peirce, a Harvard mathematics professor; Cornelius C. Felton, a Harvard Greek literature professor; and Louis Agassiz, the Swiss zoology and geology professor at Harvard. For the past few years, some members of this group of Cambridge intellectuals had been regularly traveling to Boston to dine with other poets, scientists, lawyers, and intellectuals from the city and its outlying communities. It was a tradition that had been in the works since 1849, when Emerson and Samuel Gray Ward, a young banker, began strategizing for the creation of a formal club.[10]

In the 1850s, Boston and New York City were teaming with social clubs similar to the one Emerson and Ward had been looking to form. Over the past century, clubs had been increasing in size and influence. Societies of all sorts—historical, scientific, literary, philosophical—emerged. Sports clubs, for everything from fishing to cricket, were especially popular. Not all of these clubs were exclusive, but leadership positions were usually reserved for individuals with great wealth or local prominence. Among the nonsporting clubs, wining, dining, and conversation were often what brought these men together. One such early dining club in Boston was the Wednesday Evening Club, which was founded in 1777. In Concord, out of the Committee of Safety of the Revolution grew the Social Circle. Emerson joined the Social Circle in 1840 and Hoar joined a year later.[11]

By the 1830s, some clubs had become increasingly exclusive as the aging wealthy elites attempted to stifle the advance of newcomers and reformers into high society. Such was the case with New York's Union Club, which was formed in 1836. Meanwhile, clubs such as the Sketch Club in New York and its successor, the Century Club, approached social change with less isolationism. Bryant in 1829 cofounded this club, which initially consisted of artists but later expanded to include men from other professions with artistic interests. Stuart M. Blumin has noted that the type of club Emerson and Ward went on to form was similar to the Sketch Club in that the Boston club "associated old and new men of wealth with the city's intellectual and literary leaders."[12]

Emerson had acquired a taste for social organizations and the spirited conversations they produced while in England in 1847 and 1848. Initially he had wanted a large club, but Ward convinced him a much smaller club would be more favorable. Ward was the Boston agent for Baring Brothers & Co., a major British banking firm that had not only provided the United States with credit during the War of 1812 but also helped finance the Louisiana Purchase in 1803. In 1849, Emerson and Ward began suggesting to each other the names of several men they wanted to see in their club. Those names included Lowell, Longfellow, Hoar, and Agassiz, as well as Thomas G. ("Tom") Appleton, a writer and Longfellow's brother-in-law, and Edward Bangs, a Boston attorney. During the early 1850s, Emerson and his friends held monthly dinner parties in Boston, usually at the Albion Hotel on Tremont Street. Sometime during Lowell's time abroad in late 1855 or early 1856, these informal gatherings evolved into a formal club, with a membership that initially totaled fourteen. They met on the last Saturday of each month, an arrangement that gave the group its name, the Saturday Club. The Albion dinners were later moved to the second floor of Parker's Hotel, located on School Street, which had opened in October 1955.[13]

For the most part, the club's members were literary men. No single ideology or interest brought them together on Saturdays. Richard Dana, for example, had been unfamiliar with Emerson's transcendentalism when he attended one of the club's dinners in 1855, and he never bothered to learn much more about the philosophy. By spring 1857, the Saturday get-togethers at Parker's tended to run for six hours, from three o'clock in the afternoon to nine o'clock at night. On the May afternoon of the twenty-eighth, Lowell and his party walked into Parker's to meet the other members of this club. In all, at least fourteen people were present at the hotel that afternoon. They included Emerson; Ward; Oliver Wendell Holmes; John S. Dwight, a music critic; Otto Dresel, a pianist and composer; John Lothrop Motley, the famed historian; and Edwin P. Whipple, a literary critic. Also in attendance were Dana, George S. Hillard, and Horatio Woodman, all three of whom were lawyers. At this point, Dresel, Felton, Holmes, and Hillard were "strangers" to the club, according to Emerson.[14]

Woodman was among the least eminent yet most integral to these club meetings. It was this red-haired bachelor and member of the Suffolk Bar who organized and managed the early dinner parties at the Albion and later at Parker's. He was a Maine native who had a strong fondness for the company of reputable men and an uncanny ability to unite them. The mathematician and astronomer Benjamin Gould called him "a genius broker." The last-Saturday tradition had actually begun with Woodman, who regularly encountered Emerson at the Old Corner Bookstore at the intersection of School and Washington Streets. After meeting there, the two dined at the Albion or Parker's. The club had no written rules and required a unanimous vote among its membership to admit new members. Members paid for their meals, and guests were permitted but paid for at the expense of whoever had invited them.[15]

Deviating from tradition slightly, the club's May 1857 dinner party did not fall on a Saturday. Instead the meeting had been pushed up to a rainy Wednesday to coincide with the fiftieth birthday of Agassiz, the world-renowned Swiss scientist. He was a squarely built, broad-shouldered, and somewhat pudgy man with chestnut hair. To Bostonians, the Saturday Club was actually "Agassiz's Club." Agassiz had been living in the United States since October 1846. He was then only thirty-nine years old and already one of the world's leading scientific experts on ichthyology, paleontology, and glacial movement. He had made his mark on European science at twenty-one years of age in 1828 through the publishing of his first book, which cataloged Brazilian fish. Five years later, he debuted the first installment of his groundbreaking "Research on Fossil Fish," which was fully published by 1843. However, Agassiz's crowning achievement as a young European scientist came in 1837, when he concluded that gigantic sheets of ice blanketed parts of the world extending from the North Pole to the Mediterranean and Caspian Seas. His Ice Age theory transformed the era's understanding of the earth's animal and plant life and land formations.[16]

Figure 9. Unidentified artist, *Louis Agassiz* (1807–73), circa 1860–73. Albumen silver print, 3-15/16 × 2-3/8 in. Agassiz was a prominent Swiss scientist who came to America in 1846 to study the New World's natural history. He ended up staying permanently in Cambridge, anchored by a position at Harvard, where he taught zoology and geology. He was a creationist whose beliefs significantly influenced the sciences in America. His populist appeal enabled him to pursue ambitious projects such as the creation of the Museum of Comparative Zoology at Harvard, where he taught, and the National Academy of Sciences. Harvard Art Museums/Fogg Museum, transfer from Special Collections, Fine Arts Library, Harvard College Library, 2010.94. Photo: Imaging Department © President and Fellows of Harvard College.

Initially, Agassiz had traveled to the United States to lecture and learn as much as possible during a summer about the natural history of the New World, particularly its fish. He was a rare figure who popularized the sciences among the general public, and thousands of Bostonians came out to hear his lecture series at the Lowell Institute, titled the "Plan of Creation in the Animal Kingdom." Reluctant to see Agassiz return to Switzerland, Harvard in the autumn of 1847 named him a professor of geology and zoology at its new Lawrence Scientific School. He started teaching at the college the following year and rented a house on Oxford Street, near Harvard Yard, making him a neighbor of Longfellow, Peirce, and Felton. After deciding to stay in America, Agassiz made his first of many trips to the South. It had been only a year earlier in Philadelphia that he had seen a black man for the first time. Applying his creationist beliefs to blacks, he had concluded that they did not share the same origin as whites and that both were distinct species. Southerners seized on Agassiz's racist beliefs to scientifically justify the institution of slavery, which he abhorred and said "might one day cause the ruin of the United States." While the Agassiz biographer Edward Lurie in 1955 asserted that the scientist had unwittingly or naively allowed Southerners to hijack his views on the origins of blacks, Christoph Irmscher, another Agassiz biographer, claimed in 2013 that the scientist's "obsessive" writings on the topic suggest he played a less innocent role in arming slaveholding interests with intellectual arguments.[17]

Agassiz had a passion for ichthyology, the branch of zoology devoted to the study of fish. He had spent much of the summer of 1848 studying the animals and vegetation of Lake Superior. His *Lake Superior,* cowritten with J. Elliot Cabot, published two years later, contained an extensive analysis of the lake's freshwater fish. In 1853, he set the goal of writing the definitive study of all the freshwater fish that inhabited the nation's inland streams, lakes, and rivers. To accomplish this goal he sent out hundreds of circulars calling on people throughout the country to send him specimens. After receiving hundreds of fish from around the country, Agassiz two years later decided against writing only one book on the natural history of fish of the United States. Instead, he decided to spend the next decade writing the entire natural history of the United States in a ten-volume series called the *Contributions to the Natural History of the United States.*[18]

By the time of Agassiz's fiftieth birthday on May 28, 1857, the first volume of *Contributions* was all but complete. Agassiz brought with him to Parker's the last colored plates for this initial volume. Traditionally during the club's early years, he sat at the head of the long dinner table and Longfellow sat at the opposite end. The conversation was lively and never general, and Agassiz was the most cheerful man at the table. According to Ward, "his laugh was that of a big giant." Emerson, too, would laugh heartily while smoking a cigar. At Agassiz's party, the "flower[s] of the feast," according to Emerson, were the playful poems Longfellow, Holmes, and Lowell read in honor of the great scientist.[19]

By mid-July, Lowell reunited with Stillman, who boarded with the professor at the Howe household. Lowell probably seemed like a changed man to Stillman, who had put off his Adirondack trip for about a month. The solemnity and depression that had followed Lowell from Cambridge to Germany and back again had largely subsided. He was in better spirits, mostly because a romance was budding between him and his daughter's governess, Frances Dunlap. Meanwhile, Stillman probably seemed very much the same to Lowell, still lacking direction. While living in Cambridge, Stillman told Lowell that he was considering giving up any notion of business in art and instead drifting around and working odd jobs in return for "an evangelist welcome." At the least, Stillman's brief stay with Lowell in Cambridge reminded him of what it was like to have roots. After returning to New York City, he told Lowell to tell Estes and Lois Howe that "I feel as much lost as if I had a home once more."[20]

Lowell was equally appreciative of the company he found in Stillman, so much so that he decided to join the artist on his trip to the Adirondacks. For this journey, Lowell brought with him a party of four other men whom he held dear. There were his two nephews, Charles Russell Lowell and James Jackson Lowell. There were also his fellow Whist Club members Estes Howe and John Holmes. Lowell was said to have loved John Holmes more than any other man. Howe, too, was also very close to Holmes, having frequently sat next to him at Harvard. They were said to be "lifelong cronies." Holmes was born in Cambridge and graduated from Harvard in 1832. Despite showing great promise and a keen interest in the classics, he never achieved fame.[21] He was the joker of the group—a good counterbalance to Stillman.

🌒 CHAPTER 6

Trial Run

It was toward what Stillman called "the close of a dreamy day in August." The painter and his friends were encamped near a shore of Big Tupper Lake. There, Stillman, probably with the help of guides, had built a "little house" made with fresh-peeled bark of spruces with its open side facing the lake. Already three men of the party, Holmes and Lowell's two nephews, had fallen asleep. Some guides, too, were asleep in the tent they had pitched in the area between the camp and the shoreline. Meanwhile, Stillman, Lowell, and Howe sat up and talked in hushed and tired voices. Lowell smoked a pipe as the conversation wandered from the topic of firearms to spiritualism.[1]

Stillman recounted some of his previous experiences of "presentiments" and "second-sight" in the Adirondacks. After Stillman told his stories about his spiritual moments in the wilderness, Howe suggested a row onto the lake to catch the sunset. As they got up, Lowell said, "Yes." He knocked the ashes out of his meerschaum smoking pipe. "Yes, I believe in your kind of spiritual world—but that it is purely subjective." This comment spoke multitudes to Stillman and triggered in him a series of revelations over how out of line his spiritual beliefs were with his ideas about art. Lowell made him see that his spiritualism was rooted in his inner experiences. Yet his Pre-Raphaelite beliefs, with their emphasis on detail, coupled with his formal training by devout realists, compelled him to produce works that heavily relied on objective perceptions, not subjective impressions. Stillman slowly began to realize these priorities should be rearranged. He was dumbfounded. He later said that this one sentence was "spoken like the conviction of a lifetime" and opened "a new world of marvels and mysteries."[2] Lowell's comment provided an epiphany similar to the one Ruskin had sparked in Sanford Gifford seven years earlier when he said that Turner painted not like a topographer but like a poet.

Stillman walked to the shore and joined Lowell and Howe in the lightest and slowest boat the party had. They rowed far out onto the lake and rested their oars. If Lowell or Howe talked, Stillman, still gripped by his question over subjectivity, paid no attention. "I was as one who had just heard words from the dead, and hears as prattle all the sounds of common life," he later recalled.[3] In the small and crowded boat, Stillman was likely an awkward companion. Here, his tendency to be gripped too tightly by introspection, which Norton had observed and commented on to Lowell two summers earlier, was on display.

Amid this awkward mixture of conversation and reverie, a rifle shot rang out from the shore, signaling that supper was ready. The trio headed back to shore, guided by the campfire's glow. At camp, Stillman was as unsociable as he had been in the boat. After supper, as some members of the party smoked and discussed the day's adventures, Stillman walked back to the shore, "unable to quiet the uneasy questioning" that had possessed him earlier. He got into his boat and rowed onto the lake alone. In the twilight, he observed the silhouettes of a long line of "gaunt and humanesque" northern white pines swaying in the wind along the lake's northwestern shore. It was an eerie scene. The trees were so huge that they towered over the surrounding deciduous trees and caught the full strength of the wind. They actually looked like marching giants. Frightened and excited by the scene, Stillman thought, "The procession of the Anakim!"[4]

Stillman later said he actually heard a voice say that phrase. It was spoken by "some disembodied spiritual being" in an experience spiritualists called "impressional communication." The Anakim were the biblical warlike giants in old Canaan. They so terrified most of the spies Moses had sent to Canaan that the spies' fears led to a rebellion and caused the Israelites to wander the desert for another thirty-eight years. Like the Israelites, Stillman was awed and a little fearful after his presentiment. After sitting motionless in the boat for a while, terrified by the voice he heard, Stillman returned to camp. His "attendant Daemon" followed him there and taunted him with questions regarding the subjectivity and objectivity of nature. As everyone else slept, Stillman, engrossed by his thoughts, gazed up at the stars that twinkled through the forest canopy. His daemon was something Socrates (using the Greek term *daimon*) believed to be a "sign, which is a kind of voice, [that] first began to come to me as a child." As the existential psychoanalyst Rollo May has noted, Socrates believed all men possessed a daimon, which "acted as a kind of guardian." The daimon, which often appears in the creative process, "gives individual guidance in particular situations," and communicates in dreams, conscious meditation, or moments of self-questioning. Although popularly spelled "demon," Stillman used the medieval form commonly employed by poets.[5]

So long as Stillman remained active, the daemon did not haunt him. To that end, he joined the rest of his party the next morning to hunt deer. That day, Stillman and Steve Martin boated up the dark and sluggish Bog River to drive a deer toward the other members of the party assigned to points around the lake. Stillman and Martin eventually flushed out a deer, and when they heard a single shot from Howe's double-barreled shotgun, they headed back to camp, knowing the animal had been killed because no second shot was fired. By the time Stillman and Martin returned to camp, they found two guides already dressing Howe's deer and the others preparing for supper. After supper, Lowell, his nephews, Howe, and Holmes took two boats onto the lake, and three guides took a third, leaving Stillman at the camp with two guides who played cards by candlelight. Alone by the campfire, Stillman recommenced his musings on subjective and objective natures.[6]

The next morning, the party decided to move. They decided to take advantage of what one of the guides, Sam, said was a newly opened carry that would allow them to travel from Little Tupper Lake ten miles south of camp to Forked Lake. There they could pick up the traditional route back to Martin's Hotel by rowing up Long Lake, traveling along the Raquette River, and rowing across the Saranac Lakes.[7]

After rowing and carrying their boats through miles of wilderness, they discovered the report that there was a carry between Little Tupper and Forked Lake was untrue. There was only a blazed line. Rather than turn back, Stillman and his guides spent days clearing a path along which the boats could be carried. The guides cursed Sam for giving an inaccurate report about the carry. After much effort, they arrived at Forked Lake on the afternoon of the fourth day of this trailblazing excursion and camped that night there amid a thunderstorm. The next day, they entered Long Lake and made their way back to Martin's. From there Lowell and company headed back to Boston, probably by traveling through Keeseville and catching at Port Kent a steamer on Lake Champlain. Stillman remained behind, however, opting to stay in the wilderness for several more weeks. Correspondence later that summer between Lowell and Stillman and Norton and the English poet Arthur H. Clough suggests that the artist and poet cordially parted. Despite telling Lowell before they separated that he planned to return to Forked Lake, Stillman instead went with Martin and his hound, Carlo, to Raquette Lake, believing the latter to be a better camping ground and almost as beautiful.[8]

At one of Raquette Lake's northwestern bays, Stillman built a nine-by-twelve-foot bark shanty on a bluff offshore, about thirty feet above the water. From there, he had a "charming view" of the lake's opposite shore with blue mountains rising behind it in the distance. For almost two months Stillman lived on this bluff. (The bay by which he camped to this day bears his name.) There he painted, sketched, hunted, chopped wood, rowed, and cleaned the "park" outside his woodland home. In his shanty, he made a couch out of balsam fir and hung his rifle, deer antlers, and eagle wings for decorations. There was a farm a few miles away, and Stillman could occasionally hear the tinkle of cowbells. With a sense of relief, he told Norton, "I have left no trail behind on which the days of care and trouble would follow."[9]

Indeed, by September, Stillman had lost all track of time and seemed reluctant to return. All he knew was that he had promised to be in New York City on October 1. He grew "into the spirit" of the wilderness and abandoned himself to it "more unreservedly." Stillman continued to mull over Lowell's comment on his subjective spirituality, and his understanding of himself as an artist evolved. He saw into "the true paths of study" and confessed that all his life he had been "trying to treat the face of nature objectively." He was beginning to doubt the soundness of this approach. Stillman realized that his art should not be "the clearer reflection of things around me," which was his chief complaint about the works of his mentor, Frederic Church. Instead, a painting should be "the embodiment of myself" in the things around him.[10]

Reluctantly, Stillman abandoned his outpost on Raquette Lake and arrived at Saranac Lake by September 28. Only bad news greeted him there. He received news of his "brother's failure," which probably was a result of the economic crisis that had struck the nation. A series of events had triggered the Panic of 1857, starting with the sinking of the SS *Central America* and its cargo of thirty thousand pounds of gold off the Carolinas coast in a September hurricane. After this catastrophe, the New York branch of the Ohio Life Insurance and Trust Company failed. Soon after, banks suspended specie payments and called loans, triggering more failures. On Wall Street, stock prices had plummeted, and by year's end, nine hundred mercantile businesses in New York City had failed. Even in Concord, Emerson noted the impact of the crisis, which he found perplexing. After the New York and Boston banks suspended their specie payments, he noted in his journal on October 14 that "as usual in hard times, there are all sorts of petty & local reasons given for the pressure, but none that explain it to me." What was worse than not knowing the exact cause of the panic was not knowing how inflated American investments had become during the just-popped economic bubble. Emerson believed the panic would serve as a "severer examiner than any Committee of Bank Commissioners" that would "find out how much specie all this paper represents, & how much real value."[11]

As he anticipated leaving Saranac Lake for New York City, Stillman also grew worried about Norton, who had not responded to any of the artist's letters. After returning to his home in New York, Stillman learned that Norton, like his brother Thomas, had also suffered losses in the stock panic. The panic meant that Stillman's two main supporters—Norton and Thomas—were at least temporarily financially disabled. Norton cautioned he would not "be able to earn money" for his friend. However, Stillman did not fret. After all, he had nothing to lose. Through the panic, he realized that "poverty was my best friend and my credit my weakness."[12]

By mid-October, then, Stillman was preparing for a lean existence. He expected to spend the rest of the autumn and winter painting in a new studio when not working as the vice director of a New York art gallery. He told Norton he would go in early spring to his "dear old woods," where he could live "at almost no cost." It was a sentiment he repeated to Lowell: "I wish I were buried forty miles deep in the forest where [there is] no thought of crisis or crash of fortune."[13]

By the time Stillman left the Adirondacks that autumn, his friends in Boston were already impressed by the stories they heard about the adventure, particularly its impact on Lowell. Norton, who in early August returned from Europe, encountered the professor before leaving for a vacation in Lenox, Massachusetts, later that month. Norton had last seen Lowell while abroad the previous year and had reported to Clough that he had "found Lowell very well and in capital spirits" after his "wild, camping-out journey." Indicating that Lowell was not overly upset by the long delay caused by the false report of a completed carry between Little Tupper Lake and Forked Lake, Norton enthusiastically noted that the poet "had been cutting paths through woods in which no paths had ever been made before." In the "midst of this superb and unusual scenery," Lowell also related that he had shot a bear swimming in a lake, seen herds of deer, and measured massive pine trees. In fact,

Lowell had enjoyed himself so thoroughly in the wilderness that after reading a letter from Stillman written "among the dear old Adirondacks" he became "homesick to be back again."[14]

The Saturday Club heard all about Lowell's exploits in the wilderness. According to Edward Emerson, Lowell "interested many members of our Club, and some friends." However, his tales were likely not the first ones they had ever heard about the Adirondacks. A few other men close to the club had traveled in or near the region. The most influential of these early Adirondack tourists was Samuel Ward, who had traveled to the region in August 1847. Ward had written to Ralph Waldo Emerson about his vacation in the wilderness. Emerson, who was preparing to go to England, had responded with a letter saying, "Sometimes I could wish it was the Adirondack mountains—whose summits I have repeatedly & wishfully gazed at from Vermont—a wholesomer place, no doubt, than England, and a great deal easier to live in." However, in March 1855, Emerson had declined an invitation to join an Adirondack camping party extended by Emily M. Drury, of Canandaigua, New York. Earlier in 1855, Drury had promised to send or sent to Emerson articles her husband had written about his own Adirondack adventure.[15] These inducements had not been enough to move Emerson at that time.

Ebenezer Hoar's college friend and an original member of the Saturday Club, Richard Dana, had ventured deep into New York's northern wilderness in June 1849. He had an enjoyable time traveling with three other men and a guide through the High Peaks region, rowing on Lake Sanford, and hiking up what is now known as Mount Marcy. But the trip took a turn for the worse when the guide got the party lost in the woods with no food, guns, coats, or blankets. Eventually the "worn, wearied, hungry, fly-bitten travelers" found shelter in the home of John Brown in North Elba. Brown and his large family had only recently moved to the North Elba, where the abolitionist Gerrit Smith had established a sanctuary for black families and fugitive slaves.[16]

By the time Lowell returned from the Adirondacks, Brown had become a figure of great interest to many intellectuals in the Boston area, but not because of the shelter he occasionally provided to wayward hikers. In 1855, Brown had departed from his North Elba homestead in the Adirondacks and headed to Kansas, with five of his sons, to fight proslavery forces. There he became a wanted vigilante for his involvement in the slaying of five proslavery men just north of Pottawatomie Creek in Franklin County in May 1856. Long convinced that the nation needed to eliminate the scourge of slavery and convinced that he was divinely charged to carry out that task, Brown had been harboring plans to attack the South. After the passage of the Kansas-Nebraska Act and the rendition of Anthony Burns in 1854, he became fixated on inciting a slave insurrection in the South by raiding a federal armory in Harpers Ferry, Virginia. He then planned to establish a sanctuary for these insurgent slaves in the Allegheny Mountains.[17]

With these plans in mind, in January 1857, Brown had traveled to Boston to raise funds for his holy war. He deceptively told his supporters he planned to raise an army of one hundred men who would repel proslavery forces in the Kansas territory and occasionally advance into Missouri. He made no mention of Harpers Ferry. And with the help of Franklin Sanborn, the secretary of the Massachusetts State Kansas Committee who lived near Thoreau and Hoar in Concord, Brown had been introduced to key players in New England's antislavery movement, including Thomas Wentworth Higginson and the Unitarian minister Theodore Parker, two instigators of the Anthony Burns riot.[18]

The fact that Lowell had camped about forty miles away from Brown's homestead in North Elba likely made the tale of Dana's nearly calamitous Adirondack journey of great interest to some members of the Saturday Club, particularly Emerson. Even more, Dana's story likely made an Adirondack adventure appear more appealing to the philosopher, who became interested in visiting the Brown homestead. Emerson was keenly interested in Brown since the two had met at Thoreau's house in Concord in March 1857. Emerson attended Brown's lecture at Town Hall, where the "captain" criticized the folly of Kansas's pacifist settlers. He said that "one, good, strong-minded man is worth a hundred, nay twenty thousand men without character, for a settler in a new country; and that the right men will give a permanent direction to the fortunes of a State."[19]

When Stillman returned to civilization in October 1857, he was surprised to learn that the vacation he had organized at Big Tupper Lake had doubled as a bachelor party of sorts for Lowell. Less than four years after his wife had died, Lowell married Frances Dunlap on September 16, 1857. Tellingly, during their stay in the Adirondacks Lowell had not mentioned to Stillman his intent to marry, which suggests that the artist remained more of a trusted guide than a companion or confidant. To others in the Saturday Club, Stillman would never rise above this rank. Although Stillman told Lowell he did not feel slighted at not being informed about the impending wedding, he did feel excluded and wished he had learned about it while in the woods. Nevertheless, Stillman wished his friend well and was glad Lowell had "come back into life again." Lowell not only came back to life but also returned to editing. Tired of teaching after just one year, he did not return to his classroom at Harvard that autumn. Instead, he accepted a job as the editor of the new *Atlantic Monthly,* published by Philips, Sampson & Co. Plans for the literary magazine had actually been finalized during the spring. Its first number appeared in November 1857.[20]

Harvard came close to losing another revered professor that autumn. In September, Agassiz received an offer from Gustave Rouland, the minister of public institutions of France, to serve as the paleontology chair of the Museum of Natural History, otherwise known as the Jardin des Plantes, in Paris. As Edward Lurie has noted, Agassiz by then had firmly taken root in America. He had relocated his family from Switzerland to Cambridge, and, further, had come to recognize that he could be far more influential and popular in his new home country than in Europe. However, the Jardin des Plantes offer was tempting. The Parisian museum was, after all, in Agassiz's own assessment, "the most important establishment in existence for the natural sciences." Neverthe-less, he refused the offer, citing his inability to walk away from his commit-ments in America, which included the completion of his *Contributions* series. The fact that France could not steal America's prized scientist was largely viewed as an act of patriotism by this Swiss transplant, and his letter of refusal was reprinted in newspapers nationwide. Another factor influencing Agassiz's decision to stay in America, which would not become public knowledge for another year, was that he was positioned to establish at Harvard a museum that aimed to rival the Jardin des Plantes. Shortly before dying, Francis C. Gray, Agassiz's primary benefactor, had included in his will a provision for the fund-ing of a museum of natural history. Gray died in December 1857, and this provision was not to be formally announced for two years, around the very time the Adirondack Club began to take shape.[21]

Meanwhile, by the end of the summer of 1857, the Saturday Club was shaping into a more integral part of the lives of its members. Realizing that he had not yet mentioned the club in his diary, Dana—a founding member—wrote on August 6, "It [the club] has become an important and much valued thing to us." Both the founding of the *Atlantic Monthly* and the events leading to the founding of the Adirondack Club that year provided the Saturday Club's members with "pride and pleasure," according to Edward Emerson. The extent of planning conducted by the end of 1857, if any, for the next Adiron-dack adventure is not clear. Edward Emerson claimed, "Thus the enterprise was begun and members enlisted in 1857, but the story of their first crusade will appear . . . in the following summer." It is also not clear whether Still-man, at this time, was even aware of any such enlistment for an Adirondack party for the next summer, and there is no known correspondence between Saturday Club members referencing this planned outing until June 1858.[22]

✿ CHAPTER 7

The Procession to the Pines

By early January 1858, Stillman was planning to paint for the *Atlantic Monthly*'s editor the Oaks at Waverley, the beautiful grouping of trees west of Cambridge that Lowell had first shown the artist about three years earlier. "I shall paint you something worthy [of] the feeling you have for the trees—and the feeling I have for you," Stillman promised Lowell. To produce such a picture, Stillman intended to relocate his studio closer to Waverley, though artistic interests were likely not all that drew him back to the Boston area. In the months that had passed since Stillman last enjoyed the "intellectual association" of the Saturday Club's members, he had come to long for their company. "New York seems to me after a visit to Boston as only a place to exist comfortably in and to be negatively happy," Stillman told Norton.[1]

By mid-May, Stillman declared he had completed a "dreary winter's work" and was preparing to return to painting in the outdoors. Despite the season's dreariness, Stillman had managed to paint one of his greatest works by winter's end. The painting, *The Procession of the Pines,* was exhibited in 1858 at the Boston Athenaeum. (The Athenaeum purchased the painting in 1859, but it had disappeared from the library's collection by 1870.) According to Emerson's son Edward, *The Procession of the Pines* depicted a twilight scene, with "huge Norway pines on a high promontory standing black against the orange twilight glow, and reflected in the still lake."[2] The silhouetting effect might explain why Edward Emerson identified the trees as Norway pines and not the white pines Stillman had seen swaying at Big Tupper Lake, inspiring the image of the "Procession of the Anakim."

The Procession of the Pines produced very strong reactions in many who viewed it, including Ralph Waldo Emerson. It was an effect attributable to the lessons Stillman likely had learned when painting the pine for his Ruskinian lover in 1856 and from his musings on subjectivity while in the Adirondacks with Lowell a year later. Higginson later wrote in the *Atlantic Monthly* that the painting "identified his [Stillman's] fame with that delightful forest region."[3]

Having painted one masterpiece of a grouping of trees, Stillman in spring set off to paint Lowell's beloved Oaks at Waverley. Stillman boarded at the home of David Mack III in Belmont, which is about a mile north of Waverley and four miles west of Cambridge. Mack, a Yale graduate and former lawyer, had established in Belmont a young ladies' boarding school with the assistance of his wife, Lucy. The Macks had four children, and their eldest daughter, Laura, was nineteen years old when Stillman came to Belmont.[4] She took a strong liking to the artist, and Stillman reciprocated the feeling.

FIGURE 10. William James Stillman (1828–1901), *The Oaks, Waverley,* circa 1874. This grouping of trees was one of Lowell's favorite places. He took Stillman there early in their friendship in the mid-1850s, and the painter moved to nearby Belmont in 1858 so he could paint the trees for the poet. Stillman and Lowell last walked together amid the Waverley oaks in October 1874. Courtesy of Special Collections, Schaffer Library, Union College.

By the time Stillman returned to the vicinity of Cambridge, he was, much like Lowell, a changed man. He was humbled and able to laugh more at past missteps and misfortunes. He even became remorseful over having bitterly complained about the way Lowell had neglected him during his 1855–56 European tour. "I fear I have annoyed him as much as he has done me good," Stillman told Norton, who he also feared had grown impatient with his moodiness. Even Stillman's health, while still prone to fluctuation, was slowly improving. Most important about this change of attitude was that Stillman had bucked, albeit temporarily, the self-centeredness and neediness that had defined him in his midtwenties. Such antisocial behavior had created barriers between him and his Boston friends and acquaintances, such as Lowell and possibly Longfellow. As testimony to this change in character, Stillman even managed to bring these two men to the Waverley area. He painted Lowell lying beside a bank of Beaver Brook and Longfellow sitting beneath an oak. Lowell convinced Stillman not to finish the portrait of Longfellow, probably to save the poet from the "martyrdom" of having to sit on a huge boulder to the point of clear discomfort.[5]

By mid-June, planning for the summer Adirondack camping trip was in full tilt. On June 22, Emerson visited the Boston Athenaeum, where *The Procession of the Pines* was likely still on display. From there, Emerson planned to go to Cambridge to find Stillman and Lowell. Emerson abandoned such plans when he learned the artist did not live in Cambridge, and he doubted Lowell would be home. Instead, the philosopher wrote to Lowell from the library and said, "I shall check my social zeal till Saturday." He identified Stillman and Lowell as the "heads of the Adirondac party" and made one request: that an invitation to join the party be extended to Edward Hoar. Edward Hoar, Ebenezer Hoar's brother, was a naturalist who had spent the past eight years in California. Emerson made this request shortly before Edward Hoar on July 2 embarked on an adventure to the White Mountains with his neighbor, Thoreau. Although the two men returned to Concord on July 19, Edward Hoar did not join the Adirondack party, possibly because he had had his fill of camping by that time. While there is no record that an invitation was extended to Edward Hoar, it is hard to imagine Lowell's ignoring or denying such a specific request from Emerson.[6]

As Thoreau's New Hampshire adventure illustrates, the type of trip Stillman and Lowell were planning was not uncommon in the mid-1850s. It had been a different story, though, a few decades earlier. As late as 1810, tourism in America had been nearly nonexistent, and in New England it had been largely reserved for the wealthy. The first major hotel outside an urban area was built in New York State in the early 1790s in Ballston Spa, Saratoga County, to accommodate the growing number of tourists seeking the healing powers of the area's mineral water. Fueling this rise of American tourism was the emergence of a tradition of American travel literature that had begun with writers such as Washington Irving and James Fenimore Cooper. Irving, for example, wrote about the "Style of Ballston" for the *Salmagundi* magazine in 1807, and Cooper popularized many upstate New York locations by including them in his novels. And by the mid-nineteenth century, this tourism movement had spread to other areas, such as Niagara Falls and the White Mountains.[7] Internal improvements, including road and canals (and later rail lines), made the interior accessible first to the wealthy and then, later, to more middling classes of people.

Tourism can be defined as a "kind of travel that creates an illusion of novelty while remaining within a narrow range of comfortable, socially defined boundaries." It certainly was a practice of certain socioeconomic classes and not others. But the rise of tourism in America also coincided with broader developments in national identity, and citizens were encouraged to leave their cities and villages and travel to view the nation's grand scenery and visit locations of historical significance. These literary expressions of the likes of Irving and Cooper certainly captured the imagination of Americans. Yet to head out on a tour required a plan or reliable guide. In 1821, George M. Davison provided just that by publishing the nation's first guidebook, *The Fashionable Tour, or, a Tripp to the Springs, Niagara, Quebec, and Boston in the Summer of 1821*. From their first appearance in America, these guidebooks were steady sellers. Attempting to capitalize on the travel literature trend, newspapers also regularly published articles by reporters dispatched to various tourist destinations or by correspondents who visited them. Their reports were often similar to Emerson's observation made in 1832 while touring the White Mountains that "the good of going in the mountains is that life is reconsidered; it is far from the slavery of your own modes of living, and you have the opportunity of viewing the town at such a distance as may afford you a just view."[8]

By July 1, Agassiz and his colleague at Harvard, Jeffries Wyman, had confirmed their intent to join the Adirondack party. An invitation to join the party extended by Stillman to Oliver Wendell Holmes was rejected, mainly because the doctor was not interested in trading the comforts of city life for the primitive experiences of the wilderness. While Agassiz's acceptance of an invitation could elicit much excitement among the Adirondack-bound party, it must have been especially exciting that summer given that America had again come close to losing its prized scientist to France. Weeks after Agassiz had declined Rouland's initial offer on September 25, 1857, France's minister of public instruction responded with an enhanced offer extended at the behest of Emperor Napoleon III. The emperor had ordered the Jardin des Plantes paleontology chair position to be left open for two years, providing the scientist with ample time to finish his work in America and subsequently assume the prestigious position abroad. Although Rouland's second letter had been sent in November, Agassiz did not receive it until he returned to Cambridge from Florida in April.[9]

This enhanced offer included a high-paying senatorship. Even Emerson told Arthur Clough in mid-May that "I fear we shall lose him, as the French Emperor is bidding high on him." Highlighting how Agassiz had become a source of national pride, newspapers across the country speculated about and fretted over his next move. The *Daily Ohio Statesman* feared that if Agassiz accepted the offer, "we shall lose our most eminent naturalist." However, in what proved to be a validating moment for the nation, Agassiz rejected the emperor's enhanced offer in late June. "The truth is—and we wish to have the nations of Europe, France included, to understand it—that we do not mean to let Prof. Agassiz leave America," said a *Boston Courier* report, which the *New York Times* reprinted. "We have a need for him here, and we love and honor him too much to have him go away from us."[10]

Days after it became certain the Swiss-born scientist would remain in the United States, Emerson informed his son William that Agassiz and Wyman had agreed to join the Adirondack party. Wyman was another eminent naturalist, but unlike Agassiz he was native to America. Born in Chelmsford, Massachusetts, Wyman would turn forty-four years old while in the wilderness, on August 11. Harvard-educated, he had quickly emerged as a leading expert on human and comparative anatomy and the natural history of physiology, and he was especially skilled in anatomical drawing. After teaching anatomy and physiology for four years at Hampden Sidney College's medical department in Richmond, Virginia, he joined Harvard's faculty in 1847. He was tall and slender and wore round wire-frame glasses that perched on a large nose. Even though he had been an athletic youth who served as a member of the Boston Fire Department, a bout with pneumonia during his senior year at Harvard in 1833 compromised his health for the rest of his life.[11]

The Adirondack adventure was actually one of three vacations Emerson had scheduled for that summer. The others were at the Newport, Rhode Island, home of George Bancroft, in the Adirondacks, and at the home of the railroad magnate and merchant John M. Forbes on Naushon Island off Cape Cod. The Adirondack party was set to leave on the morning of August 2 and "promises to stay out 2, 3, or 4 weeks," Emerson told Harrison G. O. Blake.

FIGURE 11. John Adams Whipple (1822–1901), *Jeffries Wyman* (1814–74), circa 1858. Salted paper print, 5-5/8 × 5-1/16 in. Wyman was an anatomist and naturalist who taught at Harvard. He was the first curator of the Peabody Museum of American Archeology. Harvard Art Museums/Fogg Museum, transfer from Carpenter Center for the Visual Arts, Gift of Arthur S. Eldredge, 2.2002.2086. Photo: Imaging Department © President and Fellows of Harvard College.

Emerson planned to send his son Edward and daughter Edith to Naushon on August 3. From Belmont, Stillman on July 22 notified Emerson of his intention to travel to the Adirondacks in advance of the party and "prepare the way, enjoying the wilderness." He said he would entrust his directions to Lowell, and he advised Emerson not to trouble himself with firearms because the artist had a "large assortment" from which the philosopher could choose. However, this advice did not stop Emerson from purchasing a firearm. On July 24, he recorded the twenty-five-dollar purchase of a "rifle & gun," along with a "box," probably of ammunition, and other items. Concordians looked at these purchases with amusement. According to Thoreau, "the story on the Mill Dam is that he [Emerson] has taken a gun which throws shot from one end and ball from the other!"[12]

On July 27, just three days after Emerson recorded the purchase of his firearm, Lowell and Stillman traveled to Nahant to visit Longfellow, who had been staying for more than two weeks at a cottage on the rocky peninsula. Stillman traveled to Nahant to complete a portrait of Longfellow. Rather than deal with the painter by himself, Longfellow had requested Lowell's company. It was likely during this visit that Stillman asked Longfellow to join the Adirondack party, which was to set out in less than a week. To this invitation, the poet asked, "Is it true that Emerson is going to take a gun?" To Stillman's yes, Longfellow replied, "Then I shall not go, somebody will be shot." Stillman, however, believed Longfellow's refusal to join the party went beyond his fear of fratricide. As the painter later explained, Longfellow "hated killing animals, had no interest in fishing, and was too settled in his habits to enjoy so great a change."[13]

Invitations for the trip went out up to the last minute. By late July, the party consisted of ten men, though the camp was expected to accommodate twelve, not including guides. The ten included Agassiz, Amos Binney, Emerson, Hoar, John Holmes, Estes Howe, Lowell, Stillman, Horatio Woodman, and Wyman. Stillman likely invited Binney partly out of obligation and partly out of gratitude for his commissions and hospitality two years earlier. Stillman and Binney would travel separately from the main party. Saying, "We all want you very much," Hoar invited Richard Dana to join "our Adirondack party." Hoar informed Dana that the party planned to set out on the Fitchburg railroad on Monday, August 2, and reach Lake George that night. Hoar informed Dana that he would need to carry a blanket, gun, and rod, and that all other supplies would be sent to the camp.[14] Either because this invitation had come with too short notice or because his 1849 Adirondack hiking trip had left him with bad memories of the region, Dana did not join the party.

Although Stillman planned to travel ahead of the party by a few days to ensure that no inconvenience would greet Boston's luminaries, by July 29 he was still in Belmont. He had not yet received a canvas from his supplier, though he could not wait longer. Stillman arranged to have the canvas sent to Howe's Cambridge home and asked Lowell to ensure it was brought to the Adirondacks. Stillman and Emerson had agreed not to hold a dinner party before the trip. Nevertheless, the Saturday Club still met at the end of the month. Longfellow noted in his journal that he had dined with the club on July 31, which was a Saturday. It is not clear whether Stillman attended this meeting, though it seems unlikely since he made no mention of it. He left for the Saranacs at least one or two days before the rest of the Adirondack party departed on August 2 so he could search for a campsite for his friends. Above all, he looked for a place "out of the track of hunters or chance tourists, but where game was still plentiful and good fishing not far away."[15]

Stillman concluded that a thousand-acre body of water named Follensby Pond satisfied these requirements. None of his earlier letters or *Crayon* correspondence from the Adirondacks mentioned Follensby, though he had many times passed by its outlet while traveling along the Raquette River. It was probably not by accident that he happened upon this lake in 1858. One or more of the region's guides likely led him to it or at least informed him about it. One such person may have been Stephen Martin, Stillman's go-to guide with a cabin along the Indian Carry, not far from Follensby.

Follensby is about three miles long and one and a half miles wide, with ten miles of shoreline. Thanks to the nearly two-mile-long outlet that distanced the lake from the Raquette, lumbermen had left its surrounding woods untouched. It was, Stillman said, "a virgin forest." Despite its size, Follensby had the word "pond" attached to it. As Stillman explained to *Crayon* readers in *The Wilderness and Its Waters,* Adirondack guides never called a body of water a lake if it was less than three miles across.[16]

FIGURE 12. Carl Heilman II (1954–), *Follensby Pond,* 2011. Digital photograph. Despite Stillman's discovery of the ravaged woods around Follensby Pond in 1884, the wilderness around the lake today is just as much of a "not too greatly changed Eden" as Stillman remembered from 1858. Reproduced with permission of Carl Heilman II.

Follensby's name has also been spelled "Follansbee" or "Folingsby." Its name originates with a hermit, Moses Follensby (or Folingsby), who had camped at the lake. He was one of the region's earliest settlers, and little is known about him other than that he hunted and fished throughout a large swath of neighboring wilderness. His name is attached to other ponds at which he camped. By one account, he was a trapper who had built a cabin at Follensby and who vanished in 1823. By another account, he had been a decorated British officer and an earl who kept a treasure chest under his cabin's hearth. The latter account was provided by the Albany poet and avid angler Alfred B. Street, who called Follensby "a haunted place" where "many the daring hunter or trapper who, laughing at every other peril, trembles as night environs him in its dreaded precincts."[17]

However, no dreadful spirit loomed around the camp Stillman built for his friends. He knew a good campground needed many components, and he found them all near Follensby's southeastern peninsula. His checklist included a natural spring; a dry and elevated plateau wooded with hardwood trees (in this case, a maple grove); level ground for the camp; and a smooth sandy beach where the boats could be pulled ashore. The artist concluded of the camp: "Ours was one of the best I have ever seen." The site Stillman selected also featured two huge maple trees rising around the center of the camp. Looking westward from the peninsula's shore, the scholars could look into a bay with a low-rising mountain behind it. With the help of some guides, Stillman constructed a small neighborhood of shanties. For the roofs of these crude three-walled dwellings, they stripped bark and fir branches from trees deep in the woods so as "not to disfigure our dwelling-place with stripped and dying trees." After blazing a trail from the camp to the shore, Stillman headed back to Martin's Hotel to meet the scholars. Eight of them reached Lake George the evening of August 2.[18]

To get to Lake George on time, the scholars skipped dinner and rode sixteen miles on a plank road from Moreau, near Glens Falls. According to Hoar, they "went down the Lake on Tuesday, took the boat from Burlington, crossed Lake Champlain by another steamer fourteen miles to Port Kent." That same night, they then caught a stagecoach that took them five miles west to Keeseville, which at the time stood as a gateway to the central Adirondacks. The party's first impression of Keeseville likely came long before they set foot in the village, either in the form of the racket from its mills or their "vomiting chimneys," as another visitor to the region that summer described them. It was an industrial village powered by the Ausable River. And the Ausable Horse-Nail Company had put Keeseville on the map as one of the nation's largest horse nail manufacturers.[19]

News of the scholars' anticipated arrival had swept through the countryside, and droves of people came out to see the star of the party—Agassiz. According to Stillman's second-hand account, the scholars' warm reception was initially tempered by the town's selectmen, who were doubtful that America's greatest scientist would actually visit such a backwoods community. Some town officials waited to receive the party formally the morning after its arrival "to pay their respects, they said, but really to see a man who had no regard for money and distinction," Stillman said. Upon seeing the party, someone emerged from the crowd and approached Agassiz. This village spokesman carried a copy of a newspaper with an etching of Agassiz and held it next to the scientist. After carefully looking at the etching and then Agassiz, the official proclaimed, "Yes, it's him!" At this, the town members swarmed around Agassiz. They wanted to shake the hand of the man who a month earlier had become the nation's adopted hero by refusing Napoleon III's offer.[20]

Meanwhile, the party's other eminent members, according to Stillman, were ignored. That is not to say that Emerson's reputation had failed to penetrate such remote regions of the country. (When Thoreau hiked up Mount Katahdin in the Maine wilderness in 1846, he had found in a loggers' camp a copy of Emerson's "An Address on West India Emancipation.") But generally Emerson and the rest of the party were left to themselves. While in Keeseville, Hoar made some last-minute purchases, which included underwear and a gauze veil to keep away black flies. The party ventured north of Keeseville to view the Ausable Chasm, which has been dubbed the "Grand Canyon of the East." In one of the notebooks in which he documented this Adirondack journey, Emerson noted finding a harebell (*Campanula rotundifolia*) on the "gorge of the Ausable River." The song of a wood thrush also made a marked impression on him. The *Essex County Republican* noted the party's passage through Keeseville and said Agassiz was "astonished at the magnificence and sublimity of the scenery." As Agassiz stood on Table Rock at the Ausable Chasm, he reportedly "could not help exclaiming, 'beautiful—grand—sublime.'"[21]

The party eventually boarded what Emerson called "strong country carts" and headed out on a road that followed the Ausable. Stillman, as planned, met the scholars at Martin's Hotel. There each man got a guide and a boat. Stillman, though, had no guide and was to serve as one for Agassiz. The names of the guides recorded by Emerson were William Preston, Marshall Brown, Stephen Martin, William Martin, Corey, Douglas ("pronounced Dooglaw"), Fuller, Ring, Bill Johnson, Chet Peck, and Sam Dunning. It is possible some these men served as guides at the Philosophers' Camp, though

William Martin remained at his hotel, and another party hired Dunning that August.[22]

The scholars ate dinner in Saranac and then took to their boats with their guides at the oars and began their journey across the lakes. However, already upset that he had missed witnessing Emerson's first impression of the woods, Stillman did not join the party on the water at midday because the boat he had been working on was incomplete. (It was not until sunset that he started rowing to catch up with the group.) After crossing Lower Saranac Lake and Middle Saranac Lake, the scholars trekked along the carry near Bartlett's as their guides hauled the boats and luggage. From there they rowed across Upper Saranac Lake to the Indian Carry, along which they found Steve Martin's cabin. There they ate supper and lodged for the night. Sleeping on the floor of the attic on a rainy night while the mosquitoes and midges thickly swarmed, the men did not undress. Stillman, who got caught in that rainstorm, arrived at the cabin around midnight "drenched like a water-rat."[23]

After leaving Martin's cabin, Agassiz boarded Stillman's boat, and every other scholar got into his own boat, each with a personal guide at the oars. They traveled along the Raquette River until they reached Follensby's entrance, which Stillman described as a "deep mysterious stream meandering through unbroken forests, walled up on either side in green shade, the trees of centuries leaning over to welcome and shelter the voyager." (A less poetic writer who two days later rowed down the same outlet said, "It was a relief to get out of the brook, which swarmed with mosquitoes and midges.") After creeping along the outlet, past lily pads and sponges, as Emerson said, they came "to Follansbee Water, and the Lake of Loons."[24]

By the morning of Friday the sixth, Binney caught up with the party. It is not clear if he caught up to the party somewhere between Martin's Hotel and Follensby, such as at Steve Martin's cabin, or at the lake. The date of the party's arrival at Follensby is also unclear, though it could not have been any sooner than August 5 because for a total of at least three nights they lodged in or around Lake George, in or around Keeseville, and at Martin's cabin. In an August 5 brief note to his family, Emerson said he had "had good luck," which suggests he may have arrived at Follensby on that date. After the scholars left Keeseville and reached Martin's Hotel, Stillman said they "started up the lakes at midday," though it is not clear if they did so after lodging at Martin's. If they did lodge there, that would have been a fourth night, meaning their estimated time of arrival at Follensby would have been August 6. The party arrived no later than August 7, which was when Emerson recorded in his journal his satisfaction with "Follansbee's Pond." The

Adirondack historian Paul Jamieson estimated the scholars reached Follensby on August 6 or 7.[25]

The fact that Binney traveled separately from the main party illustrates how much of a stranger he was among the Philosophers' Camp's members. All the same, his arrival meant the Adirondack party was united and complete. It consisted of ten men. With the exception of Agassiz, Stillman, and possibly Woodman, they had all graduated from, or at least attended, Harvard. They were all native New Englanders, with the exception of Stillman and Agassiz, though the former's family had deep roots in Rhode Island. For the most part, they epitomized what the writer William Dean Howells would describe a half-century later as the "Old American ideal."[26]

❧ Part II

The Camp and Club

❧ CHAPTER 8

Acclimating to the Wild

Follensby's ancient white pines grew in long lines along the lake's shores. The oldest of them rose up to 150 feet and 200 feet, nearly twice the height of the surrounding deciduous trees. Without the shield provided by those smaller birches, beeches, and maples, the pines were exposed to the full force of the Follensby's dominant west wind, making them lean to the east.[1]

"They seemed to be gigantic human beings moving in procession to the east," according to Stillman. Sitting in a boat on the lake with Stillman, Emerson finally viewed this procession of the pines, which had interested the philosopher ever since he had seen the painting of it at the Boston Athenaeum earlier that year. After the Adirondack party had settled in the camp near Follensby's southeastern shore, one of the first things Emerson requested Stillman to show him was the mystical scene of the swaying pines that the artist had captured on canvas. It was an unforgettable scene that made it easy to forget everything else. In the wilderness, no politics or business troubled the scholars, Emerson later said. Other members of the party felt the same way. "We seemed to have got back into a not too greatly changed Eden, whose imperious ties to the outer world were hidden for the day in the waters and woods that lay between us and it," said Stillman later, echoing the escapist themes he had used in his earlier *Crayon* essays and correspondence. "The outside world was but a dream."[2]

It might have seemed like a dream from inside the Adirondacks, but outside this dream world the nation was careening toward political, technological, artistic, scientific, and religious upheaval. Just two months after the scholars camped at Follensby, New York senator William H. Seward gave a speech in Rochester, New York, warning about the "irrepressible conflict" that would determine whether "the United States must and will, sooner or later, become either entirely a slaveholding nation, or entirely a free-labor nation."[3]

The ten scholars set their camp during the twilight of a romantic era in which they stood as representative men. Whether they knew it or not, they were drifting into a darker period of history. When he later wrote about his Adirondack adventure, Emerson raised the question, "Ask you, how went the hours?" Answer:

> All day we swept the lake, searched every cove,
> North from Camp Maple, south to Osprey Bay,
> Watching when the loud dogs should drive in deer,
> Or whipping its rough surface for a trout;
> Or bathers, diving from the rock at noon;
> Challenging Echo by our guns and cries;
> Or listening to the laughter of the loon;
> Or, in evening twilight's latest red,
> Beholding the procession of the pines.[4]

Illustrative of how lost Emerson was in the wilderness, here he incorrectly stated that they rowed south to Osprey Bay when this feature of Follensby is actually at the northern end of the lake.

Stillman did not disappoint the eminent guests to his wild kingdom. Emerson on August 7 declared in his journal, "Follansbee's Pond. It should be called Stillman's henceforward, from the good camp which this gallant artist has built, & the good party he has led & planted here for the present at the bottom of the little bay which lies near the head of the lake." That "good camp" Stillman built was dubbed by Lowell "Camp Maple" for its giant namesake trees. The camp consisted of lean-tos that stood six and a half feet high. They featured compartments in which multiple persons could "comfortably sleep." The philosopher likened sleeping in these shanties to resting "on down-beds." He welcomed the remoteness of the camp and even praised the midges, black flies, and mosquitoes that were "looked upon as the protectors of this superb solitude from tourists." It was high praise that came despite the fact that the insects "painted our necks, hands, ankles, with red bands."[5]

By the time Emerson got around to updating his notebook on the seventh, the campers had been busy. He reported seeing bald eagles, loons, kingfishers, and ducks. He was disappointed, however, not to hear again the wood thrush the company had heard during their trek to Follensby. "Not since, & no other thrush." Deer were bountiful and the most sought creature of the trip. Hoar assured his wife they had seen "no bears, panthers or wolves."[6]

Toward the northern end of Follensby, near the outlet, there was what the scholars dubbed Osprey Bay for the five or six namesake birds of prey whose screeches they heard often there. Perched atop one of the white pines along its shore was an osprey's nest. The tree stood up to 150 feet tall and was almost 15 feet wide; "60 ft. clean straight stem, without a single branch," Emerson observed. Despite these formidable obstacles to climbing, and with the help of a neighboring hemlock tree, Lowell's guide, William Preston, scaled the pine to get an egg for Agassiz. When he got to the top, he found the nest empty, though the osprey "wheeled & screamed" at him, Emerson said. Emerson watched Preston climb in amazement. Lowell later prowled around the bay and waited for a chance to shoot an osprey. However, Emerson noted, the bird "soared magnificently, and would not alight." After Preston's feat at Osprey Bay, the scholars awoke one morning to find Lowell missing at breakfast. In the capricious fashion that had ruled his undergraduate years at Harvard, he returned to Camp Maple and told Emerson he had climbed "Preston's pine tree."[7]

On days when Lowell did not disappear from camp, it was usually the guides who were the first to wake. At sunrise, Stillman explained, the morning routine involved guides refreshing the fires and going out on boats to set the lines for trout. Breakfast came at eight o'clock and dinner before sunset. After breakfast, the scholars usually fired off a few rounds at bottles for target practice. Meals consisted of venison and trout or pork and potatoes, beans, and wheat bread. For beverages, they drank ale from tin pans and a little wine. At first, the scholars were leery about this backwoods diet, fearing it would give them indigestion. But Stillman assured them in a firm voice, "No chronic dyspepsia ever came from eating indigestible food." This statement calmed the nerves of some campers, though others continued to nervously grumble about their meals. Nevertheless, in the end, "all ate heartily & laughed heartily Whilst they ate," Emerson said. For dessert or a snack, the scholars had some gingersnaps that came courtesy of Lucy Mack, in whose house in Belmont Stillman had been lodging.[8]

Also on August 7, the Adirondack party welcomed two guests. Traveling in separate boats with their personal guides, F. S. Stallknecht and Charles E. Whitehead rowed down Follensby's outlet and entered the lake at sunset that day. They rowed toward the southern end of the lake, where a boat from a sequestered nook headed out toward them. In this boat was Holmes, with whom Stallknecht had hunted at Big Tupper Lake the previous year. Following Holmes's boat was another containing Agassiz at the stern, Emerson at the prow, and Lowell at the oars. The trio appears to have been familiar with Whitehead, an artist, because they addressed him and invited him and Stallknecht back to camp. The two visitors knew they would find the scholars' party at Follensby because earlier that day they had eaten lunch at Stephen Martin's cabin along the Indian Carry, where Stillman's party had lodged a few days earlier.[9]

At Camp Maple, the visitors found Binney and Wyman. Stallknecht had met Wyman seventeen years earlier in Paris. Wyman was examining the dry stomach of a buck. Binney was hoisting an American flag, which had previously been raised on a boat he rode while traveling along the Nile River. Stallknecht and Whitehead pitched a tent a distance from Camp Maple. After eating a supper of venison they lit their pipes and returned to what Stallknecht's guide, Sam Dunning, called the Philosophers' Camp.[10] Here it is important to note that this name, as mentioned earlier, derived from the Adirondack guides, not the party's members. While the general public quickly embraced the name, the scholars were reluctant to do so. Emerson never used the term in any of his essays, journal entries, or letters, and thirty-five years passed before Stillman used it in any of his written works. By modern standards, the name is not strictly accurate because only one party member, Emerson, was a bona fide philosopher. However, by the standards of the nineteenth century, when science and letters were still united, it is a more suitable description, which is more inclusive of other members such as Agassiz and Wyman. Perhaps the party's members shunned this title because it gave the false impression that their objective in camping in the woods was to philosophize when their goal was simply to enjoy the wilderness and each other's company.

At the Philosophers' Camp, Stallknecht and Whitehead met Stillman, Howe, and Hoar, who had all returned from an outing. Then the two visitors shared with the Adirondack party a piece of news that had been telegraphed from New York to Burlington the day they passed through the latter, shortly before entering the wilderness: the Atlantic telegraph cable had finally been laid after multiple unsuccessful and costly attempts since spring 1857. It is possible Stallknecht and Whitehead, or another unidentified party, at some time shared this news with some of the scholars while they were on an excursion to Big Tupper Lake.[11]

As of August 5, a copper wire stretched approximately 1,700 nautical miles between Trinity Bay in Newfoundland and Valentia Bay in Ireland, promising to revolutionize communications between the Old and New Worlds. Two ships, the American *Niagara* and the British *Agamemnon* had laid the cable across the ocean floor. Upon hearing this news, "three hearty cheers" filled the air around Camp Maple. Mankind, in the person of New York businessman Cyrus W. Field, had now linked two continents. In announcing the feat on August 6, the *New York Herald* called it the "Great Event of the Age."[12]

Since 1854, Field and a small circle of wealthy New Yorkers had been working to lay a telegraphic wire between Trinity Bay and Valentia Bay. Their New York, Newfoundland, and London Telegraph Company, as suggested by the enterprise's name, also intended to lay a land-based cable from Newfoundland to New York. To carry out the fund-raising campaign in London, Field established the Atlantic Telegraph Company in 1856. The company had first attempted to connect the continents by having one ship, the *Niagara,* lay the first half of the cable from Valentia Bay to midocean, where it would connect with the *Agamemnon,* which would lay the rest of the cable while traveling to Trinity Bay. However, technical factors conspired against the *Niagara,* which in August 1857 botched the first half of the cable-laying exercise.[13]

In June 1858, the Atlantic Telegraph Company had tried again, this time with the strategy of having the two ships begin laying cable simultaneously at midocean. Although the second attempt had started smoothly, the *Agamemnon* was battered as it traveled to the mid-Atlantic in a ferocious, six-day storm. After the *Agamemnon* reached the rendezvous on June 25, its cable and the *Niagara*'s cable were spliced, and they headed in opposite directions. The ships had to abandon the mission after laying 112 miles of cable because the cable became damaged. Fortunately, back in London, the increasingly nervous Atlantic Telegraph Company board of directors voted to give Field another shot. By mid-July the telegraphic fleet again set sail for the mid-Atlantic. They met in the mid-Atlantic on August 2.[14]

The last piece of news the scholars probably had caught about the Atlantic cable before they headed into the Adirondack wilderness was that the American frigate and British steamer likely were at or near a rendezvous point in the middle of the Atlantic Ocean (latitude fifty-two degrees, longitude thirty-two degrees). The *New York Herald* on August 1 reported, "In all probability the Atlantic telegraph fleet are by this time at the rendezvous in mid-ocean, commencing another attempt to lay the cable." Emerson was eager to hear the "great news . . . for which the world had waited."[15]

The *Agamemnon* had reached Valentia Bay on the morning of August 5. A day earlier, the *Niagara* had made landfall at Newfoundland, though it would not take anchor at Bull's Arm until 1:45 a.m. on August 5. From Trinity Bay, Field sent a dispatch to the Associated Press saying that the "machinery for paying out the cable worked in the most satisfactory manner" and "the electrical signals sent through the whole cable are perfect." He added that "by the blessing of Divine Providence it has succeeded." Emerson was overjoyed by this "glad miracle." "We have few moments in the longest life / of such pure joy wonder" he later wrote of the event.[16]

On the night of August 7, after celebrating the laying of the cable, the scholars occupied themselves with various pursuits. Agassiz, who was wrapped in his blanket, discussed with Wyman snakes that swallow and reject their young. Agassiz abruptly broke from the conversation when he spotted an insect, which prompted him to leap up, grab his fly net, and catch it. Whitehead plucked off his coat a bug similar to the one Agassiz had just caught and gave it to the scientist. Emerson found other aspects of the camp of greater interest. He walked over to Stallknecht, shook his hand, and invited him to look upward. They gazed at the "lofty green cathedral" above them created by the surrounding pine trees and the stars twinkling behind the forest canopy. Emerson said a few words about the ecstasy of the scene. According to Stallknecht, Emerson's comments needed "no other illustration than to follow his eyes."[17]

Stallknecht and Whitehead left Follensby the next morning, on August 8. Several members of the camp saw them off. The rustling of campers in the morning produced sounds rarely heard around Follensby, the silence of which was seldom disturbed except by the whistling of pines, the laugh of the loon, and screech of the osprey. At one moment Follensby's campers were firing off rifles, hooting, and hollering, and in the next the lake's "Lethian silence lured us deeper into its magic recesses," according to Stillman. Throughout the vacation, Emerson found himself in one extreme or the other.[18]

"So fast will Nature acclimate her sons," Emerson later said. Nevertheless, the philosopher was slow to adapt to camp life. On the "eloquent urgency" of Holmes, Emerson smoked from a tobacco pipe, though "once was enough," according to Edward Emerson. The philosopher refused at first to carry a rifle, hunt, or fish. When he did take up a rifle, it was initially only because everyone else did the same, Stillman surmised. Although Emerson had been excited about the prospect of possessing a rifle—so much so that he had gone against Stillman's advice not to buy one—his hesitancy to carry it may have stemmed from an initial lack of interest in hunting. Agassiz, too, initially abstained from using a firearm.[19]

In Follensby's outlet, Agassiz discovered a previously unknown type of freshwater sponge. This discovery, however, does not seem to have elicited much excitement within the party. Emerson did not even mention it in his poem about the camping trip. Yet he probably did not consider the omission a grave oversight. Even in Concord, such discoveries were commonplace. Thoreau had repeatedly claimed, as reported in *Walden* and *A Week on the Concord and Merrimac Rivers,* to have discovered unclassified species.[20] Perhaps Emerson thought the discovery of one more unknown species needed no commemoration in verse.

Sponges were not all the scientists caught in and around Follensby. Their list of captured creatures included lizards, salamanders, shrews, crabs, snails, minnows, and moths. Many of the specimens were placed in a lead pot of alcohol, which served as "an impartial tomb to all the kinds," according to Emerson. Agassiz's activities at Follensby were as amusing as they were interesting. While at Camp Maple, Stallknecht's guide, Sam Dunning, hilariously imitated the scientist for another visitor to the camp by running around trying to catch an imaginary insect. Dunning then pretended to catch one and declared it a "fine specimen of boog—veree."[21]

When Wyman and Agassiz discussed matters as they worked together at Camp Maple, "science seemed as easy as versification when Lowell was in the mood," Stillman said. "Nothing could have been, to any man with the scientific bent, more intensely interesting than the academy of two of the greatest scientists of their day." Members of the camp occasionally gathered around the two scientists as they worked at their tree-stump dissection table. Emerson appears to have been drawn to Camp Maple's laboratory and inquired about the scientists' activities. He wrote in his notebook: "River-lake, & brook trout cannot be scientifically discriminated, nor yet male from female."[22]

This piece of information likely came from Agassiz, who in his 1850 *Lake Superior* said no genus has a species "more difficult to distinguish" than that of the lake's trout. Europe had sixteen species of trout until Agassiz's reclassifications narrowed the number down to seven. By the end of the Lake Superior expedition in 1848, Agassiz had examined only two species from the Salmonidae family of ray-finned fish in the United States: brook trout, which is actually a char and not a true trout, and Mackinaw trout. Prior to separating from Longfellow in late July, Agassiz had briefed the poet on the experiments he planned to conduct in the Adirondacks. Longfellow, while in Nahant that August, told Charles Sumner, "Agassiz is to weigh the brains of trout, which the others are to catch."[23]

With trout, Agassiz also found not only a classification challenge but also further evidence of the Creator and his role in the origin of species. When Agassiz returned to Cambridge from his Lake Superior expedition, he became more convinced of God's design of the universe. Parts of *Lake Superior* actually read like a prelude to "Essay on Classification," from his first volume of the *Contributions,* which one modern biographer described as "a last and most explicit statement of pre-Darwinism teleology." In Agassiz's assessment, God had designed various types of animals for specific types of environments; animals' development was not a "consequence of the continued agency of physical causes."[24]

In observing trout's and whitefishes' strong muscles, which enabled them to swim upstream, and their large mouths and strong teeth that helped them secure food in Lake Superior's cold waters, Agassiz was "struck by the admirable reciprocal adaptation between the structure of these animals and the physical conditions in which they live." Almost in anticipation of Darwin's evolutionary theories, he said, "Let us not mistake these adaptations for a consequence of physical causes . . . but let us at once look deeper, let us recognize that this uniformity is imparted to a wonderfully complicated structure; they are trouts with all their admirable structure." Despite all the slight variations among the trout species, inherent to their uniform structure was "the same melody, however disguised, under the many undulations and changes of which it is capable."[25] To Agassiz, it was literally a divine "melody." And it was this connection between God and science that made Agassiz's views appealing to other intellectuals, such as Emerson and Stillman. It affirmed their worldviews, to an extent. With his studies of fish, Agassiz conveyed a message similar to the one found in Emerson's lecture on "The Preacher": "Nature is too thin a screen; the glory of the One breaks in everywhere." Hudson River School artists worked this message about the divine in nature into their paintings, such as Church's *Twilight in the Wilderness* (1860), which features a cross formed by splinters of wood standing on the altar of a tree stump in the foreground. Church, who was a follower of Agassiz and believed in "a union of science, religion, nature, and art," painted this work in 1860, a year after he met the scientist.[26]

After detailing these observations in *Lake Superior,* Agassiz in the book made a final appeal to readers who doubted "the correctness of [his] views." He referred to "another material fact, furnished by the family of Salmonidae." This fact hinged on "two essential modifications": While the "true type of trouts" show the same "general characters, backbone, skull, brain, composition of mouth, intestine, gills, & c., & c." they have different mouth sizes and an "almost absolute want of teeth." To Agassiz, only a divine "discriminating power" (i.e., God) "could have introduced those differences."[27]

While Agassiz's populism buffered his creationist thesis from the mounting evidence favoring natural selection, he often presented little empirical data to support his theory. The evolutionists would eventually exploit this weakness. Agassiz's dearth of hard data is apparent in his argument for the Creator's role in designing fish in the Salmonidae family. His main case was built largely on casual observations, such as that trout have strong muscles and broad tails that assist them in swimming up streams. This "admirable reciprocal adaptation" and others pointed to nothing else but an "infinitely wise, supreme Power" that "called . . . such animals into existence under the different circumstances prevailing over various parts of the globe, as would suit best his general plan." Only after drawing these loose connections in *Lake Superior* did Agassiz introduce for his doubters the "material fact" regarding the same general characteristics (e.g., backbone, skull, brain, composition of mouth, intestine, and gills) that fish in the Salmonidae family share and the mouth sizes that differentiate them. Given that the brain of the trout provided one of the few material facts on which Agassiz could hang this particular creationist thesis, his measuring activities at Camp Maple suggest he was interested in collecting empirical data to directly or indirectly support his beliefs on God's role in the origin of species. Agassiz's trout experiments at Follensby illustrate that he was, in the words of one of his modern biographers, both a "cutting-edge practitioner of fieldwork and [an] industrious simplifier of scientific truths."[28]

While it is not clear whether Agassiz discovered any signs of divinity in the brain of a trout, he and his fellow campers did find something miraculous at Follensby, namely, health. In the months prior to the Adirondack adventure, Agassiz suffered from a series of ailments. Earlier that summer, he had complained to Spenser Fullerton Baird, an ornithologist and memoirist then based in Washington, D.C., about rapidly losing his eyesight and being unable to read letters. He hoped "something will stop the misfortune." At least in the Adirondacks, the misfortune stopped abruptly for the fifty-one-year-old scientist. He went on the trip suffering from rheumatism and overwork, but "four days sufficed to restore him to his normal condition," Stillman said.[29]

Emerson, who was the most senior member of the camp at fifty-five years of age, was familiar with the aches and complaints of waning eyesight and rheumatism. But in the Adirondacks, Emerson noted that "in the forest delicate men / Sleep on the ground nor fear rheumatic pain." Follensby that summer heard nothing of frailness. The air there provided vitality. Emerson said of his company, "Their bold minds are answered by their good & strong bodies." A swim in the lake "commenced the exercises of the day," said Hoar, who was forty-two years old. Emerson was impressed by the swimming abilities of others at camp whose "arms can swim as far as their eyes can see."

Here Emerson probably had in mind Lowell's daring guide, Preston, who responded to the philosopher's question of how far he could swim, saying, "I never swum as far as I could."[30]

Stillman, too, felt reinvigorated. Though he was the second-youngest of the party at thirty years old (Binney was the party's youngest by two years), he had struggled with bouts of poor health. He felt a "restoration to physical health" and was "much stronger, mentally, physically and even morally." Emerson certainly took note of the painter's convalescence. "Stillman made 250,000 strokes of the oar in a day." Many of those strokes were probably expended on Agassiz during their regular trips onto the lake so the scientist could scoop up specimen samples with a dredge or insect net or examine plants by the lake's marshes. The scientist seems to have spent much time on the bay viewable across the lake from Camp Maple because the scholars named the broad inlet "Agassiz Bay." Many more strokes were likely spent taking Emerson on the water at dusk to view the procession of the pines or to get the philosopher away from the rabble of the camp and find him some quiet in the remotest of the remote corners of the lake.[31]

Rowing was a way of life at Follensby. It was crucial not only to transportation but also to hunting during both day and night. Stillman noted, "We hunted only when we needed meat." By mid-August, the scholars and their guides had killed and eaten seven deer. "My own exploits in that line were limited to a charge of buckshot put into the head of *one*," Hoar boasted to his wife. Day hunting was a matter of driving the deer out of the woods and into the lake, where they would be easy targets. Initially, the hunters set out in boats for various watching posts around Follensby. A guide then searched for deer prints, and when they were found, he set his dogs on the creature's trail. Sometimes, for up to two hours, the dogs chased a deer through Follensby's woods until it sought to escape them by swimming across the lake. A boat then pursued the fleeing animal, which was shot while swimming. With their short summer coats, the deer sank immediately after being shot, so a guide in the boat alongside it had to grab the animal's tail "when the shot became a sure one," Stillman explained. Stillman reserved night hunting for dark nights and when venison was needed because of unsuccessful day drives. This type of hunting was a matter of clandestinely rowing up to a deer along the shore and using a lantern to blind and daze the deer, making it an easy target.[32]

When there were ample supplies of venison at camp and after the scholars finished breakfast and their morning exercises, they further explored the wilderness. They broke into groups, one of which consisted of Emerson, Woodman, and Agassiz, who ventured to Big Tupper Lake. To reach their destination, the trio's guides rowed up Follensby's outlet into the Raquette River and down the Raquette fourteen miles to Big Tupper Lake. Then there was a six-mile row to Jenkins's compound near Bog River Falls, which Stillman had written about in the *Crayon* in 1855. Emerson noted that Jenkins lived in Atherton, "which contains eleven souls." Emerson appears to have talked at length with Jenkins, who had recently sold his farm in Lebanon County, Pennsylvania. In the Adirondacks, Jenkins did surveying work, measuring town lines and the breadth of lakes. Hoar also took a trip to Big Tupper Lake, where he stayed overnight and went night hunting. He spent the next day rowing back to Camp Maple in the pouring rain.[33]

When the scholars could not find their destinations, they were content enough with the journey alone. In his poem, Emerson noted that parties climbed steep slopes in search of a "rumored lake" they named "Lake Probability." However, "our carbuncle," was "long sought, not found." Something else that was long sought, at least by Emerson, and seldom found around Follensby was solitude. In Concord, if Emerson needed some time away from such noble-minded men, he could easily have walked with his thoughts simply by stepping out his side door and taking a stroll to Walden. At Follensby, Stillman explained, that was not an option. Such meandering was far too dangerous in the wilderness, where it was easy to get lost and attacked by wolves.[34]

Given these circumstances, Stillman occasionally escorted Emerson to secluded areas away from the rest of the party. Stillman consequently became as much of a guardian of Emerson's solitude in the wilderness as he was a guide to it. In return, Emerson supplied the painter with something engaging, namely, himself. "To me the forest was familiar," Stillman later said. After years of painting and camping in the wilderness, summer after summer, his "sophomoric sentiment" had waned, and the forest "no longer lured me with any emotion beyond that of quiet, the charm of Lethe, the fascination of an almost complete negation of intellectual existence, and absolute rest." However, Stillman was tickled by Emerson's reaction to the wilderness—the way "he took in her influences as the earth takes the rain."[35]

One Sunday morning, Stillman took Emerson out in his boat as the guides set out for a hunt. Some scholars headed to their watching posts, but the painter and philosopher instead hunted peace and quiet. The pair landed on the lake's remotest shore, and solitude greeted Emerson there. It was a meditative moment. Then the hounds caught the scent of a deer and disrupted Follensby's hush with their barking, faint yet distinct from a distance.

Emerson's and Stillman's ears followed the chase from one end of Follensby, up its hills, to another end and back again. Finally, yielding to the thrill of the hunt, Emerson exclaimed, "Let us go after the deer!" They leapt back into their boat and flew down the lake even though neither one had brought a rifle. They headed to the part of the shore where the dogs were baying. They arrived too late, though, because Lowell had killed the deer before their arrival.[36] The scholars' acclimation to nature was complete.

🐦 CHAPTER 9

The Worthy Crew Chaucer
Never Had

Nighttime.

"Shoot," the guide whispered. The boat had glided through the darkness, creeping closer and closer to the indistinguishable landscape lining Follensby's shore. Rocks and trees blended into each other, forming a black mass. A faint glow rose from the boat, revealing three shadowy figures sitting in it. Up until that moment, the only sound had been of the water occasionally rushing beneath the boat, and then something else. The guide had heard it first: the rustling of a deer walking out of the woods toward the shore. He had pointed a lantern toward where the noise was coming; the light dazed the animal, which stood motionless twenty yards away.[1]

The signal to fire had been given. Sitting in the spot behind the guide with the lantern, Emerson aimed his rifle toward the bright spot on the shore. Just silence, which the guide softly broke with his whisper. Emerson strained his eyes to see what he was being told to shoot. It was all a blur to him, even when they got within a boat's length of the deer. "Shoot!" Stillman repeated. Seeing the creature bolt for the woods, the painter let go a hasty shot. *Crack.* Then the quiet again, disrupted by the rustling of foliage as the deer galloped away, crying, "Ahaish! Ahaish!"[2]

Emerson was stupefied. A deer? "I knew not whether it were a rock or a bush." The boat followed the shoreline of Osprey Bay, near the outlet. It was not long until Follensby offered Emerson a second chance. This time, the deer was already at the water feeding on lily pads or drinking. The boat glided closer and closer. The boat got even closer to this deer than to the one that got away. It stood in the shallow water broadside to the philosopher, yet he could not make out his target and pull the trigger. Fearing a repeat of what had happened moments earlier, Stillman took no chances and raised his rifle. *Crack.* A kill. Then the quiet returned to the endless shadows. "Well," Emerson said to Stillman, "if that was a deer, I shall fire at the first square thing I see."[3]

After days in the wilderness, "the survival of the earliest passion of the primitive man, the passion of the chase, overcame even the philosophic mind of Emerson," Stillman said. Once that passion awoke, there was little Emerson could do to shake it. ·A series of unsuccessful daytime hunts only stoked his desire to kill. The deer, however, always eluded him; they always appeared at someone else's watching post. "I must kill a deer before we go home, even if the guide has to hold him by the tail," Emerson told Stillman. The night hunt on which Emerson went "jack hunting" and saw only the "square mist" was the painter's last-ditch effort to satiate the newly savage bard. Yet the only game Emerson bagged at Follensby to appease his passion was a "peetweet," a type of spotted sandpiper. He gave the blasted peetweet to Agassiz.[4]

Eventually, the morning shooting range became a little more crowded. Emerson and Agassiz joined Lowell, Hoar, Stillman, Woodman, and others in taking aim at some bottles. There was plenty of ammunition to go around. Several pounds of lead were cut from one tree, which probably stood behind the bottles or mark at which the scholars shot. In Agassiz's case, he apparently participated in the target practice under peer pressure. One morning, someone in the camp asked the scientist to try to hit the mark. Agassiz's initial hesitation prompted the rest of his companions to prod him to take a shot, claiming that a man "with such excellent eyesight must be a good shot." Eventually, Agassiz picked up his rifle, took aim, fired, and hit the bull's-eye. Agassiz's marksmanship earned the cheer and applause of the party, but he declined to take a second shot.[5]

Wyman was as much of a crack shot as Agassiz. According to Emerson, Wyman's "level gun will hit the white." Hoar was probably not much of a marksman. During his Harvard years in the early 1830s, he had had to sit out on the primitive "Massachusetts game" of baseball because of his nearsightedness. When encouraging Richard Dana to join the Adirondack party, Hoar had said he wanted at camp a "friend, with a lively imagination, to make fun of my shooting. It will doubtless set you up with a new comic stock." Emerson, too, did not have the best eyesight, so he took his shots at six rods.[6]

Nearsighted or not, Emerson could see clearly enough the clothes some men at camp wore. They were hard to miss. "In sooth, red flannel is a saucy test," Emerson noted, "which few can put on with impunity." His "polished gentlemen" from Boston were to "bow to the stalwart churls in overalls . . . doctors of the wilderness." Emerson brought with him a cloak and shirts to don in the wilderness. Nevertheless, with or without flannel shirts, the scholars "were a remarkable looking set, considering who they were," Hoar said to his wife. "And I think any one of them would have been convicted on very slight evidence, especially Mr. Emerson." Emerson, meanwhile, saw himself "dressed, like Nature, fit for her own ends."[7]

With a vermilion pencil, the scholars marked the number of days they spent in the wilderness. As the number of pencil marks grew, the scholars adopted the rugged looks of their guides. The comparison, though, ended there. As Emerson noted, "We flee away from cities, but we bring / The best of cities with us." While they did not find the high culture of Boston in the Adirondacks, they brought with them their knowledge of literature and art and science. That is not to say the wilderness was entirely bereft of culture. Somewhere during the journey, "on the verge of craggy Indian wilderness," Emerson heard someone playing Beethoven on a piano in a log cabin. The music was, they jested, something to keep the bears "at bay."[8]

Although the guides were no match for the scholars intellectually, for the most part, the polished gentlemen got along well with their flannel-clad companions. There was at least one exception: Lowell. In October 1871, after giving a lecture in Medford, Massachusetts, Higginson encountered a guide who called Lowell "a d—d ignorant cuss." Higginson identified the man as "H.'s guide in the Adirondacks," but it is not clear whether he was referring to Hoar's, Howe's, or Holmes's guide or whether he served as a guide during the 1858 Adirondack trip or during the preceding or follow-ing years' adventures at Big Tupper Lake or Ampersand Pond. In contrast, Agassiz was as wildly popular with the camp's guides as he was with the residents of Keeseville. "His inexhaustible *bonhomie* won even the guides to a personal fealty they showed no other of our band," Stillman observed. Even the painter confessed to falling under the "magic of his colossal individual-ity." The scientist made less of an impression on Sam Dunning, Stallknecht's guide, however. Dunning challenged the theory supported by Agassiz that female trout deposit their eggs in males, who then impregnate them with their milt. The guide later told Stallknecht, "He may be a nice man and pleasant enough, and I might be willin' to guide with him, but it must be great consolation for a man to come far away off here in the woods to catch boogs and mice; I should think he might find enough of 'em where he came from; but if you tell me he knows anything about breeding trout, I tell you he don't know nothing about it. Pshaw!"[9]

Agassiz gave lessons to his guides and fellow scholars on everything from fish to the Laurentian range, which was a belt of Paleozoic rocks "in one of whose hollow we lay," Stillman said. Here, teaching the cultured man and the common man at camp about fish and lake formations, Agassiz was in his element. In the Adirondacks, instead of lecturing to the guides, Emerson talked to them and studied them. He conversed with Preston and Jenkins. Emerson was fascinated by how the guides reversed social customs by putting their coats on when they went to sleep and taking them off after waking; they wore their hats in camp but not while on the lake. Wielding an ax and helping out around camp, even Stillman found himself under Emerson's microscope. "[N]ow he found a man who could be taken up as a specimen and studied as an individual, as Agassiz would have studied a fossil, and all this was new," the painter said.[10]

Stillman's comparison of Emerson to Agassiz is fitting. Over the previous two decades, both men had been building elaborate systems of classification. Agassiz's classification contributions covered fish from around the globe, most notably Brazil; Emerson's included addresses and essays such as "The American Scholar" in 1837, "Man the Reformer" in 1841, "The Transcendentalist" in 1842, and "The Poet" in 1844. With each address or essay, Emerson constructed a classification system built around virtues and skills. The reformer was the "renouncer of lies; a restorer of truth and good, imitating the great Nature which embosoms us all." The scholar was the "world's eye" and the "world's heart"; he "raises himself from private considerations and breathes and lives on public and illustrious thoughts."[11]

Emerson's studies of men had reached their zenith in 1856 with the publication of *English Traits.* In the book, he detailed an array of traits inherent to Englishmen, such as their ability, manners, and wealth. However, two years after the publication of *English Traits,* in the Adirondacks, Stillman that observed Emerson had become "weary" of such studies of society in general. Nevertheless, the philosopher displayed an "insatiability in the study of human nature . . . in our first summer's camp."[12]

As the philosopher studied the men around him, he saw himself fulfilling a tradition in English literature. The Philosophers' Camp, to him, was an American version of Chaucer's *Canterbury Tales* except that the Adirondack party, guides included, was smaller than the thirty pilgrims who had ventured to Canterbury in the fourteenth century. Stillman could easily pass as Chaucer's knight, Woodman as the merchant, and Howe as the physician.

Given Lowell's and Hoar's testy dialogue around the campfire, they could be viewed as nineteenth-century versions of the friar and the summoner. Emerson, naturally, could have played the part of Geoffrey Chaucer. Like the Middle English poet, Emerson saw it as his responsibility to describe his company. In this context, he studied the men around him not to classify them or to reveal some truth about human nature but simply to tell a tale. Emerson later wrote in his notebook the following lines, which became the motto for "The Adirondacs":

> Wise and polite
> And if I drew
> Their several portraits you would own
> Chaucer had no such worthy crew,
> Nor Boccace in Decameron.[13]

In a way reminiscent of Chaucer's prologue to *The Canterbury Tales,* Emerson went on to write in his notebook the portraits of his companions at Camp Maple. He started briefly with Agassiz: "The Doctor with whose fame / Both worlds are filled, whom France / Grudges to us." He then wrote seven poems, each of which initially bore the title of its subject: "Hoar," "J. Holmes," "Wyman," "Woodman," "Howe," "Stillman," and "Lowell." Tellingly, Emerson wrote no poem for Binney, the stranger of the group. He never published these biographical sketches in his lifetime, though there is evidence he had considered publishing the lines on Holmes and Lowell. Edward Emerson more than a half century later included verses he edited about Wyman, Woodman, Stillman, Lowell, and Howe in his *Early Years of the Saturday Club.*[14]

It is hard to date these character sketches. The Emerson biographer Ralph H. Roth estimated they were drafted at the latest by February 22, 1859, when Emerson read the first draft of "James Russell Lowell" to the Saturday Club on the day of the namesake poet's birthday. In all likelihood, he completed these poems before a lecture tour started in November 1858. While some of the poems describe their subjects in general terms and cannot be connected to a specific time or place, others are clearly based on observations Emerson made in the Adirondacks.[15]

Hoar's four lines are an example of the former. In the judge's poem, Emerson recalls his "keenest wit" and calls him "A champion of the state / A giant of the law." Likewise, Howe's verses feature no specific reference to the Adirondack trip, although they suggest the party at Follensby could have been indebted to his "Generous heart & solid sense," which guaranteed that "Where though art, society / Still will live and best will be." Meanwhile,

Wyman's performance at Camp Maple's shooting range—and probably at dinner table debates—earned him the lines about his "level gun" hitting "the white" and "his cautious tongue [that] will speak the right." Woodman's poem seems to be as applicable to the gathering at Follensby as to the Saturday Club meetings at Parker's Hotel. At both locations, he played the role of peacekeeper. In his poem, he reconciled a "Scientific feud" by pacifying "the injured heart" and mollifying "the rude." He was a "Man of affairs / Harmonizing oddest pairs / With a passion to unite / Oil and water."[16]

While Woodman kept the group's affairs civil, Holmes kept its members merry in "a rude and savage place," which could be the Adirondacks or Parker's. Holmes, according to Emerson, was the group's self-deprecating "humorist" who caressed "his infirmities / As cossets for his play." He filled "Saxon minds / With his redundant fancy & his wit." Lowell's gallivanting up giant pine trees and around Follensby, along with his wit and humor at the dinner table, likely influenced Emerson's sketch of him. Emerson painted him as a ball of energy, teeming with vitality and playful trouble. He was "Most at home in mounting fun / Broadest joke and luckiest pun / in the mantling tones / Of his rich voice / Speeding troops of social joys / And in the volleys of his mirth." The phrase "Strength for the hour" is repeated in the poem.[17]

Finally, there is Stillman's poem. It is pure Adirondacks. And in the poem Emerson leaves no doubt as to who was in charge of camp. Stillman was "Easily chief" and "admiral of all the lakes," though Emerson crossed out the latter rank.[18] It is quite clear from this sketch that the painter was the one who held the camp together. According to the poem, it was Stillman who planned out each day's duties and who gave the guides orders. Again, he was the camp's

> Gallant artist, head and hand
> Adopted of Tahawus grand,
> In the wild domesticated,
> Man and Mountain rightly mated
> Like forest chief the forest ranged
> As one who had exchanged
> After old Indian mode
> Totem and bow and spear
> In sign of peace and brotherhood
> With his Indian peer.
> Easily chief, who held
> The key of each occasion

In our designed plantation,
Can hunt and fish and rule and row,
And out-shoot each in his own bow,
And paint and plan and execute
Till each blossom becomes fruit;
Earning richly for his share
The governor's chair,
Bore the day's duties in his head,
And with living method sped.
Firm, unperplexed,
By no flaws of temper vexed,
Inspiring trust.
And only dictating because he must.
And all he carried in his heart
He could publish and define
Orderly line by line
On canvas by his art.
I could wish
So worthy Master worthier pupils had—
The best were bad.[19]

Although Emerson wrote highly of Stillman in this poem, it does not mean the philosopher believed himself to be subordinate to this "chief," at least outside the wilderness. Stillman's high standing in Emerson's eye existed only in the woods and the studio. Unlike the poems about the camp's other participants, Stillman's does not place him in the social settings of a more civilized environment. Emerson did not portray him as an integral player in any court, intellectual debate, or the liveliest and best society. Stillman remained an outsider. In Boston he was not an equal, but in the wilderness he was superior.

As Emerson observed these men, he grew fonder of their company and the way the wilderness made it sweeter. Others in the party shared this sentiment. In reference to Lowell, Stillman said, "We were nearest each other in our Adirondack life, in which he had all the zest of a boy." Although Emerson had spent countless Saturday afternoons at Parker's Hotel with many of his fellow campers, the wilderness unlocked aspects of their characters he had never seen. Stillman recalled Agassiz commenting one day about a realization he had during his experiences in the Alps. Agassiz found, Stillman said, "when the company was living on terms of compulsory intimacy, . . . men found each other out quickly." Miraculously, what the scholars found out about each other in the Adirondacks only strengthened their camaraderie.

At some point, they began to talk of making such summer vacations a tradition. As Emerson explained, the scholars planned to build a "spacious lodge" where they could take their sons, "willing they, and more adroit."[20]

About a week into the scholars' retreat from civilization, the civilized world learned where they had gone into hiding. Emerson's family heard the news first. On August 5, Emerson sent a brief note to Concord saying he "had good luck" and he invited his family to write to him. Emerson's nineteen-year-old daughter, Ellen, had actually been working on a letter to her father since August 3, the day after he left for the Adirondacks. Over the following six days, she kept her father abreast of the happenings around the home, such as a caterpillar infestation at their Concord house; the departure of Edward and Edith, who were sent to the Forbes estate on Naushon; and the receipt of an invitation to lecture in Albany from A. D. Mayo, a Unitarian preacher. Additionally, there was the news about the laying of the Atlantic cable. When Ellen received her father's short note on August 9, her sweet letter turned bitter. "We were all indignant enough before at your not writing a word, but now the word has come, you don't tell us anything and I don't think that's pretty. . . . I will set your tiger loose on you the moment she gets home."[21]

Given the tone of this letter, it is not surprising that Emerson later said in his poem about the trip: "Nay, letters found us in our paradise." The *New York Evening Post* was among the first publications to break the news about the Philosophers' Camp, reporting that Agassiz, Lowell, "Dr. [Oliver Wendell] Holmes," Emerson, Wendell Phillips, Hoar, Stillman, and "Dr. S[amuel]. G. Howe" were in the Adirondacks for a month. Correcting the *Post,* the *Hartford Daily Times* on August 10 reported that Phillips was to lecture in Amherst on the next day. Suggesting how the popularity of the camp threatened to undermine the remoteness of the outing, the *Daily Times* noted, "There are one or two more in the party, whose names are not mentioned by the *Post,* and they are glad of it."[22]

It is no surprise that a band of ten New England intellectuals could not anonymously pass their days in the wilderness. The Adirondacks that summer were teeming with journalists. In addition to Stillman and Stallknecht, the *New York Times* also had a correspondent in the region that month, as did the *Evening Post.* In August, the *Times* began printing a travel series titled "Letters from Summer Resorts: Life in the Adirondacks," based on a series of letters written by a correspondent identified only as "H.," and who may have been Samuel H. Hammond. Hammond was an Albany attorney who in 1857 had published *Wild northern scenes; or, sporting adventures with the rifle and the rod.* On July 9, 1858, he had sent a letter to the *Times* from Lower Saranac

Lake. Don Carlos was the *Post*'s correspondent who visited the Adirondacks at the suggestion of Stallknecht. Carlos and a friend had stopped at Martin's Hotel to pick up supplies. William Martin commissioned the pair to deliver additional supplies to the scholars at Follensby Pond, some of whom Carlos knew. With two hired guides, Carlos and his companion headed deeper into the wilderness. At Little Tupper Lake, they encountered two old sportsmen friends, a Mr. Dibblee of New York, and a Mr. Bradish of Flushing.[23]

Carlos's next stop was at Follensby Pond. Finding Camp Maple would not prove to be a difficult task, regardless of the time of day. At night a fire served as a beacon and during the day it raised a pillar of smoke. Binney's American flag also "waved in sublime ostentation" over the roof of a shanty. To Carlos, the camp looked like a permanent one with complete arrangements. It included a butchery, a kennel, a covered kitchen, and a landing for boats. Carlos stayed at the camp long enough to observe Agassiz catching insects "with an industry and enthusiasm" that astonished the guides, "who were more bent on getting rid of the same insects than in securing them." Wyman collected the anatomical parts of animals he dissected; Holmes shot his rifle and wrote; Emerson read and watched Stillman fish. After they had finished their supper, the party gathered around the big fire for lively conversations. After leaving Follensby, Carlos found at Forked Lake another big camp built by the philanthropist Charles L. Brace, the founder of the Children's Aid Society, whose so-called orphan trains took thousands poor urban children to rural communities. At night a large tent covered his camp, which consisted of four men and four women, including himself and his wife and son.[24]

Around the time news about the Philosophers' Camp began appearing in newspapers, Longfellow, still at Nahant, was surprised not to have heard news of Emerson's shooting anyone. On August 12, he informed Sumner about the Adirondack party and the gun Emerson had bought. "They have been out ten days, and so far we have not heard of anybody's being shot." Even without any casualties reported, Longfellow did not express any regret for not participating in the Adirondack party. Yet he longed for the isolation Emerson was then enjoying. He said, "We are leading an idle life here at Nahant; and the little leisure I can contrive to secure to myself is filched away from me by unmeaning letters;—invitations to lectures; requests to do some thing or other for somebody I never heard of. Most of them I feel bound to answer."[25]

By mid-August Norton was in Newport preparing to receive as his guest Oliver Wendell Holmes, who had declined Stillman's invitation to join the Adirondack party. Norton told Arthur Clough, "Lowell, Emerson, and Agassiz, and two or three more are out camping in the Adirondack Mountains—shooting deer, and perhaps a 'b'ar' or two, catching trout, cutting their names on birch trees, and having a general good time. They will soon be at home again." Even without the company of Oliver Wendell Holmes and Longfellow, the spirit of the Saturday Club thrived in the wilderness. Stillman's description of the gatherings at Camp Maple is reminiscent of those at Parker's Hotel. Those outdoor meetings were "symposia to which fortune has invited few men." At camp, Lowell, with his "unceasing play of wit and erudition," and Hoar, with his "pyrotechnical wit," engaged in their usual game of "matching table-talk." Agassiz and Emerson sat as "umpires" of the debate. "Holmes and Estes Howe [were] not silent in the well-matched contest, the forest echoed with such laughter as no club ever knew," said Stillman.[26]

When the conversation died and darkness fell, the camp remained something at which to marvel. When Emerson looked around, he saw stars peeping through the maple boughs, which "overhung, like a cloud" when lighted by the campfires below. In the dark surrounding woods, decaying tree trunks appeared to be swarming with glowworms or "phosphoric crumbs."[27] These glowing crumbs Emerson saw alight in the forest were the byproduct of the oxidation process of hyphomycetes, a type of fungus. The fungus produces light when it comes in contact with oxygen and then goes dim as it is removed, an effect similar to the glowing of a firefly.

As this phosphorescent flashing continued around him, one evening in mid-August Emerson sensed a change in the wind. "One August evening had a cooler breath," he wrote, and "intruding duties crept" into his mind. Other members of the camp, too, sensed that their vacation was coming to an end. Hoar was among the first to go. By August 15 he was in Saratoga Springs, where he wrote to his wife. He told her, "I came in from the lakes and mountains yesterday—considerably browner and wiser than I went. Neither Mr. Emerson nor I have shot the other, and Mr. Emerson has passed for a very credible woodsman. I think all of our party have had a good time." Emerson, too, "was one of the first to turn back to the sterner use of time," Stillman said. On Emerson's last full day in the woods, Stillman rowed him onto the lake at twilight one last time. There they watched "the glow dying out behind a noble line of marching pines on the shore of Follansbee Water."[28]

This bittersweet moment aboard the boat demonstrates how deeply moved Emerson was by the enchanting procession of the pines and how grateful he was to Stillman for introducing it to him. After spending two weeks camping together, as his character sketch suggests, Emerson admired the artist far more than he had before leaving Boston. Stillman was equally intrigued by Emerson, particularly his perpetual wonderment and lack of vanity and self-importance. But it is hard to say whether Stillman admired Emerson more by the time they sat together that last time on the boat. From his observations of Emerson in camp, Stillman concluded that the philosopher "had no self-sufficiency," and he "lived and felt with the minimum of personal color." Stillman recognized that Emerson categorized men into "two classes" those with whom he formed "personal attachments" and others who were "objects of study." Stillman knew he did not fall in Emerson's first class of personal attachments. He knew he was an object, an outsider.[29]

One thing the scholars made certain to do before leaving the Adirondacks was to send their gratitude to Lucy Mack for the snacks she had made for the party. From Saranac Lake, they sent her a note written on birch bark in Agassiz's handwriting. It was dated "Camp Maple Aug 16 '58" and noted that the party had voted to extend its thanks to Mrs. Mack "for her contribution of ginger-snaps." The note was signed by Emerson, Woodman, Wyman, Lowell, Howe, Stillman, Hoar, and Binney.[30] Hoar's signature on the August 16 note is odd because he had left the Adirondacks two days earlier. Emerson, too, likely left before the sixteenth. He arrived home in Concord the next day. This note signed by such influential Boston men also likely served the purpose of elevating the standing of Stillman before Lucy and David Mack. The painter had fallen in love with their daughter, and, much like Lowell the previous year, would propose to his love shortly after returning from the Adirondacks.

When his company left the Adirondacks, Stillman stayed behind to paint. "They left me in the early stages of a picture on which I worked as hard as I knew how," he told Norton. However, Stillman said he opted to leave this painting rather than finish it. Before the party left, he did work on a study of camp and its inhabitants performing various tasks one morning. He planned to work on it further when he returned home. Usually Stillman had ended his summer vacations in the Adirondack or White Mountains with multiple paintings that he later displayed at the next spring exhibition hosted by the National Academy of Design. But this summer his not yet completed study would be the only such landscape to be shown there in 1859. At this event he did show two other paintings, titled *Sunset* and *Harvesting,* but these works likely had no connection to the Adirondack adventure.[31] It is possible that Stillman's duties as chief guide kept him from devoting more time to painting.

After leaving Camp Maple, Emerson may have passed by John Brown's farm in North Elba. Brown, with whom the philosopher had been intrigued since they met in Concord in March 1857, was in Kansas at the time. Members of his family were then still living at the homestead, but Emerson never mentioned meeting them. Either way, the philosopher was not impressed by the sight of the farm. He later said he had "once passed by the farm when it did not look attractive to a settler."[32] The fact that no other members of the party mentioned this trip to the Brown homestead suggests that Emerson went there while traveling alone or with a smaller group, which had not been the case when he was en route to Follensby.

In Concord, Emerson did an accounting of his vacation. In his account book, he noted arriving home on the evening of August 17. He had been gone for fifteen days. For expenses, Emerson registered $71.15 plus $3.50 for "a few purchases." Not long after Emerson's return, other campers, too, came home and began readjusting to civilization. By August 19, a delighted Agassiz was back in Cambridge, spending the evening at Longfellow's house. When Thoreau heard of Emerson's Adirondack exploits, such as his shooting bottles, he said, "It sounds rather Cockneyish." Emerson arrived home just in time to catch the newspaper reports of the successful transmission of Queen Victoria's Atlantic cable message. Cyrus Field returned to New York from Newfoundland on September 1 and received a hero's welcome. However, during the festivities he received the devastating news: the cable had died. A public outcry erupted over the cable's failure. *The Boston Courier* called the entire project a scam meant to enrich Field.[33]

Emerson's summer was far from over. He told John Forbes to expect him and his wife at Naushon on August 31. Ellen would also join them. Edward and Edith had been sent to the island earlier that month. Prior to making the journey, he told Forbes, "Your island has such a fame in these parts, that my children think one may well go to the Adirondac by way of study & preparation for Naushon." One evening at the Forbes house Ellen noted, "We talked awhile and Father read 'Adirondac' after which I went to bed."[34] She was probably referring to what would eventually become Emerson's epic poem on his Adirondack journey.

Just before the Emersons left for Naushon, the *New York Evening Post* on August 30 printed a letter Don Carlos had written on August 16 at Raquette Lake. The letter detailed his adventures in the Adirondacks, including his discovery of the Philosophers' Camp. Carlos provided a description of the camp and the activities of its ten members. After describing how the scholars gathered around the campfire after supper, Carlos said, "It would not be amiss to affirm that no such coterie of minds is assembled at one

FIGURE 13.   William James Stillman (1828–1901), *The Philosophers' Camp in the Adirondacks*, 1858. Oil on canvas, 30 × 19 in. When Stillman showed this painting at the National Academy's 1859 exhibition, the work was initially titled *Morning at Camp Maple: Adirondack Woods*. To the right are Hoar, Lowell, Stillman, Binney, and Woodman; and to the left are Holmes, Howe, Agassiz, and Wyman. Emerson, holding a pilgrim staff, stands between the two groups. Courtesy Concord Free Public Library.

hearthside from the land of the chivalry to where 'the fisher baits his angle and the hunter twangs his bow' on the larchen banks of the Temiscouta." From this point onward, the Philosophers' Camp was to be recognized as an unprecedented gathering of intellectuals in the Adirondacks that represented a unique interaction of culture with the wilderness. Within a week, the Carlos report about the Philosophers' Camp had spread as far as Minnesota. On September 7 the *St. Paul Daily Minnesotian* reprinted an excerpt of his letter.[35]

By early October Stillman was back in Belmont and busy working on his own contribution to the rapidly evolving Philosophers' Camp reputation. He informed Norton that work had begun on what was to become his most famous painting, *Morning at Camp Maple: Adirondack Woods.* "I am painting a picture of our camp and its inhabitants," he said. The painter called this work an "experiment in historical painting with which I have every reason to be pleased." This painting grew out of the study of a Camp Maple morning Stillman had worked on while he was with the scholars in the Adirondacks. He divided the study into the various morning activities. On one side stand Lowell, Hoar, Binney, Woodman, and Stillman engaged in or watching target practice; on the other stand Agassiz and Wyman dissecting a trout with Howe and Holmes watching. Somewhat lost in the middle is Emerson, who is holding a pilgrim staff and watching the firing exercises near a huge boulder. All around the scholars rise massive tree trunks. At the insistence of his fellow campers, Stillman included himself in the painting. He painted his figure from a photograph and was disappointed with what appeared on the canvas.[36] Although this painting is better known today as *The Philosophers' Camp in the Adirondacks,* it does not appear to have acquired this title until sometime after 1895.

By October 22, Stillman reported to his old colleague at the *Crayon,* John Durand, that "the portraits in the camp picture seem to give universal satisfaction to the friends of the parties, particularly those of Agassiz Emerson and Lowell. Emerson is pronounced *perfect,* by everybody." Stillman noted at this time that the portrait of Agassiz was "not quite finished," and he already had an order for duplication of this work. Stillman later said he had planned to turn this study into "a picture which should commemorate the moment; but, owing to changes in my plans, it remained a study."[37]

On October 11, Lowell wrote to a friend about the Saturday Club's latest dinner, which was held in honor of Stillman. Lowell recounted an amusing anecdote from that gathering during which Hoar had given a speech. Lowell expressed his desire for Hoar to continue speaking so he could propose Stillman's good health. Hoar, however, declined this request, saying he believed he had already spoken "the sentiments of every gentleman present." While it is not known what Hoar said in his initial remarks, his refusal to propose Stillman's health suggests that club members remained hesitant to embrace the painter too strongly.[38]

On October 13, Stillman finally told Lowell in a letter what he had been reluctant to tell the poet a day earlier when the two were together. "I am engaged to Miss Laura Mack, a charming little body whom you don't know but whom I hope you will know and like as she deserves." Stillman assured Lowell his intentions were as noble as they were practical. Indicating that he considered himself a member of a class lower than that of the company he had just kept in the Adirondacks, he told Lowell he had chosen "one from my own level."[39]

Many of Stillman's friends warned him that he had "thrown away chances of advancement by matrimonial alliance" by taking for a wife a woman as simple as Laura. Certain that the world could offer no wealth greater than Laura's "lavish love" and "purity of heart," Stillman declared, "Come what may." He was certain that he had chosen "the eternal" over "perishing Fortune." He concluded that it was "wiser as an artist to stay in my native atmosphere."[40] It was through this same wisdom that Stillman managed to accept himself as a subordinate to the men at the Philosophers' Camp.

❧ CHAPTER 10

Ampersand

It was November. Winter made its traditional early debut in the Adirondacks. In the Adirondack woods, Stillman faced a northwesterly wind carrying a cold fog, which crystallized on every tree. As far as he could see, the painter saw a "forest of frosted silver." As the wind swirled around him, Stillman marveled at the scene. "It was a spectacle for a lifetime, and has never been offered to me again," he recalled late in life. And this spectacle came close to being the last thing Stillman ever saw. Stillman trudged through the icy wilderness, likely coughing as much as he was freezing. Before venturing back into the woods, the painter had caught a severe cold in New York City. He had considered it a "trivial matter to notice, but one which narrowly escaped that gravest consequences to me." The cold turned into "bronchial attack," but the painter continued with his journey, and he found shelter at Martin's Hotel at Lower Saranac Lake. He was dangerously chilled. It was "the closest shave to death" he had ever experienced.[1]

It was Stillman's fellow campers back in Boston who had sent him to the Adirondacks' crystal forest. At a late-autumn meeting in Cambridge, members of the Follensby party called for the formal organization of a club. Stillman never fully identified who attended this meeting, short of saying the club's most ardent supporters included Boston's and Cambridge's most prominent intellectuals who had also stayed at Camp Maple, such as Emerson, Lowell, and Hoar. The group decided to purchase a tract of land in the Adirondacks—"the less accessible the better"—and build a permanent clubhouse there. Stillman was appointed the club's secretary. The idea for the clubhouse likely originated with Stillman, who in 1855 had expressed to Norton his desire to build an Adirondack cabin that could house a dozen of his friends.[2]

A day after arriving at Martin's Hotel, Stillman gathered several guides and trappers for a consultation meeting about a tract of land he was eyeing for the club. He focused their attention on a remote body of water at the base of a mountain and east of Follensby. Its name: Ampersand Pond. It is possible Stillman had learned about this pond during his 1855 Adirondack adventure, when his planned fishing trip to Ampersand Brook had been abandoned because of flooding. Given his illness, the storm, and the fact that there was not a house within fourteen miles of the pond, Stillman did not then venture into the woods to survey the tract as he had initially planned. Fortunately, many of the guides he called to Martin's Hotel were familiar with the tract—some had even participated in a recent official survey of Ampersand's woods. With their assistance, Stillman drew a map of the pond, which sat in the northwest quarter of Township Twenty-Seven of Great Tract One of Macomb's Purchase, with the pond's eastern side almost abutting the border of the northeast quarter. Macomb's Purchase was series of massive land transactions that had occurred over several years in the 1790s. It had provided Alexander Macomb and two wealthy investors, William Constable and Daniel McCormick, with four million acres of Adirondack wilderness previously owned by New York State. The acquisition included six "great tracts," which were divided into smaller sections dubbed "townships."[3] Follensby ended up in Township Twenty-Six. Townships Twenty-Six and Twenty-Seven were both located in southern Franklin County.

With the map in hand and the guides' testimony detailing the tract's features, including the depths of the water, the lay of the land around it, Ampersand's inlets and outlets, and its wildlife and vegetation, Stillman's mission was complete. Before leaving for New York, he even managed to initiate preliminary negotiations for land around Ampersand. He believed the club would be able to purchase the tract for ten cents per acre. From Lower Saranac, Stillman went to New York City to visit a doctor, who advised the ill painter to go home and get in bed as quickly as possible. Stillman then went to a hospital in Plainfield, New Jersey, where he had family and his brother Charles lived and practiced medicine. From there, Stillman briefed Lowell on the Adirondack scouting mission. He reported having returned from the Adirondacks "somewhat the worse." The club's secretary provided Lowell with an overview of his meeting with the guides and their discussions about

Plate 1. Charles C. Ingham (1796–1863), *The Great Adirondack Pass, Painted on the Spot, 1837.* Oil on canvas, 48 × 40 in. Charles Ingham was among the first wave of nineteenth-century artists who ventured into the Adirondacks to capture on canvas unique wilderness scenes. Ingham in 1837 joined the renowned geologist Ebenezer Emmons on the New York Natural History Survey, during which the artist painted *The Great Adirondack Pass, Painted on the Spot, 1837.* The Adirondack Pass, also known as the Indian Pass, is in Essex County. Courtesy of the Adirondack Museum.

Plate 2. Thomas Cole (1801–1848), *View of Schroon Mountain, Essex County, New York, After a Storm*, 1838. Oil on canvas, 99.8 × 160.6 cm. Thomas Cole and other landscape artists, such as Stillman, often overlooked the "ravages of the ax" so they could convey in either paintings or written works the idea of a pristine American wilderness. The art historian Nicolai Cikovsky Jr. has noted that Cole did not include in *View of Schroon Mountain* the tree stump and felled trees found in an earlier sketch of this scene ("'The Ravages of the Ax': The Meaning of the Tree Stump in Nineteenth-Century American Art," *Art Bulletin* 61 [December 1979]: 611–26). The Cleveland Museum, Hinman B. Hurlbut Collection 1335.1917.

Plate 3. Sanford R. Gifford (1823–1880), *Morning in the Adirondacks*, 1854. Oil on canvas, 40-7/8 × 36 in. Stillman in his autobiography claimed he learned from Sanford Gifford, a Hudson River School painter and fellow Ruskinian, how to navigate the central Adirondacks. Gifford executed *Morning in the Adirondacks* the same year Stillman embarked on his first painting expedition in New York's northern wilderness. During the summer of 1854, Stillman lodged in a farmer's cabin near Upper Saranac Lake. Property of the Westervelt Collection and displayed in The Tuscaloosa Museum of Art in Tuscaloosa, AL.

Plate 4. William James Stillman (1828–1901), *Study on Upper Saranac Lake,* 1854. Oil on canvas, 30-1/2 × 25-1/2 in. Stillman produced this work during his first Adirondack painting expedition in 1854. By the time he showed it at the National Academy of Design's 1855 exhibition, he had earned a reputation as the American Pre-Raphaelite for his attention to detail. Photograph © 2015 Museum of Fine Arts, Boston. Gift of Dr. J. Sydney Stillman.

Plate 5. Sir John Everett Millais (1829–96), *Christ in the House of His Parents (The Carpenter's Shop),* 1849–50. Oil paint on canvas, 864 × 1397 mm. From an organizational standpoint, Stillman's *Morning at Camp Maple: Adirondack Woods* resembles Millais's *Christ in the House of His Parents.* Stillman, like Millais, divided the figures into two groups at opposite ends of the canvas, with the focal point on Emerson or Christ between them. ©Tate, London 2014.

Plate 6. William James Stillman (1828–1901), *Mount Chocorua,* 1856. Oil on canvas, 12 1/8 × 18 in. After leaving the *Crayon,* Stillman resurrected his painting career and traveled to North Conway in New Hampshire's White Mountains to hone his skills with his brush. Courtesy of the Smithsonian American Art Museum, Washington, DC / Art Resource, NY.

Plate 7. Frederic Edwin Church (1826–1900), *Twilight in the Wilderness*, 1860. Oil on canvas, 101.6 × 162.6 cm. In the mid-nineteenth century, artists, writers, and scientists praised the divine in nature. Frederic Church, the leader of the Hudson River School's second generation, hinted at the divinity in nature by placing a cross formed by splinters of wood on the tree stump in the foreground of his *Twilight in the Wilderness*. The Cleveland Museum of Art, Mr. and Mrs. William H. Marlatt Fund 1965.233.

Plate 8. William James Stillman (1828–1901), *The Philosophers' Camp in the Adirondacks*, 1858. Oil on canvas, 30 × 19 in. When Stillman showed this painting at the National Academy's 1859 exhibition, the work was initially titled *Morning at Camp Maple: Adirondack Woods*. To the right are Hoar, Lowell, Stillman, Binney, and Woodman; and to the left are Holmes, Howe, Agassiz, and Wyman. Emerson, holding a pilgrim staff, stands between the two groups. Courtesy Concord Free Public Library.

Plate 9. Asher Durand (1796–1886), *Woodland Interior,* circa 1855. Oil on canvas, 24 × 18-1/4 in. Stillman's *Morning at Camp Maple: Adirondack Woods* is a woodland interior scene reminiscent of those by Asher Durand, a leader of the Hudson River School movement. A *Crayon* critic, probably Stillman, had called Durand's *Woodland Interior* one of the "leading attractions" of the National Academy of Design's 1855 exhibition. Photograph © 2015 Museum of Fine Arts, Boston. Bequest of Mary Fuller Wilson, 63.269.

Plate 10. Asher Durand (1796–1886), *Forest in the Morning Light*, 1855. Oil on canvas, 24-3/16 × 18-3/16 in. In the mid-1850s, Durand painted *Forest in Morning Light* and *Woodland Interior*. The latter was displayed at the National Academy of Design's 1855 exhibition and received a positive review in the *Crayon*. Although it is not clear whether Stillman ever viewed *Forest in the Morning Light*, there is a restriking resemblance in the way morning sunlight cuts through the forest interior in Durand's painting and Stillman's *Morning at Camp Maple: Adirondack Woods*. Courtesy of the National Gallery of Art.

Plate 11. Frederic Rondel (1826–92), *A Hunting Party in the Woods/In the Adirondac*, 1856 . Oil on canvas, 22 × 30 in. Two years before Stillman painted *Morning at Camp Maple: Adirondack Woods*, Frederic Rondel painted *A Hunting Party in the Woods/In the Adirondac*. The two works are similar, though the latter lacks the identifiable and representative men found in the former. Courtesy of the Adirondack Museum.

Plate 12. Sanford R. Gifford (1823–1880), *A Twilight in the Adirondacks*, 1864. Oil on canvas, 24 × 26 in. Sanford Gifford's emphasis on light in paintings such as *A Twilight in the Adirondacks* lent emotional power to his landscapes. The art historians Kevin J. Avery and Franklin Kelly have noted that Gifford's luminism helped him weather the nation's shift in taste to "more subtly suggestive styles of landscape painting" in the post-Civil War years (*Hudson River School Visions: The Landscapes of Sanford R. Gifford* [New York: Metropolitan Museum of Art, 2003], 230). Courtesy of the Adirondack Museum.

a place called Ampersand Pond. He assured Lowell, "I shall be able to satisfy the club as well as if I had seen it myself. I am certain it is far beyond all compare the best place for our purpose in the whole vicinity."[4]

Stillman asked Lowell to notify the Adirondack Club's executive committee that he planned to present his report on December 11, a Saturday. The exact makeup of the executive committee is unclear. At the least, it consisted of Emerson, Lowell, Ward, and Hoar, all of whom were kept abreast of Stillman's activities on behalf of the club in late 1858. The secretary added that he would bring a duck for dinner and "the report will be satisfactory." Lowell got out the word of the forthcoming club meeting. In Concord, Emerson on December 6 told Ward that "Stillman seems to have had the laboring oar at the Hills." Ward, who had played a key role in establishing the Saturday Club a few years earlier, would become just as integral to the formation of the Adirondack Club. Given the Saturday dinner plans, Stillman likely delivered his report to the executive committee at Parker's Hotel, where the Adirondack Club occasionally met. There the secretary, far from recovered from his sickness, gave his report, "drank a glass of champagne to the future lodge, and went to bed in the early stages of pneumonia," which kept him bedridden for six weeks.[5] He sought health and comfort at his fiancée's home in Belmont.

Stillman believed the club would be able to cheaply acquire Ampersand because, he explained, the land had been "forfeited to the state at the last tax sale, and was for sale at the land office in Albany." In the second half of the nineteenth century, New York employed an administrative tax sale process through which landowners' failures to pay taxes could result in the loss of their property. Under this process, the state foreclosed on tax liens on nonresident lands. How the Adirondack Club learned of the tract's anticipated tax sale is unclear. Headley suggested Agassiz may have learned about the sale through the state comptroller's statutorily required advertisement or by inquiry, or "was informed of the circumstances of the case by friends."[6]

By 1859, deeds to lands in Township Twenty-Seven had passed through several hands since the death of William Constable, a key investor in Macomb's Purchase who had died in 1803. Much of the land had been dispersed among Constable's children and their descendants, who by the 1850s had sold their shares in chunks of the township to the Saratoga & Sackets Harbor Railroad Company. In October 1855, John Augustus McVickar (sometimes spelt McVicker) and his wife conveyed to the railroad the township's northeast quarter. McVickar was the son of John McVickar and Eweretta McVickar, one if Constable's heirs. That same month saw the execution of a warranty deed for the nearly fifteen thousand-acre southern half of the township, which had belonged to Constable's wife, Mary E. Constable

The legislature had chartered this railroad in 1848, and it was incorporated four years later with the intent of developing a railroad from Sackets Harbor, Jefferson County, to the Saratoga and Schenectady Railroad in Saratoga Springs or nearby Milton, Saratoga County. The rail line was to run 140 miles through seven counties. Franklin County was not among those counties, meaning the company was likely interested in Township Twenty-Seven for its natural resources since they would not be directed affected by the railroad. In 1857, the railroad was reincorporated as the Lake Ontario and Hudson River Railroad Company, which received ownership of three quarters of Township Twenty-Seven.[7]

Meanwhile, the township's northwest quarter, which contained Ampersand, similarly had been subjected to multiple transactions between Daniel McCormick, another key investor in Macomb's Purchase, and other parties. By midcentury, the quarter's largest landowner was Enoch H. Rosekrans, a New York Supreme Court justice. In 1852, a warranty deed conveying to Rosekrans 4,933 acres in the northwest quarter was executed. Some of the most coveted properties in this quarter were the four lots that were part of a 1,561-acre parcel running along the township's northern border. Lots One and Two of the parcel adjoined Ampersand while Lots Four and Three were positioned to their west, respectively. In 1858, several buyers were involved in the conveyances of these lots via quitclaim deeds. Each lot totaled 390.5 acres.[8]

Planning for a club with a "spacious lodge" had begun the previous August at Follensby. It is not clear when the scholars worked out the details of the club's organization, but it appears to have been similar to that of the Saturday Club. There was no written constitution and there was no hierarchical leadership. Rules were few and do not appear to have been written. It was agreed upon that for six weeks each summer, the club's executive committee would use this Adirondack property exclusively for their own leisure and that of their guests. Before or after this six-week period, club members were free to invite whomever they wanted and stay there for however long they pleased. Each person was promised his own guide and boat. They were free to explore the forest or remain at camp as they pleased, "forming parties or moving independently, lapsing as far as might be into the original state of society," according to Stillman. Adirondack Club members likely had to pay for their guests, as Saturday Club members had also done at Parker's. Last, there was a club assessment, which for Emerson totaled fifty dollars. The assessment was probably the same amount for other club members, as suggested by an 1876 letter Ward sent to Emerson.[9]

Stillman's report convinced the club's executive committee to pursue the plan for establishing a permanent retreat in the Adirondack wilderness. He had briefed them on a mile-long, crescent-shaped pond that sat at an elevation of 1,875 feet and just south of a mountain that shared its name: Ampersand Mountain. This mountain stood south of the head of Lower Saranac Lake. Its 3,352-foot summit offered panoramic vistas of the wilderness, including those of Mount Seward and the Saranac Lakes. Ampersand Pond contained four small islands. A branch of Ampersand Brook flowed eight miles from the pond's western shore to confluence with the Raquette River.[10]

As the superintendent of the Adirondack Survey, Verplanck Colvin, explained in an 1897 report, Ampersand Mountain's name referred to the resemblance between the pond at the mountain's base and the character "&" ("and"). Colvin believed it was the Philosophers who had coined the name Ampersand Pond, but Stillman's December 1, 1858, letter to Lowell indicates that the name had been established before the scholars knew the pond existed. Colvin initially had doubts that the "ampersand" explanation was correct. In an 1870 report, he instead attributed the name "to the bright, yellow sandy shores and islands, which make it truly *Amber-sand lake.*" But his 1897 report suggests he eventually subscribed to the ampersand connection. The writer Henry Van Dyke also asserted in 1885 that, of the mountain, pond, and brook, the last was the first to be named Ampersand because it was so "bent and curved." He claimed the early explorers of this "crooked stream" "christened it after the eccentric supernumerary of the alphabet which appears in old spelling-books as &."[11]

Long before the pond received its English name, Saranac Indian magicians reportedly had performed mystic rites there to raise the spirits of the dead. An Indian legend also tells of two Indian newlyweds, a maiden named Wah-loon-dah (Rippling Water) and a brave named Os-sa-wah (Plumed Eagle), who honeymooned at Ampersand Pond. According to the legend, Os-sa-wah went hunting and fell off a cliff while chasing game. Finding him dead, Wah-loon-dah performed a burial rite and then killed herself by thrusting a knife into her chest. "Now, when other mountain lakes are lashed by Storms, Ampersand Pond moves but gently, as if the calm spirit of Rippling Water still lived in its depths." The authenticity of these Indian legends is uncertain, and they may have been the creation of guidebook writers wanting to romanticize the region. While Alfred Donaldson cast doubt on a majority of claims that Indians had occupied the central Adirondacks, except for the temporary settlement along the Indian Carry, he was familiar with five Indian legends "worthy of that name." These credible legends were set around the Indian Carry and mention the Saranac Lakes. The legend of

Wah-loon-dah was not among the five Donaldson recounted in his *History of the Adirondacks,* but there are indications Stillman was familiar with this tale.[12]

Public interest in the Adirondack activities of Agassiz, Emerson, and Lowell continued during late 1858 and early 1859, largely through the efforts of the *New York Evening Post,* whose reports about the event were noted in newspapers nationwide. For example, the *Freedom's Champion* in Atchison, Kansas, reported on a *Post* article that recounted Longfellow's refusal to join the Adirondack Party because Emerson had purchased a rifle. The *Champion's* headline read, "A Poet Afraid of Philosophers." The *Macon Weekly Telegraph* in Georgia similarly picked up a *Post* story about how Agassiz had emerged as "the best shot in the party" despite not being a sportsman and never practicing with firearms. The newspaper attributed his excellent marksmanship to his "long practice in the use of the microscope." The *Crayon* reported that Stillman was working on a "picture suggested by an excursion of distinguished literary and scientific characters to the Saranac region the past summer." It noted that Agassiz, Emerson, Lowell, Holmes, Woodman, and others appeared in this landscape painting's foreground "in the picturesque and becoming costumes of hunters."[13]

Stillman, however, was not the first artist to show the American public what the Philosophers' Camp looked like. On November 13, 1858, *Frank Leslie's Illustrated Newspaper* published F. S. Stallknecht's account of his Adirondack sporting tour in August 1858. Prominently featured on the first page of the article was an engraving of the Philosophers' Camp by Stallknecht's camping companion, Charles Whitehead. The picture shows a spacious campground composed of two large lean-tos and amid some huge tree trunks. Four men and two dogs stand in the foreground, three of whom were identified in a caption as Agassiz, Emerson, and Lowell. The man swinging a butterfly net is presumably Agassiz. In the middle distance, two unidentified men sit behind a log and before a campfire, near the lean-tos. In the corner of the engraving a dinner table is set. A sea of trees swallows the picture's background.[14]

Lowell, too, made sure his *Atlantic Monthly* did not miss out on the sensation his Adirondack exploits were stirring across the nation. Instead of having the magazine feature an article about the Philosophers' Camp, he printed a story about the camping adventure that preceded it. In December, the *Atlantic Monthly* published an essay by Stillman titled "The Subjective of It," which provided an account of his 1857 camping trip at Big Tupper Lake with Lowell, his nephews, Howe, and Holmes. However, Stillman (or Lowell) was coy about the true identities of the characters in the essay. Stillman was not listed as its author, though the essay's authorship was not entirely unknown.

FIGURE 14.   Charles E. Whitehead (1829–1903), engraving of the Philosophers' Camp, 1858. This engraving was the first public depiction of the Philosopher's Camp. Prominently featured on the front page of a *Frank Leslie's Illustrated Newspaper* article by F. S. Stallknecht about his August 1858 Adirondack adventures with Whitehead, the engraving shows "how Professor Agassiz, Ralph Waldo Emerson and James Russell Lowell amuse themselves in the summer." Agassiz is the figure holding the butterfly net. From F. S. Stallknecht, "Sporting Tour in August, 1858," *Frank Leslie's Illustrated Newspaper,* November 13, 1858. Courtesy New York State Archives.

A *New York Times* article identified Stillman as the author in March 1859.[15] Lowell was identified in the essay as "J." and Howe as "the Doctor." Readers would have to wait almost forty years before the true identities of these characters were revealed when a revised version of "The Subjective of It" was included in Stillman's *The Old Rome and the New: and Other Studies,* which was published in 1897. Stillman's essay on the trip is more introspective than many of its predecessors, even those published in the *Crayon.* Most important, the essay detailed the types of philosophical conversations Stillman held in the wilderness with his distinguished literary friends. It also retells his first impressions of the procession of the pines.

As news about the Philosophers' Camp spread across the country, Agassiz emerged as the scholar who captured the most publicity around the end of 1858. On December 29, William Gray carried out the instructions outlined in the will of Francis Gray by informing the Harvard Corporation that his uncle's will had bequeathed $50,000 for the establishment of a Museum of Comparative Zoology. The museum would be separate from Harvard but subject to the college's oversight. According to will's instructions, the museum's first faculty was to feature Agassiz as director and include Harvard

President James Walker, Jacob Bigelow, Oliver Wendell Holmes, and Wyman. This was the day Agassiz had anticipated for the past two years. His plan for founding in America a science museum on a par with those in England and France had finally hatched.[16] Soon some of Massachusetts's wealthiest and most powerful men were rallying behind what they dubbed The Agassiz Museum. Over the course of the next two years, the museum would consume much of Agassiz's time.

In early January 1859, the Adirondack Club began emerging from a nearly monthlong hiatus. Although Stillman's early December briefing to the club's executive committee had ended promisingly, the newly formed club briefly went inactive partly because of members' illnesses. On January 8, after being bedridden with pneumonia for weeks, Stillman emerged from the Mack house in Belmont and went to Boston. Riding on the train that day was Hoar, who did not realize Stillman was on board until one of them was getting off the car. Since the December briefing, Hoar had wanted to investigate Stillman's condition personally, but his own illness ("something like a lung fever") prevented him from doing so.[17]

In the midst of his convalescence, Hoar intended to purchase from Stillman a "picture," which probably was the sketch he had made of the party at Camp Maple. Hoar offered to lend Stillman $250 for the painting. It does not appear that *Morning at Camp Maple* was completed at this time, because in a January 8 letter Hoar said, "You can do what you choose with the sketch until you are ready to have me take it." While Hoar waited for Stillman to finish the painting, the judge made his own contributions to the lore of the Philosophers' Camp. He had been busy telling a tale of Stillman's marksmanship in the Adirondacks. To Stillman's dismay, Hoar had embellished the story of a challenging shot. When the painter tried to set the record straight, Hoar refused to hear anything of the sort. Stillman's explanation "about the shot," Hoar said, "comes altogether too late." The unapologetic judge continued, "I misunderstood at the time it was done with a single ball; and I have told the story to [sic] many times, that to attempt a contradiction would merely unsettle the community, and perhaps injure *your* reputation for veracity. You had better let it go, and balance it with some care where you did not get half your deserts."[18]

In the end, Hoar refused to change the opinion he had stated publicly and promised to "go on telling the story the same way." While Hoar's infamous stubbornness probably frustrated Stillman a little, the painter could take heart in the former judge's eagerness "to know what is to happen next in Club arrangements."[19]

Whatever Stillman included in his report in early 1859 on the Adirondack Club's arrangements must have made a strong impression on its executive committee, which was keen on purchasing the Township Twenty-Seven
tract. Despite the fact that the club could purchase large swaths of wilderness
for pennies at tax sales, such transactions were riddled with risks. Edward S.
Godfrey, a legal scholar, has noted that the purchase of tax titles after 1850
was a "hazardous business," and courts heavily leaned in favor of original
property owners. There were many ways original owners could challenge
long-completed tax sales, including pointing out official errors in assessments, levies, or collections. Another tactic involved noting failures to provide
proper redemption notices.[20] Stillman probably warned the club's executive
committee of these dangers. The likely purpose of his negotiations with the
agent of Ampersand's owner during the fall of 1858 and summer of 1859
was not to arrange for the direct purchase of the land but to gauge the risk
of the proprietor's redeeming the tract after the club bought it at a tax sale.

By mid-March, news about the club had spread to New York City. A *New
York Times* correspondent in Boston reported, "Of course you have heard
about the Adirondack Club—the congregation of philosophers, *savans,*
authors, artists, and ordinary human beings who every summer proceed to
the wilds of the Adirondack on a few weeks' visit to Nature." The correspondent, Jack Robinson, said the club's membership included Emerson, Stillman,
Lowell, Agassiz, Wyman, and "a number of gentlemen whose names I have
never heard or have forgotten." The *Times* article also mentioned the club's
plans to purchase twelve thousand acres in the Adirondacks, where it would
build a "commodious camp-house." However, this purchase would have to
wait until after the 1859 tax sale commenced on November 10 at the capi-
tol building in Albany. Robinson added, "The expedition last summer gave
birth to two memorials of these unique excursions, both children of the same
brain." These memorials included Stillman's *Atlantic Monthly* essay "The
Subjective of It" and his painting *Morning at Camp Maple: Adirondack Woods.*
Agassiz's experiments in the Adirondacks also gained some notoriety. The
correspondent noted that the scientist "devoted his attention and weighing
and measuring the brains of fishes, and . . . some very curious discoveries
were the result of his investigations."[21]

To much fanfare, Stillman displayed *Morning at Camp Maple* at the National
Academy of Design's 1859 exhibition. Both the *Crayon* and *Harper's New
Monthly Magazine* took note of the painting at the exhibition. Robinson praised
the artist, who "excelled himself." In describing the painting, Robinson managed to identify Stillman, Lowell, Agassiz, Wyman, and Emerson. He incorrectly
referred to Hoar as "Judge Story," while Woodman, Howe, and Binney assumed

FIGURE 15. Asher Durand (1796–1886), *Woodland Interior,* circa 1855. Oil on canvas, 24 × 18-1/4 in. Stillman's *Morning at Camp Maple: Adirondack Woods* is a woodland interior scene reminiscent of those by Asher Durand, a leader of the Hudson River School movement. A *Crayon* critic, probably Stillman, had called Durand's *Woodland Interior* one of the "leading attractions" of the National Academy of Design's 1855 exhibition. Photograph © 2015 Museum of Fine Arts, Boston. Bequest of Mary Fuller Wilson, 63.269.

the anonymity that history has largely bestowed upon them. Robinson said, "Mr. Stillman has expressed that peculiar sonority which the forest possesses. One feels the detonation of the rifle about to be fired will roll from trunk to trunk and die in gradually weakened vibrations in the lonesome distance."[22]

Although a modern critic has called *Morning at Camp Maple* the "antithesis of Pre-Raphaelite art," Stillman did not stray far from his Pre-Raphaelite roots to produce this painting. Stylistically, according to William A. Gerdts, its fluid brushstrokes are more impressionistic than Pre-Raphaelite.[23] However, from an organizational standpoint, the painting very closely resembles John Millais's *Christ in the Carpenter's Shop,* the painting that Stillman had viewed at London's Royal Academy exhibition in 1850 (see figures 2 and 13). It was this painting, by one of the founders of the brotherhood, that had revolutionized Stillman's artistic beliefs and transformed him into the "American Pre-Raphaelite." Given that *Morning at Camp Maple* represented an "experiment in historical painting," it should not be surprising that Stillman would return to his roots and look to Millais's historical work for inspiration.

Stillman, like Millais, divided his painting's characters into two groups at opposite ends of the canvas, with the focal point resting on the individual standing between them in the center. Whereas Stillman placed a rather lost-looking Emerson at the center of the Philosopher's Camp, Millais placed a vulnerable looking Christ at the center in the carpenter's shop. Both individuals are surrounded by their preoccupied disciples or followers: Emerson by his friends who greatly admired him, and Christ by Joseph, the Virgin Mary, Saint Anne, and John the Baptist. Hudson River School influences are also apparent in Stillman's painting. The painting's forested background, which swallows the echo of the rifle's blast, is reminiscent of the interior forest scenes by Asher Durand, namely, his *Woodland Interior* (circa 1855). Writing for the *Crayon* in an unsigned review, a critic (probably Stillman) called this painting one of the "leading attractions" of the National Academy of Design's 1855 exhibition. Another Durand painting that may have influenced Stillman is *Forest in the Morning Light* (1855). Although it is not clear whether Stillman viewed *Forest in the Morning Light,* there is a striking similarity between the sunbeams that cut through the forest interior in this work and those in *Morning at Camp Maple.*[24]

Such paintings of Adirondack camp life were not uncommon by the late 1850s. Replace the massive maples around Camp Maple with smaller deciduous trees and change some of the activities in camp, and Stillman's painting almost mirrors Frederic Rondel's *A Hunting Party in the Woods: In the Adirondac* (1856). Style aside, however, what differentiates *Morning at Camp Maple* from the era's romanticized campsite paintings is its subjects. They are identifiable men, excluding Binney, Howe, and Woodman, as the *Times*

FIGURE 16.   Frederic Rondel (1826–92), *A Hunting Party in the Woods/In the Adirondac,* 1856. Oil on canvas, 22 × 30 in. Two years before Stillman painted *Morning at Camp Maple: Adirondack Woods,* Frederic Rondel painted *A Hunting Party in the Woods/In the Adirondac.* The two works are similar, though the latter lacks the identifiable and representative men found in the former. Courtesy of the Adirondack Museum.

article demonstrated. They are not just ten nameless sportsmen or hunters enjoying a morning in a sheltered sliver of wilderness. Stillman's painting features characters, just as the travelers in *The Canterbury Tales* were characters. Their identities—tightly bound to their associations of nature study, politics, philosophy, science, or poetry—lend significance to a narrative that grips the imagination. Stillman created the visual for this story of great men camping in the Adirondacks. Over the next forty years, the painter and Emerson followed up on this visual story with written narratives.

Still recovering from pneumonia, Stillman had to leave New York before the National Academy of Design hung *Morning at Camp Maple* at its spring exhibition that started in April. His doctor ordered him to recuperate in Florida. On top of this directive, Stillman was advised to stop painting. Still needing some type of creative outlet, he purchased a "photographic apparatus." In late March he embarked via boat on his first visit to the Deep South. The trip, which was funded by Norton, afforded him a view of the region before the Civil War, "with slavery and its patriarchal system at its perfection." Adirondack Club matters were put on hold until Stillman's return in May or early June.[25]

By the end of June, Stillman was preparing for the Adirondack Club's membership elections. However, before the club added new members, it again temporarily lost one, this time for the summer. On June 15, a day after ground was broken for the Museum of Comparative Zoology, Agassiz sailed for England, from where he made his way to Switzerland to see his mother at Lausanne. It was the scientist's first trip back to his homeland in thirteen years. On June 24, nine days after Agassiz had set sail for England, Stillman informed Longfellow that at the last regular meeting of the Adirondack Club he had been elected a member. The next meeting was scheduled for June 29 at Parker's House. "Your attendance particularly is wanted," the club secretary said. It is not clear whether Longfellow attended that meeting. Longfellow was not the club's only new member. Stillman wrote to the poet again to notify him of an election meeting on July 9 at one o'clock in the afternoon in Samuel Ward's office on State Street in Boston. Candidates included John Forbes, Theodore Lyman, Thomas G. Appleton, Edward Bangs, and Horace Gray Jr. Since 1857, Gray had been Hoar's law firm partner. However, Hoar gave up his legal practice in 1859 because on April 12 Governor Banks appointed him an associate justice on the Supreme Judicial Court of Massachusetts.[26] Lyman was one of Agassiz's star pupils, who graduated from Harvard in 1858. Appleton was Longfellow's brother-in-law, and Bangs was the Boston attorney whom Emerson had nominated to the not-yet-formed Saturday Club a decade earlier.

As for the camping expedition Longfellow's friends were planning, it suffered from its first of a series of setbacks on July 8. Emerson on that day badly sprained his ankle while walking down Wachusett Mountain in Princeton, almost forty miles west of Concord. The injury put him on crutches, and it was far worse than he initially thought. Although the sprain severely limited his mobility over the next few months, he had optimistically told Ward a day after the stumble, "I hope for my feet again tomorrow or Monday." With the Adirondack Club's elections scheduled for the ninth, he told Ward "to give my vote at the Adirondac meeting as you give your own for J[ohn].M[urray]. Forbes, of course, if there be another vacancy for Edward Bangs or for Theo Lyman as you see best."[27]

The sprain undoubtedly spoiled Emerson's summer, though he did not appear to be resolutely set on attending the Adirondack Club's inaugural gathering at Ampersand. He wanted to again sever ties with the outside world as he had done at Follensby, but this summer he wanted to be with his family in Maine. The Emersons were supposed to leave on July 15. Forbes tried to coax the family back to Naushon, too, but Emerson told him, "You are bent on stirring a mutiny in my troop,—what with your Faerieland of Naushon." The sprained ankle, however, put all plans on hold. Ellen Emerson lamented to a friend about the abandoned Maine vacation. She said the family had a "plan of hiding ourselves in the back-woods of Maine for six weeks, to feel entirely disengaged from home and all belonging to it, and try a new kind of life, keeping house for ourselves in a nice little house among the mountains, close to the woods." While the Maine woods lacked the drives and walks and waters of Naushon, Emerson explained to Forbes, "the Maine solitude has its good side & I shall let Ellen explain it to Mrs. Forbes."[28]

By the time of Emerson's injury, plans for the Adirondack trip were quickly materializing even though the club had not yet purchased the Township Twenty-Seven tract. However the July 9 vote turned out, the Adirondack Club's membership for that summer was firmly established. According to Ward, the club membership reached its cap of twenty, with Forbes and Lyman being the last two additions. My attempts to locate a comprehensive list of the club's membership were unsuccessful. Only thirteen probable club members could be identified through a review of executive committee members' correspondence and the published works of Stillman and Edward Emerson. These probable members included Emerson, Lowell, Hoar, Ward, Howe, Stillman, Forbes, Longfellow, Wyman, Lyman, Gray, and Norton. According to Edward Emerson, Woodman was another member of the club. Longfellow once saw Agassiz and Edmund Quincy, an abolitionist and the son of a Harvard president, en route to an Adirondack Club meeting with some executive committee members, suggesting those two men may have been members.[29] Assuming John Holmes, an inaugural meeting attendee, was a member, and if Bangs and Appleton were accepted into the club during the July 9 vote, that would push its identifiable roll call to eighteen.

It is not clear whether Longfellow participated in the July 9 election, but he did partake in an Atlantic Club dinner at the Revere House in Boston also on that date. There he was joined by Lowell, Oliver Wendell Holmes, Stillman, John Greenleaf Whittier, Edwin P. Whipple, Edmund Quincy, Higginson, Woodman, Calvin E. Stowe, John Wyman, and Francis H. Underwood. Although Higginson concluded he did not care very much for the Atlantic Club dinners, it proved to not be a wasted night. It is likely that at this gathering he received an invitation from Stillman to visit the Adirondack Club's camp at Ampersand. Higginson later identified Stillman as "the artist, who had invited us all."[30]

After the membership elections, the Adirondack Club's next order of business involved inviting guests. By mid-July, Lowell was in Newport. He considered inviting to Ampersand a man named Torrey, possibly the Harvard historian Henry W. Torry. "I think Wyman would be more likely to go if *he* does, and besides, he is a capital fellow," Lowell told Emerson. Despite Emerson's injured foot and his original plan to spend the summer in the Maine woods, Lowell did not stop pressing for the philosopher's company at Ampersand. "Pray, for all our sakes," Lowell said, "do not give up on the Adirondacks." By July 25, Emerson was still toying with the idea of going to the Adirondacks. He responded to Lowell's entreaty, saying, "I am not without appetite and, I thought at one time, a degree of necessity, of going. At all hours, the invitation has a kind of mountain echo." Lowell's entreaty was not the only one Emerson reluctantly rejected that summer. Forbes on August 6 likewise received news that Emerson's summer plans were off indefinitely: "I fear I cannot hope to go to Naushon or Ampersand."[31]

Lowell sent Emerson a list of invitees. Highlighting Stillman's subordinate role in the Adirondack Club, Lowell said, "We are the Committee, you remember, with Stillman who consents to whatever we do." The list noted that Horace Gray had withdrawn the invitation he wanted to extend to "Mr. Howe," and Emerson had accepted the withdrawal. It is not clear whether the Mr. Howe in question was Estes Howe, the abolitionist Samuel G. Howe, or someone else. Lowell's brother-in-law did travel to Ampersand that summer. "In the present state of the tribe & the wigwam, one member should not ask more than one guest," Emerson said. On July 25 he approved of the other names on the list. He asked Lowell why no boys were on the list, noting that "three or four were on fire to go."[32]

Two boys were already playing in the Adirondacks. By July 20, Ward, his son, Thomas, and Emerson's son Edward had left for the Adirondacks, according to Emerson. On July 21—one day after Emerson said Ward, Thomas, and Edward were bound for the Adirondacks—Stillman from Belmont wrote to Longfellow that an upcoming Adirondack Club dinner party had been canceled. It is not clear when or where Stillman met with Ward and the boys. But after they regrouped, they headed for New York's northern wilderness "to prepare the ground," Stillman said.[33]

❧ CHAPTER 11

The Inaugural Meeting

Click. The rifle did not discharge, and alarm shot through Stillman. He sat in a boat along with Ward, his son Thomas, and Edward Emerson. They had arrived at Ampersand Pond late in the day and with no food except the bread they had packed, so they went hunting the next morning. The boat had drifted closer to what Stillman hoped would be his party's dinner: a young buck grazing near the sandy beach at the foot of the pond. The creature had been about fifty yards away when Stillman first attempted to shoot it. Now closer, he slowly exchanged his rifle for another, and the deer took no notice of him. Stillman took aim, and this time his rifle discharged properly, killing the deer. He was astonished: "I have often paddled within easy shot of a deer on other waters, but only by remaining motionless when he was looking round, for the movement of a hand would send him flying in panic; but this poor deer might have been reared in Eden."[1]

Stillman and Ward had traveled to Ampersand to prepare a campsite for the Adirondack Club's inaugural meeting, which was to take place in August. At the time, Stillman and Ward were little more than acquaintances. It is not clear whether the banker partook in these preparations so he could supervise the club's secretary or so he could enjoy the wilderness with his son. Thomas and Edward likely tagged along for these premeeting activities so they could fish and play and not disturb the club's members when their vacations began.

Ward, too, did not plan to stay for the club's inaugural meeting. He had to ensure the boys' safe return home.

In the 1850s and for decades later, Ampersand was an isolated pond in the Adirondacks. The easiest way to it involved rowing up Cold Brook and then traversing a carry for five miles that led to Ampersand's eastern shore. Having not been able to view Ampersand the last time he was in the vicinity in November 1858, Stillman was relieved by what he found. "It was certainly the most beautiful site I have ever seen in the Adirondack country," he said. A guide who later visited Ampersand described the pond as "completely embosomed in the forest . . . at the feet of mountain peaks (Seward, Ragged, Seymour and Ampersand) that guard it on every side like faithful sentinels." Amid this beauty, there were noticeable patches where hunters and trappers had cut wood for campfires, Stillman observed. By July, the club had not purchased the Township Twenty-Seven tract, but it appears at this time to have been conducting its due diligence. Sometime that summer, D. M. Arnold of Port Henry, almost thirty-seven miles south of Keeseville, conducted a survey of Ampersand. In mid-August, the surveyor delivered a map of Ampersand to Silas Arnold. This was likely the same "Uncle Silas" Arnold who was a Keeseville attorney and who held a small mortgage on Martin's Hotel. This map, which ended up in the Hoar family's possession, identified an "Old Camp" near the pond's eastern shore and a "New Camp" at its southeastern shore. It is not clear whether these camps were associated with the Adirondack Club. This map shows the middle of the township dividing Ampersand in half, meaning the northeast quarter contained the pond's east half. But an 1895 Franklin County map in the *Atlas of the State of New York* shows Ampersand entirely in the northwest quarter.[2]

Stillman pitched camp near a crystal spring and amid a grove of deciduous trees. It was "a repetition slightly enlarged of that on Follansbee Pond," he recalled. He never specified how many lean-tos he constructed near Ampersand's shore, but it was probably several because he was expecting a larger party than the one he had hosted a year earlier. Ward and the boys camped there for two weeks. They likely left Ampersand around the time the Adirondack Club's members began trickling into their new Eden. For Stillman, the week before the inaugural meeting showed great promise. At any time of day, deer were seen feeding on the shore of the pond. Stillman had brought with him painting and photography equipment and materials, counting on the wilderness to again reinvigorate his creative spirit. He enjoyed his pre-club meeting company and later told Norton, "I like Ward even better than before we came up—he stands the test of camp life well."[3]

Much like his father, Edward Emerson carefully studied Stillman. But the son's main objective was to learn all he could about camping and not to gain new insights into human nature. "Mr. Stillman's wonderful prowess as a woodsman kept my ears open, if my mouth shut," he recalled. By August 5, Ward and the boys returned to Concord. Along with a warm welcome, Emerson sent to Ward an "Adirondac club assessment" of fifty dollars, to which he added ten dollars for Edward's blanket and because twenty-five dollars did not cover his road expenses. For the rest of that summer, Edward and his "Adirondack Blanket" were inseparable as he and friends went on numerous camping trips in Massachusetts.[4]

Undoubtedly, Edward's pleasure in his camping experiences that summer surpassed Stillman's. A smaller-than-expected party came to the Adirondack Club's inaugural meeting. Most of the club's members likely arrived at Ampersand around August 8, which according to Emerson was when Forbes was "promised to the Adirondack Party." Norton was expected there by August 18, though he never came. He had traveled as far as the "edge of the woods," but he became ill at that point and returned home.[5]

Initially, the roster of "Amperzanders" that August included Lowell, John Holmes, Howe, Hoar, Forbes, and Gray. Holmes began the expedition in his classic comical fashion. Into the deep woods he bought to Ampersand an armchair with the help of four men. To the guides it was hard work, but Holmes was all jokes. This merriment, however, was short-lived. The Adirondack weather that August was wet and the deer were scarce. What exactly happened at the club's inaugural meeting is not known. Stillman, perhaps ashamed of his moody behavior at Ampersand, did little to preserve its memory in his published prose. But we do know that Lowell for one enjoyed himself, reporting at the meeting's conclusion that he "had a good time and stiff work which set me all right again."[6]

"The club meeting has not been as satisfactory as I hoped," Stillman reported to Norton in late August, after the Adirondack Club's members had left him alone at Ampersand. Forbes was the last to depart. Although there had been an abundance of deer around the pond in the week before everyone arrived, the group members saw only one while they were there. And as a cruel irony, once everyone left, the deer came out in force. "Since they have been away, I have killed two very fine bucks with first-class antlers," Stillman said. Moreover, Ward and Forbes left him with two commissions for scenes on the pond.[7]

For most of that summer, Stillman sulked around Ampersand like the gloomy clouds that hovered over it. Over the previous five years, he had grown accustomed to using his summers in the Adirondacks to restore his "equilibrium" after winters of working. He also appears to have employed this strategy to counter the effects of his anxiety disorder by achieving the

FIGURE 17. William James Stillman (1828–1901), *Rustic Lean-To*, 1859. Photo—mounted in album, albumen, sepia. Stillman likely took some of the photographs in *Photographic Studies Part 1. The Forest. Adirondack Woods* around Ampersand Pond in 1859. This lean-to may have been built for the inaugural meeting of the Adirondack Club that August. Courtesy of the Adirondack Museum.

serene state of meditative awareness. But it was only after the club had left that he began "to feel at home." Partly as a consequence of this delayed decompression, he had been moody and socially detached while the club was at Ampersand, more so than he had been when his "attendant Daemon" had troubled him at Big Tupper Lake two years earlier. He was anything but a model host. "I have been able to do little all this summer save make the party uncomfortable by my restless (and angry) humors," he told Norton.[8]

With his company gone, Stillman slipped back into a solitude "you never could have dreamed of." He reflected on his behavior with the club and turned remorseful. "I am still only well enough to see how far from well I have been. I am only sorry in that I . . . did much to make the party less pleasant and perhaps decidedly unpleasant in some respects," he told Lowell. Lowell and Norton, in particular, were familiar with Stillman's moodiness, which in years earlier had been the source of considerable tension. He did not elaborate on how he discomforted the club's members, but he seemed anxious or depressed, or a little of both. How the club reacted to Stillman's behavior is not known, but they were likely not overly disappointed with him. After all, he had successfully secured and prepared a beautiful campsite in accordance with his duties as the club's secretary. And after the party left Ampersand, he continued to dutifully fulfill these duties as he negotiated the property's purchase. Despite Stillman's rude temperament that August and its negative effects on the club, he still felt justified in having chosen a spot so inaccessible and of unrivaled beauty. The mountain air reinvigorated him, as it always had. He chopped a half cord of wood at one chopping. He painted for an hour or two at least every afternoon when it did not rain. He took photographs around the camp in the intervals between showers.[9]

One September afternoon, Stillman was sketching on one of Ampersand's islands while his guides were driving deer. The pond's quietude was then disturbed by the crack of three rifle shots. Stillman immediately sent a guide to find out who had fired the three shots—a signal for distress in the wilderness. Standing by the mainland shore and carrying a smoking rifle was Higginson. From there Higginson watched a red-shirted woodsman paddle toward him from the island. Accompanying Higginson were Marcus Spring—a Quaker philanthropist—and their guide.[10]

Higginson's visit to Ampersand was one of his last stops on a nine-day tour through the Adirondacks with Spring, Thomas Earle, a friend from Worcester, and possibly a few others. Higginson left Worcester, Massachusetts, in early September and followed the footsteps the ten scholars had taken the previous year, making it one of the earliest, if not the first, documented post-1858 accounts of a quest for the Philosophers' Camp. Higginson and a few others had visited Keeseville, Martin's Hotel, Steve Martin's cabin along the Indian Carry, and even Follensby, where the party found a group of men and women from New Haven, Connecticut, who were camping and hunting there. After Higginson's party camped and hunted at Big Tupper Lake, most of the group headed home. Higginson and Spring stayed behind "to penetrate to the new Philosophers' Camp at Amperzand Pond."[11]

Ampersand, to Higginson, "seemed an enchanted lake." In Stillman, however, Higginson observed the behavior that weeks earlier had disturbed the Adirondack Club's members. The painter, according to Higginson, declared that "Nature was pressing upon him to an extent that almost drove him wild." A remote and questioning look filled the painter's eyes. The Worcester pair hesitated to ask Stillman "to come out of his dream" and offer them dinner, but he eventually became more hospitable and attentive to his guests. They dined on boiled and broiled venison, cranberries, and guava jelly. Stillman also served an Indian meal-based concoction of his own creation that he tried to pass off as dumplings. Higginson said he and Spring "preferred the venison, but the host showed a fidelity to his invention that proved him to be indeed a dweller of an ideal world."[12]

While Higginson and Spring felt awkward before dinner, they were awestruck by the end of it. They were all on the island on which Stillman had been sketching. As Higginson and Spring undressed to bathe in the pond, Stillman shouted instructions to a red-shirted guide who was heading for the mainland to make dinner. "Ben!" Stillman said, his voice echoing around the pond. The guide paused in his boat. "Remember to bo-o-oil the venison, Ben. And Ben! Don't forget the dumplings!" Upon hearing these commands, the loons around the pond broke out in a fit of laughter. They "took up the strain with vehemence, hurling their wild laughter at the presumptuous mortal who thus dared to invade their solitude," Higginson recalled. The loons repeated their heckling over and over, for more than two hours. "They could not get over it," said Higginson, who ate his dinner at camp to the sound of this cacophony.[13]

For days after the Worcester party left Stillman, the loons around Ampersand continued to laugh uncontrollably. Some of the noises they made Stillman had never before heard. He surmised they were "first lessons to the young." Because he expected more people to arrive by September 15, he kept some guides at camp. While they waited, Stillman had the guides build roads to camp from Cold Brook and to lookout points dubbed Sunset Ledge and Tip Top Ledge. Higginson had told his mother in a September 11 letter, "Emerson and Longfellow and others are now coming."[14] But no one else came.

Emerson was resigned to his foot injury and accepted the fact that his summer would be spent in Concord. On August 20, he wrote in his journal, "Home is a good place in August." Meanwhile, Longfellow had already written off his friends' new club. On August 9, he informed Ward he did not want to be a member of the Adirondack Club. Initially he had been drawn to the club for the sake of his sons. However, the poet explained, "I am not a sportsman, and probably should never join one of the expeditions, though they are very charming to the imagination."[15]

With the prospects dimming of any other Adirondack Club arrivals, and with theories about art brimming in his head, Stillman turned restless. "To use my brains much is still a source of trouble," Stillman told Norton. Alone at Ampersand, Stillman devoted much of his time to painting a massive dramatic scene. On a twenty-five-by thirty-inch canvas, he painted the scene of a hunter and buck lying dead at the bottom of a cliff, off which they had fallen after engaging in hand-to-hoof combat. It was a scene reminiscent of the Indian legend of Os-sa-wah, who had died after falling off a precipice in the pursuit of his game. Stillman spent two months working on this picture titled *Bed of Ferns,* believing it to be his finest. He told Norton on September 30 he liked "something in it more than anything that I have done," and he wanted to complete it before leaving.[16]

Aside from painting, Stillman had two other matters of business to complete before he could return home. He set sable traps for miles throughout the woods, intent on catching the mink-like creatures and giving their pelts to his fiancée as gifts. In the end, he caught several "prime" sables. At this point, Stillman had been engaged to Laura Mack for almost a year, but no wedding date had been set. For half of that time, he had been in either Florida or Adirondacks. The delay in getting married, however, was not entirely his fault. Laura had gotten cold feet, and she did not consider herself a worthy bride. Laura's indecision, however, may not have stemmed entirely from her insecurities. Her father, David Mack, was deeply concerned about Stillman's financial situation—namely, his massive debt.[17]

Stillman's other task involved negotiating a land deal for the Adirondack Club. In Higginson's September 11 letter to his mother, he said the club was "just buying up the pond and its whole surroundings, to keep them sacred from lumbering and injury." Stillman's negotiations with the landowners and their agent did not go smoothly. A little over a week after Higginson left Ampersand, Stillman reported to Lowell that he had made inquiries about "the falls," but these questions only piqued the landowners' appetite for speculation. It is possible Stillman here was referring to the falls in the vicinity of the Duck Hole and Preston Ponds, in the southeastern corner of Township Twenty-Seven. The owners thought that "if anyone wants to buy there must be a good reason and they will look into it first," Stillman said. "I am stale-mated."[18]

On September 29, Stillman told Ward he was waiting for the "knowledge of our purchase and its prospects." He mentioned the possibility of a railroad company's wanting the land, "but they buy to sell." Additionally, he believed the railroad's pursuit of the property seemed unlikely because the tract was mostly swamps and water. If the company did buy, he expected to receive news about it sometime soon. Stillman had spoken to the proprietors' agent, who concluded, "the land was worthless to them."[19]

According to the comptroller's list of lands to be sold for arrears of taxes for that year, all of Township Twenty-Seven would be put to bid at a tax sale. The township contained a total of 29,980 acres. Stillman informed Ward the southern half and the "section which includes the Eastern junction of the pond" were to be sold for taxes. The unpaid taxes on 22,500 acres of the township totaled $400. Here, Stillman appears to be referring to the 7,495-acre northeast quarter and 14,990-acre south half owned by the financially troubled Lake Ontario and Hudson River Railroad Company, which was months away from foreclosure. The railroad company's holdings in the township totaled 22,485. Stillman also hoped to secure part of the northwest quarter, bringing the club's potential land holdings to 23,000 acres, from the northern side of Ampersand to over the summit of Mount Seward. He described this property in the northwest quarter as the "section of the town which includes the w. half of the lake." Here he may have been referring to the 390-acre Lot One or Two. While Stillman handled the land negotiations, Norton provided him with funding for work around Ampersand. Norton gave Stillman a note for $629.03, though by late September $150 of that had been expended on the men for a survey, Forbes's expenses, and roadwork. Stillman apologized to Ward for not consulting with him in drafting a contract for the hired men and promised to reduce some of their daily wages from $1.50 to $1.00. "I have no business education, but *I am* not too old to acquire one," Stillman assured Ward. Norton also covered Stillman's expenses, which included supplies and a hired man.[20]

Both Higginson and Headley identified Agassiz as a key player in the land acquisition. Higginson said the tract "was bought by Professor Agassiz and his friends." Meanwhile, Headley claimed that it was the scientist who "either accidentally or on inquiry" discovered there were delinquent taxes on the property and who "bought it for a mere song." However, it is uncertain how involved Agassiz could have been in the deal because he did not return to Cambridge from Europe until late September 1859. Agassiz, along with his wife and daughter, had left Liverpool aboard the *Arabia* on September 10, 1859, and arrived in Halifax, New Brunswick, on September 20. By September 22, Longfellow was eagerly anticipating the return of Agassiz, who

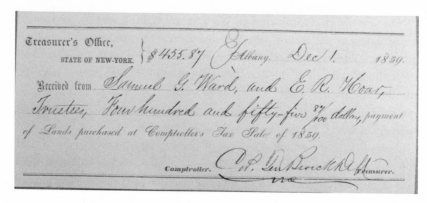

FIGURE 18.   Receipt of payment for Township Twenty-Seven property. The New York State Treasurer's Office on December 1, 1859, issued this receipt after Ward and Hoar submitted a winning bid at a tax sale for most of the land in Township Twenty-Seven, where the Adirondack Club planned to build a permanent encampment near Ampersand Pond. Receipt from "Payment receipts for lands purchased at tax sales, 1859–1926," Records Relating to Comptroller's Sale of Non-resident Lands for Unpaid Taxes, 1799–1928, New York State Archives, Albany, New York. Courtesy New York State Archives. Photo by James Schlett.

was expected to come "back in the steamer of this week" and attend the Saturday Club's meeting two days later, along with Emerson.[21]

By October, a well-rested Agassiz had immersed himself in developing his museum's operation plan. And November also saw the beginning of what became the public debate over Agassiz's creationist beliefs when he received a package from Charles Darwin containing the English naturalist's newly published *On the Origin of Species*. In the book's margins Agassiz wrote, "This is truly monstrous!" and "What is the great difference between supposing that God makes a variable species or that he makes the laws by which species vary?"[22]

The tax sale started on November 10, 1859. It was Ward and Hoar who together put in a bid of $455.87 for the Township Twenty-Seven tract. This purchase price was 25 percent less than the widely cited $600 that Stillman years later cited in his autobiography. The New York State Treasurer's Office issued a receipt for the pair's payment for the tax sale purchase on December 1. They were identified as trustees. On or after November 28, Ward sent Hoar an envelope on which was written "Adirondack Club" and "certificate of purchase of Land at Tax Sale."[23]

This certificate likely detailed the club's acquisition of the 22,500-acre tract and should have clarified whether part of Ampersand was technically in its confines. The purchase excluded the 500 acres (possibly rounded up from the 390 acres of Lot One or Two) that Stillman had wished to acquire because taxes had been paid on that property. The exact date and land included in the tax sale purchase could not be ascertained because the envelope was empty when it was donated to the Concord Free Public Library. My attempts to locate a copy of the certificate of purchase of land at tax sale in the comptroller's tax sale records at the New York State Archives were unsuccessful. The receipt of the certificate did not mean the club absolutely possessed the deed to Ampersand. The Tax Law of 1855 (Laws of 1855, chap. 427) afforded owners and occupants a two-year redemption period from the sale's last day. The comptroller could only deliver a deed for the premises after that period expired and an application from the purchaser was received.[24]

Having wrapped up as much of this business as possible from the wilderness, Stillman planned to leave Ampersand by the end of October. "I shall probably not be in next summer," Stillman told Lowell in an October 13 letter. Within three months, the painter would set sail for England. It was a decision that on its face ran contrary to all he had been working toward over the past four years. Soon the club would have the Adirondack cabin he had long desired. Stillman later claimed his "principal reason" for going to Europe was to give his indecisive fiancée space so she could decide whether to go through with the wedding.[25] He also had other motives for traveling abroad, particularly so he could reunite with Ruskin and other artists in London and submit his works to exhibitions in that city and Paris.

As for the Adirondack Club, at least in the short term, Lowell and Ward oversaw any unfinished business. Stillman likely informed William Martin of these matters, which included the construction of the club's lodge. Before leaving the Adirondacks for Cambridge, Lowell gave Stillman his rifle to sell. Lowell's relinquishment of his rifle, however, did not mean he was through with the Adirondacks. Within four months he would return to the region. Stillman offered to sell his boat to Lowell, who while at camp had wished he had his own. Stillman assured him, "If you want it I will have it put in order for next summer." Reluctantly, Stillman returned to "the state of civilization." When he left Ampersand, the gallant artist closed the chapter on his final "serious experience of woodland life."[26] Meanwhile, the civilization to which he returned that October had just taken a leap toward civil war when John Brown and eighteen of his men raided the federal arsenal at Harpers Ferry on the sixteenth of that month.

In the aftermath of the standoff, which had concluded on October 18 with a group of marines storming an engine house into which Brown had retreated from the main arsenal building, seventeen people were dead. They included two slaves, three townsmen, a slaveholder, one marine, and ten of Brown's men. Only five months earlier, some members of the Adirondack Club, including Hoar, Emerson and Forbes, had seen the "Old Captain" while he was on a final fund-raising push in the Boston area.[27]

The consequences the raid would have on the nation were not lost on these acquaintances of Brown in or around Boston. On October 31—shortly after Brown's trial had begun in Charlestown, Virginia—Hoar told Amos Lawrence, "If they hang him after . . . a trial, Virginia will never get over the disgrace of it." After a five-day trial and forty-five minutes of deliberation, a jury found Brown guilty of all charges, and on November 2 he was sentenced to hang. Higginson, one of Brown's covert sponsors (known as the Secret Six), had contemplated rescuing the Old Captain. Instead, he returned to the Adirondacks to fetch Brown's wife so she could be taken to Virginia and see her husband before the hanging. With a November 8 lecture in Boston titled "Courage," Emerson identified in Brown a paradigm for courage. Longfellow called the day of Brown's execution in Virginia, December 2, "the date of a new Revolution—quite as much needed as the old one." He prophesied that the hanging was "sowing the wind to reap the whirlwind, which will come soon." [28]

Less than a month after Brown's hanging, on Christmas Eve, Stillman and the portrait painter George Fuller boarded an old sailing ship bound for England. Ten years had passed since Stillman had first sailed to England. He had been twenty-one years old at the time of that first overseas journey, with his "heart and brain full of enthusiasm of art." But by 1859, that enthusiasm had been exhausted. By mid-January, Stillman had settled in England. The voyage marked a close to what Stillman considered "the American period of my life." His "warming, adventurous feeling" and "childlike love of nature life for very life's sake" were gone. [29]

Stillman had left Belmont with his engagement to Laura Mack on "uncertain" terms, and although he had heard no word from his fiancée by mid-February, her parents informed him she was "very unhappy." Laura failed to overcome her indecision over getting married. Either before leaving for London or shortly after arriving there, Stillman proposed calling off the engagement, but that proposal made her "wretched." Meanwhile, Stillman felt trapped. "She cannot marry me and she cannot bring herself to say she will not," he told Norton. Complicating matters further was David Mack's requirement that his daughter not wed until Stillman paid off his debts and he had a career lined up. By April, Stillman was $700 in debt. He owed Lowell $320. By May, Laura agreed to go through with the wedding, but Stillman did not plan to return to America until he had satisfied her parents' demands that he pay down his debts and was "in a condition to much the requirement of her parents." [30]

Prior to leaving America, Stillman had also entered some type of business "arrangement" with Binney. After a month in London, he learned that that their business had "exploded." He took this setback as a sign that he should

Figure 19. William James Stillman (1828–1901), *Photographic Studies Part 1. The Forest. Adirondack Woods*, 1859. Photo—mounted in album, albumen, sepia. A few months after the Adirondack Club's inaugural meeting in 1859, Stillman traveled to London. His parting gift to the club's members was a collection of photographs he had taken at or around Ampersand Pond in 1859. The photographs in this collection, including this one used on the title page, are among the earliest of those taken in the central Adirondacks. Stillman dedicated the book to the Adirondack Club. Courtesy of the Adirondack Museum.

not "waste energy on schemes and diversions." He intended to focus squarely on painting, though he did express an interest in writing articles on "rifle-shooting and the Adirondacks" for "Macmillan," a possible reference to the new *Macmillan's Magazine* in London.[31]

Stillman's parting gift to America in 1859 was a book featuring twelve albumen photographs he likely had taken around Ampersand during the summer and fall. The book, *Photographic Studies Part I. The Forest. Adirondac Woods,* was published by J. W. Black of Boston. The photographs were mostly studies of trees, ferns, and foliage. One showed a forest interior with a body of water glistening behind fir trees, and another showed a lean-to probably leftover from the Adirondack Club's inaugural meeting. These photographs were among the earliest known to be taken in the central Adirondacks. The January 1860 edition of the *Atlantic Monthly* reviewed Stillman's new book. The magazine's critic concluded, "One may study these pictures till he becomes as familiar as a squirrel with fern and tree-bark and moose-wood and lichen, till he knows every trunk and twig and leaf as intimately as a sunbeam."[32] *The Forest's* title page featured a photograph of a moss-covered boulder sitting on a leaf-strewn forest floor. The page also featured a dedication to the Adirondack Club.

For at least the period immediately after Stillman's departure, the Adirondack Club remained active. On December 17, 1859, Emerson, Lowell, Agassiz, Holmes, Norton, and Edmund Quincy gathered at Parker's. According to Longfellow, they "came in by accident, thinking it the Adirondac Club." Instead, they had walked in on a meeting of the Atlantic Club, which they joined. According to Longfellow, it was a "very agreeable dinner." In February 1860, Lowell and Ward returned to the Adirondacks, possibly to oversee preparations for the Adirondack Club's cabin at Ampersand. According to Ellen Emerson, the pair went to the Adirondacks "for fun with fur bags such as Artic travelers use, to sleep in."[33]

PART III

Campfire Lore

❦ CHAPTER 12

War

The whirlwind Longfellow had predicted would follow John Brown's hanging tore through the nation within two years of his death. Stillman was in Europe when the Civil War broke out. Although he never saw combat, by 1861 he had already been wounded in spirit. Stillman's European journey, which began in December 1859, was far less fruitful than he had hoped for his artistic aspirations. He spent much of the first half of 1860 in London, calling on the British friends of the Adirondack Club's members and visiting the Rossetti family. Stillman also explored a publishing opportunity in England for Lowell with Macmillan & Co.[1]

Stillman had brought with him to London his *Bed of Ferns,* the massive dramatic scene he had spent three months painting at Ampersand Pond the previous summer and autumn. Although the painting received the praise of Dante Rossetti, Ruskin, who visited Stillman at his studio in London, was put off by the depiction of the dead man and deer. Ruskin's critique of Stillman's work was cutting: "What do you put that stuff in for? Take it out; it stinks." Stillman in his autobiography claimed the Royal Academy refused to hang *Bed of Ferns* in its exhibition and he later burned it, though there are indications he first sent the painting back to Boston with instructions for Norton to sell it. Although Ruskin's blunt criticism had wounded Stillman's ego, he did not lose his confidence in the critic's "judgment and correct feeling for art." A decade had passed since they first met, and Stillman remained Ruskin's pupil. Much of his sense of worth as an artist continued to hinge on the master's opinion.[2]

Wanting to keep his expenses down so he could pay off his debts, Stillman became Ruskin's guest in early June. The two painters that summer embarked on a sketching expedition in the Alps, and Ruskin likely covered most of Stillman's traveling expenses. The trip had begun with much promise, but tensions between the artists quickly rose as Ruskin vacillated from scolding Stillman to praising him over the quality of the sketches he executed. The Alps did not impress Stillman as much as the Adirondacks had. Like Niagara Falls in western New York, the Alps awed him but "they left me cold," he said. Stillman later told Woodman he had tried "in vain" to lure Ruskin to America, but the English critic wanted his pupil to stay in Europe. Ruskin relentlessly chipped away at Stillman's artistic practice, saying his method for painting scud clouds was "incorrect" and that he should end a work after painting little more than the foreground. At one point, Ruskin, fed up with his pupil, separated from him and went to Geneva. On top of this disillusionment, while working in Neuchâtel on a sketch of a castle, Stillman temporarily lost his vision. He attributed this malady to the strain from overwork, coupled with his "anxiety to lose none of my time and opportunities." Although his sight partially returned a few days later, a more severe onset of blindness struck him in Basel, where he also suffered from an "incessant headache and obstinate indigestion."[3]

After Stillman's second outbreak of blindness, Ruskin, oblivious to how hurtful his criticisms had been to his pupil, decided to return to England. Meanwhile, Stillman retreated to St. Martin de Belleville, France, and waited for his vision to return. He was in more ways than one a crippled artist. "Ruskin had dragged me from my old methods, and given me none to replace them," Stillman lamented. He lost faith in himself and in Ruskin as "a guide to art." The two never reconciled, though Stillman tried to salvage their friendship. It was not long before Ruskin was avoiding Stillman because "many melancholy things" made it hard for the critic to write to his former protégé.[4]

During the autumn following his Swiss adventure, Stillman made a quick return to Massachusetts to marry Laura Mack, who over the spring or summer apparently again had lost her resolve to go through with the wedding. Stillman said he "ended the vacillation by insisting on being married at once." They wed two days after he landed in America and planned a Parisian honeymoon. However, before setting sail, Stillman attempted to put his fledgling family's future in order. The painter on November 29 solicited the support of Charles Sumner for a diplomatic appointment under the new

Lincoln administration. The Massachusetts senator had already left Boston for Washington, D.C., by that time, so Stillman was not able to make his request in person. In a letter, Stillman expressed his interest in a position at the U.S. consulate in Venice, and he cited the support of "some of our leading Republicans in Boston." He also hinted at an art-related alternative motive for the appointment.[5]

About a week after writing to Sumner about the Venice appointment, Stillman and Laura sailed for France. In Paris, they spent much time with the family of the famed English poets Robert and Elizabeth Barrett Browning. The Stillmans and Brownings intended to spend the summer of 1861 together at Fontainebleau, but those plans were dashed by Elizabeth's respiratory illness, from which she died on June 29. Not wanting to intrude on the Brownings' tragedy, the Stillmans alone went to Normandy. Before leaving, Stillman attempted to firm up his bid for the appointment to the consulate at Venice. At the onset of the Civil War, he was more interested in going to Venice than in going home to fight for the Union. On April 20—eight days after shots were fired at Fort Sumter—Stillman again petitioned Sumner for the appointment. He explained that he was no "ordinary" applicant for office. "I am an artist," he declared, and he urged his appointment to one of the world's great art centers "in the interest of the arts."[6]

Stillman's interest in Venice appears to have been part of an effort to salvage his artistic passions by merging them with his stronger journalistic skills. In Venice he planned to write a book on the history of Venetian art. It would have served as a follow-up to Ruskin's *Stones of Venice,* which examined Venetian architecture and was published in three volumes in 1853. Stillman's eagerness to travel to Italy marked a significant change in his attitude toward the country since 1856, when he had told Lowell he wanted to remain at home to work on the *Crayon.* At that time, he had not wanted to travel abroad, particularly not to Italy, which was inhabited by "a lazy people."[7]

The Adirondack Club rallied behind Stillman in his bid to secure the consular appointment. In an undated letter to William Seward, Lincoln's secretary of state, Agassiz, Lowell, Benjamin Peirce, Norton, Longfellow, Ward, Forbes, and Horace Gray recommended Stillman. Gray drafted the letter. It identified Stillman as "an accomplished scholar and artist, an experienced traveler, [and] an earnest and consistent Republican who will perform the duties of the office with . . . attention." Hoar included a short personal note recommending Stillman's appointment, and so did Charles Sumner. This endorsement from the club indicates that its members continued to hold Stillman in high esteem, regardless of the outcome of the 1859 meeting at Ampersand. A similar letter of recommendation for Stillman's appointment came from a New York contingent led by the artist's former employer at the *Evening Post*, William Cullen Bryant. Another came from Charles Baldwin Sedgwick, a Syracuse lawyer who two years earlier had been elected a U.S. representative from New York. He was also a friend of the Mack family. Sedgwick noted that, with the consulate's annual compensation totaling $750, "there will probably be little competition for the place."[8]

Stillman's bid for the consulate put him in competition with William Dean Howells, an Ohio newspaper reporter. Around 1860, Howells had begun submitting poetry to the *Atlantic Monthly* and corresponding with its editor, Lowell. Howells was far better positioned to secure the position from the new administration, having earlier been commissioned by the Republican Party to write a biography of Lincoln. The Venice affair became a matter that pitted Lowell's old pupil against his new one. Indeed, from the first time they met in August 1860, Lowell took Howells under his wing. He introduced Howells to Boston's literary social circles, as the editor had done for Stillman five years earlier. At a dinner party that Oliver Wendell Holmes threw in honor of Howells, Lowell's affection for the younger writer had been so apparent that the doctor said, "Well, James, this is something like the apostolic succession; this is the laying on of hands." Lowell told Nathaniel Hawthorne that Howells has "more in him than any of our younger fellows in the way of rhyme." Around the time Stillman was vying for the Venetian consulate appointment, Lowell was reeling from a series of loses he had suffered in early 1861. His father had died in January, and in the spring Lowell resigned as editor of the *Atlantic Monthly*. The magazine had recently been acquired by Ticknor & Fields in Boston following the death of the magazine's owner, Moses Phillips, and the bankruptcy of his Phillips, Sampson & Co. James T. Fields succeeded Lowell as the magazine's editor, while Lowell continued to submit essays to the magazine and provide Fields with consulting services.[9]

Shortly after Lincoln's March 4, 1861, inauguration, Howells went to Washington, where he applied for a position at the U.S. consulate at Munich. He was instead offered a job at the consulate at Rome, mostly as payback for his work on Lincoln's biography. Finding the Roman consul's income too low, Howells rejected the offer, prompting Lincoln's private secretaries to offer him the consulate at Venice with a salary doubled to $1,500. It is not clear whether Stillman knew with whom he was competing for the Venice appointment, but he did acknowledge in his April 20 letter to Sumner that "it may be that the appointment will have been determined on before this reaches you."[10] Either way, Stillman and his wife went through with their summer vacation as planned.

It was a "quiet and happy life" for the Stillmans in Normandy. However, the eruption of war in their homeland cut the couple's vacation short. In Paris, Stillman agreed to return to America with William B. Greene. A West Point graduate and a native of Haverhill, Massachusetts, Greene had been living in Paris for some time before the war broke out. With the expectation to be appointed colonel of a regiment, which ended up being the Fourteenth Massachusetts infantry, Greene offered Stillman a position on his staff. They had agreed to sail home together, but Greene grew impatient to return and left for America without Stillman. About a week before the Union suffered a devastating defeat at the Battle of Bull Run on June 21, the Stillmans caught the next available transatlantic steamer, the *Fulton*. Before leaving Paris, Stillman told Norton he was "sick at heart with this insatiable longing to be with and part of my country in her hour of strength." If Stillman could not serve the Union by volunteering for military service or making use of his knowledge of small arms, he envisioned himself becoming a war nurse.[11]

Despite his agreement to join Greene's staff, Stillman was in no rush to volunteer for active duty, partly because he was in no condition for field service. His health was failing him again. Upon landing at Sandy Hook, New Jersey, in July 1861, Stillman felt compelled to travel to the Adirondacks to convalesce. Greene's regiment of Essex County volunteers would not wait for the frail painter to recover. By June 25, the Fourteenth had been mustered and ordered to Fort Warren, at Boston Harbor. The regiment was included in the national service on July 5.[12]

"Tell me if any body is going into the woods," Stillman asked Norton after the *Fulton* landed off Sandy Hook. It appears Stillman hoped the Adirondack Club had remained active during his months abroad. Suffering from weakness and a slight cough—but no longer the vision problems that had afflicted him in the Alps—he hoped a few weeks in the open air and exercise would "break me in" for military service. While in the wilderness, Stillman planned to serve as a guide for Edwin James, a London man of questionable reputation who had also made the transatlantic journey aboard the *Fulton*. Stillman also planned to recruit outdoorsmen for a company of sharpshooters.[13]

Stillman spent most of August in Plainfield as he waited to begin his Adirondack guide work. He did some freelance journalism work for the New York newspapers, and he felt out his options for military service. With his health putting his usefulness to the Union in question, he did not take well to waiting and slid back into depression. Either in late July or early August, Stillman attempted to visit Greene at his headquarters, probably at Fort Warren. But he was "too late for Greene," and he could not pass medical inspection. On August 7, Greene's regiment was ordered to Harpers Ferry, though the Fourteenth never made it to this destination and was instead redirected to Washington. Probably a few weeks after his unsuccessful rendezvous with Greene, Stillman investigated a company of sharpshooters that Colonel Hiram Berdan was raising in New York. Stillman dismissed the idea of serving in such an outfit, despite his excellent marksmanship skills. Berdan was a "humbug," and Stillman refused to trust his honor to the "riff raff" recruiters he encountered in New York.[14]

Eventually, Stillman received word from Greene, who said the painter was not healthy enough to be of any use. This order likely did not greatly disappoint Stillman, who still hoped he could secure an appointment to a diplomatic position far away from the front. Probably after he left Plainfield for the Adirondacks that August, he took up an offer for assistance that had been extended years earlier to him by his mentor at Union College, Eliphalet Nott. Nott, the college's longtime president, wrote on August 29 a letter of recommendation to Seward. Unlike the letters drafted by Stillman's other supporters, Nott's did not specifically request an appointment in Venice. Instead, he said Stillman was a "deserving young man; and who you may rest assured will fill with honor to his country any office that may be assigned him." However, Eurania E. Nott, the president's wife, was blunter in her letter of recommendation sent to the Seward's son, Frederick, who served as his father's assistant secretary of state and oversaw the Union's consulate services. Of Stillman, she said, "He is an Artist and not an idler—and as such ought to be at Venice."[15]

When Stillman ventured into the Adirondacks, he notably did so without the company of his wife. The condition of his marriage at this time is unclear. Stillman's accounts of his European honeymoon make little mention of Laura. However, the couple appears to have been faring well enough for Laura to become pregnant in or around August, as she would give birth nine months later.

By mid-September, Stillman had served out his approximately two-week stint as a guide. He boarded at Martin's Hotel, the spot from which he recruited scouts and sharpshooters and did odd jobs to pay his keep. On September 16, he attempted to secure another guide position by writing to the famed Hudson River School painter Albert Bierstadt and inviting him to take photographs of the Adirondacks. Stillman offered Bierstadt, who had just started a painting expedition in the White Mountains, his services as guide. He also offered to supply camping equipment, including a boat and tent. "I can show you some magnificent bits," he said.[16] Bierstadt did not take up the offer, and Stillman's recruitment plans also backfired. His backwoodsmen were eager to fight, but they wanted to be part of a specially armed unit designed to "shoot secesh" (i.e., Confederate soldiers). Union officials, how-ever, wanted to use Stillman's men for infantry.[17] With no guide job and no sharpshooter company, Stillman slipped back into his backwoods routine of physical exercise paired with solitude. His work was done, but he could not leave the Adirondacks without checking up on one place dear to his heart.

It was all the same. The pond. The surrounding forest. Still "a most charm-ing place." On October 1, shortly before leaving the Adirondacks, Stillman returned to Ampersand Pond to see if all was right there. "Everything almost is as the club left it," he reported to Norton. All that was different was that near the pond's shore stood a cabin, which the club had contracted William Martin to construct. Minus the liquors, all the provisions were still there. Martin had built the cabin near the termination of the carry from Cold Brook.[18]

While the Adirondacks' lakes and rivers were frozen, probably during the winter of 1859–60, Martin had moved logs and other materials for the cabin to Ampersand. Lowell and Ward had been in the Adirondacks in February 1860 and may have supervised this phase of the project. Martin built the cabin at Ampersand the following spring. Inside, the cabin consisted of one large room with two narrow rooms partitioned off it. These two side rooms, which ran the length of the house, contained two staterooms, or private compartments, that each featured two bunk beds made of boards nailed to posts. Piled hemlock boughs were to be used as mattresses. The cabin also contained an iron stove.[19]

Looking at it, Stillman thought the cabin was not what he had designed, but it was a "pretty house nevertheless." More important, the pond remained "the gem of our country." Yet it was one the Adirondack Club never fully utilized. With its "admiral of all the lakes" abroad, the club became a rud-derless organization. Aside from Ellen Emerson's February 11, 1860, letter mentioning Lowell and Ward's winter trip to the Adirondacks, no other doc-umentation detailing any small or large club gathering at Ampersand after that date apparently exists. If any members, aside from Stillman and possibly Wyman, returned to Ampersand, none of them appear to have thought such a visit worth mentioning.[20]

It is not clear whether any Adirondack Club members bunked in the cabin in 1860, and Stillman's solemn journey into the wilderness suggests the clubhouse went unused the following year. A lecture Emerson gave earlier that year suggests that he also was not keen on returning to camp life. On April 9, he had delivered his first lecture in his *Life and Literature* series at Mei-onaon Hall in Boston. This lecture, "Genius and Temperament," examined the origins and qualities of genius—a theme that Emerson had woven into earlier essays such as "Nature," "Self-Reliance," and "The Poet." At Meionaon Hall, he stressed the distinction between talent and genius. Talent, he said, was vital to the act of creation, whether it be in a poet composing a poem or in an architect such as Frederick L. Olmstead, who was constructing New York City's Central Park. However, while talent sprang from "a temporary and personal origin" and grew out of "the severalty of man," genius grew out of a "universality" and worked for all men.[21] To highlight these creative powers, Emerson described a camp—reminiscent of the Philosophers' Camp at Follensby Pond—as a symbol for an environment that fosters talent:

> Men of talent create a certain artificial position, a camp in the wilderness somewhere, about which they contrive to keep much noise, and firing of guns, and running to and fro of boys and idlers, with what uproar they can. They have talents for contention, and they nourish a small difference into a loud quarrel, and persuade the surrounding population that it is the cause of the country and mankind. But the world is wide; nobody will go there after tomorrow. The gun can defend nothing but itself, nor itself longer than the man is by.[22]

Although Emerson had recorded in his journal his amazement with the Adirondacks in 1858 and his delight in the company he kept there, he revealed with this lecture the aspects of camp life he found least palatable. Just as he stands lost at the center of Stillman's painting *Morning at Camp Maple,* Emerson in this lecture distanced himself from the firing of guns by emphasizing not the enjoyment of shooting but the racket it created. He also appears to discredit the national attention the Philosophers' Camp attracted, saying that the "surrounding population" was persuaded, perhaps improperly, into believing the campers' "loud quarrel" represented "a cause of the country and mankind." Emerson may have been suggesting that an issue over which the campers argued—and that they believed to have been important—was actually less so to others outside of the camp. Despite the fun such campers had, "nobody will go there."

In referring to the camp as an "artificial position," Emerson also predicted the arguments of the transcendentalists' critics, who would contend that these idealistic men lived not as naturally as a bird dwells in a nest or an Indian in his hut. Instead, the outdoor haunts of the transcendentalists were far more civilized than wild. Much of this criticism was directed at Thoreau, who had tried to pass off his home at Walden as a link between nature and society. Stillman, for instance, called Thoreau's stay at Walden a "barn-door backwoods." A growing number of Americans, however, did not share Stillman's attitude toward tamed experiences with nature. They eagerly pursued such experiences, whether they were in Central Park or at an Adirondack hotel. In January 1861, Higginson rallied for such civilized experiences with the wild in an *Atlantic Monthly* essay titled "Barbarism and Civilization." He said, "In the wilderness and on the prairies we find a frequent impression that cultivation and refinement must weaken the race. Not at all; they simply domesticate it. Domestication is not weakness."[23]

Back at Martin's Hotel in early October 1861, Stillman wondered what the more civilized world had in store for him. A few weeks' worth of mountain air did not restore as much strength as he had hoped it would. A day before leaving Martin's, Stillman asked Norton to tell him what he could about a consul position—not at Venice but at Rome.[24] By this point it had probably become known to Stillman that the position in Rome that Howells had passed up for Venice was the artist's last shot at a diplomatic appointment abroad.

Upon returning home from Lower Saranac, Stillman visited his doctor in New York. By this time, the wearied painter was so debilitated that he needed to use "stimulus" to keep active for more than a half hour. The doctor diagnosed Stillman with "exhaustion of the brain" and advised him to go to Rome. Stillman was told to "give up all headwork" for three or four months and devote himself to exercise. Upon his doctor's recommendation, he gave up all military aspirations. He then went to Washington, where he learned there was a good chance a position would soon become available at Rome, especially in the event of Italy's capital being changed from Florence to Rome. Stillman received a conditional promise to be appointed to the position at the consulate, and this assurance was enough to convince him to go to Rome. Stillman late in life identified the letter to Seward by Nott—who did not specify a consulate in his request for Stillman's appointment—as having great influence in Washington. As it turned out, collegiate ties trumped literary and political influences. Seward had graduated from Union College in 1820. He was also one of Nott's favorite pupils, and up to the Civil War he regularly had sought the college president's advice before taking any step in politics.[25]

While in Washington, Stillman saw Charles Lowell, Lowell's nephew, who had participated in the 1857 camping trip at Big Tupper Lake. Charles had joined the Union army and was commissioned captain in the cavalry. Stillman told Lowell that Charles "will make a splendid soldier." After receiving enough assurances about the consul position in Rome, Stillman left Washington and visited Fort Albany, located north of the Potomac. Greene's regiment was stationed there. One cold night with the soldiers camped out at Fort Albany convinced Stillman "that was not the place for me." He returned to Plainfield, and he hoped to leave for Rome immediately, or at least by mid-November.[26]

Before leaving for Rome, Stillman went to Cambridge for information and advice. While visiting Lowell at Elmwood, he for the first time met Howells. Lowell's two pupils each offered the other "condolence for the other's disappointment" at not getting the diplomatic appointment he most desired. While the two diplomats-to-be got along congenially, their predicament was greeted less warmly in the Lowell household. Either before or after Stillman made this visit to Elmwood, Howells was having dinner with the Lowells when the poet said half teasingly to his wife, Frances, "Think of his having got Stillman's place! We ought to put poison in his wine." Lowell added that he wished Stillman had received the Venice appointment so he could follow up on Ruskin's work there. Lowell did not try to make Howells feel guilty about the consul arrangements, and it would not have mattered if he had. Howells, meanwhile, did not possess a shred of "any personal regret for my good fortune."[27]

Torn between his belief that Stillman was more deserving of the Venetian appointment and his fondness for Howells, Lowell attempted to establish a position of neutrality on the issue. While Lowell had signed the Adirondack Club's letter recommending Stillman for the appointment, he likely did so before he—or Stillman—knew Howells was also in the running for that position. It is hard to say whether Lowell would have knowingly sided with Stillman over Howells. A year earlier Stillman had complained to Norton that "Lowell has no faith in what I do." The artist opined that because Lowell's "ideas of art" were "so incompatible" with his own, he could not "write with any abandon for the Atlantic."[28] The bitterness that had tainted Lowell and Stillman's friendship after the poet went to Europe in 1855 returned.

Howells left the United States that November and arrived at Venice a month later, though he did not assume his position at the consulate until February 1862. Stillman left the United States without his wife—then about four months pregnant—around the same time. He arrived in England in November or December 1861 and reached Rome just before Christmas. The city, he said, "was still decaying, picturesque, pathetic, and majestic."[29] This is where Stillman, for the most part, spent the rest of the war years.

✖ CHAPTER 13

Peace

The Adirondack Club did not survive the war. Stillman never wrote in detail about the club's demise. Toward the end of his life, he made only two slightly different comments about the dissolution of the club, with one placing its demise in 1861 and the other suggesting it may have come at a later date. In 1893, he claimed the club "expired when the war broke out." Five years later he said that the club "existed until the war absorbed all the thought of its members, and the estate of 20,000 acres . . . was allowed to be re-conveyed to lumber cutters." After learning of the growing popularity of the tract, Township Twenty-Seven's original proprietor reportedly had redeemed the land by paying past dues on it.[1]

It is not clear who redeemed the club's Township Twenty-Seven lands or when, though the two-year redemption period should have contained that loss to the early 1860s. According to Headley, the original proprietor had offered to give Agassiz the land on which the cabin sat and that surrounded its immediate shores. Recognizing that the proprietor's speculation plans would infringe on the club's privacy, Agassiz reportedly rejected the offer. Thus the club abandoned the camp. My attempts to locate the original proprietor's petition for redemption in the New York State Archives were not successful. Additionally, the comptroller's index of redeemed tax sales lands does not list any redemptions in Township Twenty-Seven during the early 1860s, but several books are missing from these records. In March 1876, Emerson received from Ward "a surprising note and cheque on amount of the Adirondac Club, a piece of property long ago forgotten by me." As Ward explained, Emerson, as an original subscriber to the club, was entitled to a one-eighteenth share of a fund that totaled $910.84. Emerson's check totaled $50, which equaled the amount of the assessment he paid in 1859. (Ward in 1859 had told Norton the club's membership had reached twenty, so it is possible two people withdrew their membership, as was the case with Longfellow, resulting in eighteen original club members.) In a responding letter to Ward, Emerson said, "Such a windfall ought to be used to a rare & even romantic need." The fund's balance appears to have represented the assessments of the club's original membership for one year, plus almost $11 in interest. The balance may have represented unused funds from 1862, which was the last year Emerson had paid his club assessment. Assessments from years leading back to the club's creation in 1859 appear to have been expended, though that does not necessarily mean some or all members enjoyed the club's services in the Adirondacks over the intervening years.[2]

Continuing efforts to develop an Adirondack railroad network—more than speculation—likely had been what drove the redemption of Ampersand. After the Lake Ontario and Hudson River Railroad Company defaulted on its interest obligations and had a foreclosure judgment entered against it in early 1860, a court-appointed referee had sold its assets at various public auctions. Alrick Hubbell, of Utica, Oneida County, purchased the railroad company's entire rail line along with the right, interest, and title to the company. He also purchased its Franklin County lands, including the south half and northeast quarter of Township Twenty-Seven.[3]

These assets had been reconveyed to Adirondack Estate and Railroad Company, but this enterprise also failed after a key financier withdrew. In 1862, Albert N. Cheney purchased the assets of this company. Some funding for the acquisition came from Enoch Rosekrans, the judge who about a decade earlier had acquired nearly five thousand acres in the northwest corner of Township Twenty-Seven. In 1863, Cheney and Rosekrans conveyed their Adirondack Estate and Railroad Company assets to the Adirondack Company. This company was created by Thomas C. Durant and others associated with Union Pacific, which was about to begin work on the transcontinental railroad. In 1863, Rosekrans separately conveyed his 4,933 acres in Township Twenty-Seven's northwest quarter to the Adirondack Company. So by the early 1870s, most of the township was in the hands of railroad interests, with the main exception being the four lots in the 1,561 acres at the northern end of the northwest quarter.[4]

The abandonment of the clubhouse had not deterred at least one club member from returning to the Adirondacks in the mid-1860s. In August 1866, Wyman had vacationed in the Saranacs region, where he encountered the Boston abolitionist Henry I. Bowditch, who was staying at Bartlett's. Wyman, according to Bowditch, was staying at a "pretty camp" where the scientist and his wife in 1863 had passed "one of the happiest weeks of his life." It was a bittersweet memory, though, because his wife, Anna W. Whitney, died the following year after giving birth to a son.[5]

By the time Bowditch encountered Wyman in the Adirondacks in 1866, the region had already taken on a character far different from the one the scientist had first encountered eight years earlier at Follensby. A thriving tourist industry had developed, and the Adirondacks region was in the midst of its evolution from a wild land to a vacationland. This transformation had actually begun to take hold shortly after the Philosophers' Camp convened. A hunting trip that Apollos "Paul" Smith took in September 1858 with a Boston lawyer later convinced him to relocate his primitive retreat called the Hunter's Home, near Loon Lake, to Lower St. Regis Lake. Initially, Smith erected a seventeen-bedroom hotel at Lower St. Regis, north of Follensby. Business boomed during the Civil War, and Paul Smith's hotel grew into one of the region's premier resorts. Following Smith's success at Lower St. Regis, several other entrepreneurs opened hotels in the Adirondacks. Among them was one of Smith's earliest patrons, Daniel S. Hough, who built the lavish Prospect House (later known as the Saranac Inn) at the north end of Upper Saranac Lake. In 1865, Martin C. Lyon built the North Elba House (also known as Lyon's). Martin Moody built the Tupper Lake House in 1868.[6]

Luring Americans to these hotels were piles of literature highlighting Adirondack experiences and destinations. As the Adirondack Club had held its inaugural gathering at Ampersand, *Harper's New Monthly Magazine* in August 1859 had published the first of an illustrated two-part series recounting an Adirondack hunting and sketching adventure around the Saranac region. The series was titled "A Forest Story," by Thomas Addison Richards, a New York City painter and former *Crayon* correspondent. Richards, like Stillman, had displayed paintings at the Boston Athenaeum, including one titled *View among the Adirondacks*. They both enjoyed hunting, but Richards took the sport to an extreme. "Day after day we came back to camp laden with trophies of victory until the sport began to weary from its very ease and success," Richards said.[7] The entire tone of Richards's "A Forest Story" is starkly different from that of Stillman's yet-to-be-told "The Philosophers' Camp," and not only because the latter lacked the careless slaughter of deer. Like the countless other Adirondack travel essays that followed Richards's,

"A Forest Story" follows a simple plot. The travel routes are more important than the travelers. Richards does not even say much about the members of his party. In the late 1850s and early 1860s, stories about men camping in the Adirondacks and men building camps were plentiful. What was missing, however, was the story of a camp composed of great men. Here, eventually, Stillman and Emerson stepped in to fill the void.

Alfred Street, the official New York State librarian and a poet from Albany, had sought to produce a story about such a great camping trip with his *Woods and Waters: or, The Saranac and Racket*. The book, which was published in 1860, details the woodland adventures of Street's Saranac Club, whose membership was far more corporate and less literary than that of the Adirondack Club, consisting of the librarian, at least three lawyers, and a banker. This Albany crew explored the Saranac region, and Street even visited Follensby Pond and Ampersand Pond. In addition to the regular hunting and fishing stories, Street's book features many interesting stories of Adirondack history. It even includes the tales of "Captain Folingsby" and the Saranac Indian wizards at Ampersand Pond.[8]

Just as the Adirondacks had changed during the war, so did the lives of the Adirondack Club's members. At the war's onset, Agassiz had applied for U.S. citizenship. He spent the rest of the war years devoting himself to enriching the American sciences. He gave lectures aimed at defeating the advancement of Darwin's theories, cofounded the National Academy of Sciences in 1863, and vastly expanded his goal of collecting every fish specimen in North America to including every fish in the world. Agassiz's fame peaked in the early 1860s, and from there his influence began to decline. Even his pupils who rose to prestige at his Museum of Comparative Zoology turned on him and subscribed to Darwinism.[9]

Along with returning to poetry with a new *Biglow* series, Lowell had emerged from a two-year hiatus from editing. Along with Norton, Lowell in 1863 became a joint editor of the *North American Review.* Norton went on to cofound a weekly magazine in New York City called the *Nation* in 1865. Lowell lost three nephews to the war, including the two who had camped with him and Stillman at Big Tupper Lake in 1857. William Lowell died at Ball's Bluff in 1861, James Lowell during the Seven Days' Battles a year later, and Charles Lowell at Cedar Creek in 1864.[10]

Stillman had found much wanting in Rome. He was as put off by the American and English tourists who flocked to the city as he was by the Catholic Church. In July 1863, he made a brief trip to America to see his son—named after John Ruskin and nicknamed Russie—for the first time.

He landed in New York the day after the battle of Gettysburg ended. Before leaving Boston, Stillman encountered Woodman, who tried talking him into investing in a business enterprise or supporting some type of venture. Stillman expressed to Norton his reluctance to accept the offer. He returned to Rome with Laura and Russie and discovered to his dismay that while he was away, Rufus King, a former brigadier general for the Union and the minister to Rome, had circumvented the power of the consul at Rome through his appointment of Vermonter James Clinton Hooker as an unofficial secretary of the legation. Hooker had convinced the Roman Ministry of Foreign Affairs to eliminate the visa requirement on American passports. This maneuver robbed Stillman of his primary power as consul, namely, his ability to control the movement of Americans by endorsing their passports.[11]

Displeased with his situation in Rome, Stillman in 1865 managed to get a transfer to the consulate at Crete, with the help of George G. Fogg, a friend of Lincoln and the minister to Berne. Fogg had initially lobbied his friends in the House of Representatives to restore Stillman's powers in Rome, but Secretary of State Seward refused to take action. Instead, Stillman saw his funding under a consular and diplomatic appropriation eliminated. Lincoln later approved the transfer order, as Stillman was later told by one of the president's Illinois friends, "as the recognition of the injustice with which Seward had treated my case." Stillman in his autobiography surmised that his commission was one of the last Lincoln signed because he received it after the president's assassination on April 14, 1865. However, one of Lincoln's secretaries had signed Stillman's commission to Candia, Crete, on January 16, 1865—almost four months before the assassination.[12]

A year later, Stillman's brother Thomas died in Plainfield of pneumonia on January 1, 1866. Thomas was the Stillman family's successful businessman who for years had financially supported his artistic brother so he could pursue his passions. Although Stillman had been told he would be provided for after his brother died, Thomas in his will left his younger brother nothing, instead bequeathing everything to his wife. His death pushed Stillman to pursue practical means through which he could make a living, whether it was in diplomacy, photography, or journalism. Placing more pressure on Stillman was his growing family, which a few days before Thomas's death added a daughter, Eliza (Lisa). Stillman's family joined him in Canea. At the consulate at Crete, Stillman had expected to do little more than issue quarterly reports. Instead, he found himself navigating through a war zone. In April 1866, an insurrection erupted after an assembly of Christian leaders met at Omalos. Crete's Christians sought greater independence from the sultan of the Ottoman Empire. The sultan responded by calling Crete's Muslims into the shelter of three fortresses and then sending troops to the island to forcibly disperse the assembly. Hostilities ensued, and eventually total war broke out. Ottoman atrocities met the Cretan resistance. In the spring and fall of 1867, six hundred villages were destroyed.[13]

From openly opposing the sultan's plan to disperse the assembly at Omalos to providing safety behind the doors of his consulate to the Christian Cretans who could not seek refuge in Greece, Stillman stood as a guardian of the Cretan Christian cause. In Boston, some of the Adirondack Club's members rallied behind him in this effort. Although the Adirondack Club had long been inactive by this time, its members maintained a sense of community, mostly through their monthly meetings at Parker's on the last Saturday of the month. Despite the ocean between them, Stillman remained part of this community, primarily through his connection with Norton, to whom he continued to write on a regular basis. But since leaving America to assume his position at the Roman consulate in late 1861, Stillman had rarely corresponded with Lowell. Toward the end of the Civil War he had told Lowell, "I think of a visit to you all some day—a call to see how the old ideals keep their gold, but Cambridge to me now is a dream . . . and pleasant it is true but no more a reality to take hold of at last."[14]

In March 1867, the executive committee of the Boston Greek Relief Committee petitioned Massachusetts's senators to introduce in Congress a resolution declaring the United States' "sympathy with the heroic struggle in Crete." The committee consisted of Samuel G. Howe, former Massachusetts governor John A. Andrew, Amos Lawrence, Hermann J. Warner, and Woodman. Howe, along with Oliver Wendell Holmes, raised a substantial amount for the Cretan cause. Despite having a price put on his head, Howe in 1867 also visited Crete. Forbes, too, was involved in this aid effort. He told Stillman in a letter that food was being gathered for the Cretans, and he also had a supply of Sharpe rifles and was more "inclined to turn the committee, at least part of the way, on to powder instead of flour.[15]

For siding with Crete's Christians, Stillman became a political target of the Turks, who lobbied in Washington for his removal from the consulate. And after three years of war, his Cretan appointment took its toll on his family, which had grown to include another daughter, Bella, born in 1868. A year after Bella's birth, while in Athens, Laura killed herself, unable to bear the "anxiety and mental distress of our Cretan life," Stillman said. He partly blamed himself for Laura's death, owing to the fact that he had been too indebted to move her out of the environment that wore her down. Making matters worse, Russie started to limp after taking a heavy fall. It became an ailment that haunted his young life.[16]

Stillman was not the only Adirondack Club member recruited to serve the federal government. On March 5, 1869, President Ulysses S. Grant appointed Hoar the U.S. attorney general. Grant, skeptical of Washington insiders, embraced the recommendation of Hoar for the position of attorney general almost entirely on the basis of his reputation. In September 1869, when a vacancy emerged at the Supreme Court, Grant recommended Hoar to sit on the highest court, but the Senate defeated the nomination. Stillman had counted on Hoar to protect his position at the consulate at Crete. However, Rufus King and Turkish officials demanded the appointment go to someone else. While Hoar did fight for Stillman's position, King's friend, Hamilton Fish, who became Grant's secretary of state in March 1869, managed to circumvent the attorney general. Grant appointed Hugo Hillebrandt, a major with the New York Thirty-Ninth Regiment Volunteers during the Civil War, as the consul at Crete. According to Stillman, Fish pushed the appointment through a cabinet meeting at which the attorney general was absent, and Hoar was unable to reverse it at the next meeting. On March 4, 1870, Hoar told Stillman, "You were removed in company with a great many excellent officers of various kinds, for the removal of some whom there was no earthly reason . . . except that they held office for some term, and others wanted the places."[17]

Less than two weeks before the end of the Civil War with Confederate General Robert E. Lee's surrender at Appomattox, Virginia, Emerson found himself again testing out his own contribution to the growing literature paying homage to the Adirondacks. On March 27, 1865, probably at an engagement with Samuel Ward, he "read 'Adirondac,'" which was likely a version of the poem he had read seven years earlier at the Forbes summer home at Naushon. Seven months later, in November 1865, Emerson found himself gazing on the mountain ranges that had inspired this poem. After giving a lecture in North Adams, in the northwestern corner of Massachusetts, Emerson hiked into Vermont. From a hill near Bennington, he viewed the Green Mountains before him, "& chief & grand the Adirondac ranges in New York bounding our western line."[18] In seven more months, news originating from the barren Newfoundland coast would send Emerson into an even deeper Adirondack reverie.

After the failure of the first Atlantic cable in September 1858, Cyrus Field and the Atlantic Telegraph Company had spent the next six years preparing for another shot at laying a line between the Old World and the New. By 1864, Field had secured not only enough funding for another cable-laying enterprise but a new ship as well: the British *Great Eastern,* the largest vessel of its day. This ship would do the work of both the *Niagara* and the *Agamem-non* and make a single run from Valentia to Trinity Bay. Because of its massive size, the *Great Eastern* would not be able to make it to Bull's Arm, forcing Field to search Newfoundland for an alternative place for the ship to bring the cable ashore. He had found such a spot at the small, secluded fishing village of Heart's Content.[19]

On July 13, 1866, the *Great Eastern* again embarked on a voyage for Trinity Bay—one year after it was forced to abandon a similar mission when the cable snapped 1,200 miles into the journey. The cable was brought ashore at Heart's Content on July 27, though it took two days for the news to reach New York because the submarine cable that ran across the Cabot Strait from Newfoundland to Nova Scotia was malfunctioning. By July 30, news of the *Great Eastern*'s arrival at Heart's Content with a working Atlantic telegraph cable splashed the front pages across the country. The headlines echoed those from eight years before: "Successful completion of the Great Work" and "The Old and New Worlds Joined." The recovered cable from the 1865 mission was brought to Heart's Content in September. In Concord, the news took Emerson back to simpler times. On July 30, he wrote in his journal, "This morn came again the exhilarating news of the Atlantic cable at Heart's Content, New Foundland, and we repeat the old wonder and delight we found on the Adirondac, in August, 1858. We have grown more skillful, it seems, in electric machinery, and may confide better in our lasting success."[20]

Less than four months after the *Great Eastern* made landfall at Heart's Content, Emerson was readying what became his first book of poetry in twenty years. In November 1866, news spread that Emerson was reading proof sheets for a volume of poems to be published by Ticknor & Fields.[21] The new book, *May Day and Other Pieces,* contained poems on nature, life, and the elements, occasional and miscellaneous pieces, translations, and quatrains. The book began with two long poems that celebrated experiences with nature: "May Day" and "The Adirondacs."

It does not appear as though Emerson included "The Adirondacs" in his new book to advance the story of what had become popularly known as the Philosophers' Camp. Not once in the poem did he refer to the camp as such. He did not describe those who had joined him at Follensby as philosophers. Instead, they are "Fellow-Travellers," "scholars," and "polished gentlemen." His subtitle to the poem, "A Journal," indicates that he viewed the outing as a personal occasion he wished to share. Although Emerson had begun writing "The Adirondacs" either during or shortly after the Philosophers' Camp in August 1858, the poem was a work in progress up to the very point of printing. Lines of the poem were scattered throughout his notebooks, and its only

complete text is the printer's copy, although after that copy ι
Emerson sent to the printer a blue sheet of paper containing th
fourteen lines.[22] They read:

> The holidays were fruitful, but must end;
> One August evening had a cooler breath;
> Into each mind intruding duties crept;
> Under the cinders burned the fires of home;
> Nay, letters found us in our paradise;
> So in the gladness of the new event
> We struck our camp, and left the happy hills.
> The fortunate star that rose on us sank not;
> The prodigal sunshine rested on the land,
> The rivers gamboled onward to the sea,
> And Nature, the inscrutable and mute,
> Permitted on her infinite repose
> Almost a smile to steal to cheer her sons,
> As if one riddle of the Sphinx were guessed.[23]

It was with these last lines that Emerson provided closure to a long journal entry put to verse. Without this addition, the poem's ending would have seemed abrupt, like a journal awaiting the next day's entry. More important, it shows that even after the demise of the Adirondack Club, Emerson still believed his "Fellow-Travellers" to whom he dedicated the poem had found something truly extraordinary in New York's northern wilderness. Namely, they found a "paradise" and something "fruitful." Whatever joys the scholars had found in the Adirondacks, Emerson acknowledged they could not be kept, whether they were undisturbed connections with nature or carefree lifestyles usually reserved for children. Try as Thoreau did to nurture this harmony and innocence for more than two years at Walden, such experiences are designed to come and go, and they repel attempts to keep them fixed. The Adirondack Club's cabin at Ampersand would soon become symbolic of this point as it fell into disarray. Indeed, the holidays "must end."

It is important to note that in the last fourteen lines the Sphinx's riddle was "guessed," not answered. Additionally, the juxtaposition of "the gladness of the new event" and the striking of the camp poses a problem that makes the riddle harder to unravel. Because of the proximity of these lines, some people have interpreted the Sphinx's riddle as relating to the laying of the transatlantic cable. However, the scholars had initially rejoiced over the news of cable on August 7, and about a week passed before they had started to leave Follensby. These two events are not as chronologically linked as they appear in the poem. William W. Stowe has interpreted the poem's last line as relating to the news the scholars received in the wilderness about the trans-atlantic cable. "Man thinks that in shrinking space by harnessing electricity, he has solved one of the Sphinx's riddles, thus empowering him to impinge on her prerogatives," said Stowe. "Sphinx-like nature humors him, smiling at his impertinence and settling back, her mystery intact." Stowe said this ending to "The Adirondacs" "revises the final pronouncement" of Emerson's 1841 poem, "The Sphinx," through the former's declaration that "one technological triumph is not sufficient to decode and subdue nature in its grand entirety." However, this reading of the poem's ending portrays nature as relishing man's ignorance and allowing him to stray further from the truth, even though it cannot be known. This view runs contrary to Emerson's long-held belief that nature guides men to truth. "A life in harmony with nature, the love of truth and of virtue, will purge the eyes to understand her text," he said in "Nature."[24]

Instead, the Sphinx-like nature in "The Adirondacks" appears to have more in common with the Sphinx invoked in the 1852 poem "Questions of Life" by John Greenleaf Whittier, who became a member of the Saturday Club in 1858. Whittier's Sphinx "propounds / The riddle of her [nature's] sights and sounds." With the poet unable to determine "Nature's cypher" and answer the questions of life, Whittier's Sphinx "mocks" him. Here, Whittier's Sphinx, unlike the one described by Stowe, is more amused than threatened by man's "vain" attempt to crack its unbreakable code. However, Emerson's more compassionate Sphinx-like nature smiles on scholars and their hopeless guesses because, although their knowledge is incomplete, their experiences in the wilderness have nonetheless brought them closer to her and her mystery. Emerson's ending to "The Adirondacs" suggests the scholars did not—or could not—fully fathom what they experienced in the wilderness.[25]

To Emerson, the wilderness was enigmatic, and to encounter it was to receive a lesson in befuddlement—both perplexing and astonishing. This befuddlement might explain why he uncharacteristically did not attempt to define or categorize the wilderness in the poem. It would also explain how he could go from disparaging the experiences at "a camp in the wilderness" in his 1861 lecture "Genius and Temperament" to publishing a poem praising Adirondack camping. In the years to come he would return to his critical viewpoint of such primitive experiences. Emerson, whose transcendentalism was fueled by the powers of perception, did not know what he perceived in the Adirondacks. His ending to the poem makes his conclusions about those perceptions more along the line of speculation than of statement. It was as though he was still standing in Stillman's painting *Morning at Camp Maple*, lost in the middle.

The Adirondack historian Philip G. Terrie has also noted Emerson's ambiguous feelings toward the wilderness. He noted that when writing "The Adirondacs," Emerson did not join his contemporaries in developing belief systems under which the primeval forest became acceptable. Instead of embracing the wilderness's "mystical medicine," Emerson believed primeval nature accepted mankind's progress. Terrie said the philosopher suggested as much in "The Adirondacs," when neither cheers of men elated over news about the transatlantic cable nor the sound of Beethoven played on a piano seems out of place in the deep woods. However, by not taking into account Emerson's post-1867 writings addressing wilderness experiences, Terrie overestimated Emerson's acceptance of the wilderness, or his hesitation in accepting it. In his analysis of "The Adirondacs," Terrie did note that Emerson unfavorably viewed camping in the wilderness because of the wedge it formed between man and the "momentous achievements of the modern world."[26] But over time Emerson's opinion on primitive experiences became less ambivalent and more pessimistic.

In reviews of *May Day,* "The Adirondacs" was largely overshadowed by the book's title poem. As a critic for the *Boston Radical* explained, "'May Day' contained a richness of color and a fine flow of movement which he [Emerson] has never attained." Despite hearing at length about Adirondack camping trips from Stillman, Norton did not even mention "The Adirondacs" in his first review of *May Day* in the *Nation* in May. However, in another review of the book for the *North American Review* in July, he said the poem "reads like an American episode out of the best part of Wordsworth's 'Prelude.'" In a review of the book for the *Atlantic Monthly,* William Howells, whose tenure at the consulate at Venice had ended in 1865, said he did not regard "The Adirondacs" "as of great absolute or relative value." In a rather obtuse criticism, Howells said, "For a professedly out-of-doors poem [it] has too much study in it." The Philadelphia *Christian Recorder* panned the subject of "The Adirondacs" as being widely different from that of *May Day.* The newspaper nevertheless added that the former had "some fine passages." Instead of highlighting the experiences at Camp Maple or hunting around Follensby at night, the *Recorder*'s critic found greater value in the part of the poem furthest removed from the Adirondacks. He said the joy Emerson expressed in the poem from learning the transatlantic cable had been laid successfully "can now be read with greater appreciation than any of the intervening years since the time of which the poem treats."[27]

According to the American transcendentalism historian Joseph Jones, modern critics and commentators have continued not to think much of the poem, which "has little canon to offer." He criticizes the poem for weak blank verse, poetical diction "with an overburden of gratuitous classical allusions," and arbitrary changes in tense and calls it a "somewhat prosy, heigh-ho account." The poem's literary noteworthiness lies primarily in its inclusion of other literary figures.[28]

Strangely, nineteenth-century critics did not find the experiences of ten scholars shedding their city clothes and behaving like "Sacs and Sioux" noteworthy. This oversight might be explained by the fact that such outdoors excursions were not uncommon in the 1860s and over the prior four decades had become an American tradition. But in the coming years some American tourists increasingly found the primitive experiences Emerson described in "The Adirondacs" especially appealing. During the postwar years, as the frontier closed, overcrowding in urban areas became common and public disgust with political corruption was piqued. A few Americans increasingly longed for simpler times—even primitive times. To experience this primitiveness, many turned to the nation's rapidly disappearing wilderness, where they could get a taste for the type of life the Indian or frontiersman had once lived. But that is not to say that tourists who traveled to the Adirondacks wanted to live like Indians or frontiersman.[29]

This primitivism movement is summed up by Emerson's statement in "The Adirondacks" that "we flee away from the cities, but we bring / The best of cities with us." The primitivism of the second half of the nineteenth century sought to stimulate the "savage" feelings that overcame Emerson at Follensby. The thrill of the hunt, whether with a rifle or a rod and reel, and any direct experience of nature were usually the key objectives of these Adirondack trips. According to the historian Roderick Nash, primitivism also reflected Americans' awareness of the growing distance between themselves and the wilderness and their attempt to close this gap. It resulted in what Theodore Roosevelt described as "over civilized" people who had lost touch with their "great fighting, masterful virtues." By retreating to the wilderness and living as simply as possible, some sought to restore these virtues and a degree of self-reliance. This "cult of the primitive," as Nash called it, grew out of an antimodernism movement that was largely driven by white upper- and middle-class Americans. As the historian T. J. Jackson Lears has noted, the antimodernist impulse stemmed from a distrust of liberalism and dissatisfaction with modern culture, which became detestable in its "overcivilization." Europeans and Americans both recognized that "the triumph of modern culture had not produced greater autonomy (which was its official claim) but rather promoted a spreading sense of moral impotence and spiritual sterility." These antimodernists, however, represented only a minority of Americans, with the majority rallying behind the march of capitalism, economic growth, and technological advancement.[30]

Emerson in "The Adirondacs" did not attempt to gloss over his fellow campers' cultivated backgrounds and pass them off as rugged men who just happened to live in the city. The two doctors could not abandon their affinity for scientific experimentation any more than the scholars could forget their fondness for books or the strains of Beethoven. "Look to yourselves," Emerson said, "ye polished gentlemen!" Nevertheless, at the same time he was not coy about what the scholars were after: a primitive experience in which they could live like Indians and play like boys. Emerson did not view this reversion to a purely primitive state as the panacea for a troubled nation, however. What was needed was not wild men but civilized men—free men. Humanity's salvation, he said, rested not in the primitive "Iroquois or cannibals" but in "the free race with front sublime."[31]

This position differs from that of other Adirondack writers, such as Street, who were more skeptical of what they saw as the overcivilization of the age. Street questioned whether the "trophies won by that civilization" (e.g., the "treasures of science" and "enchanted realms of painting, poetry, sculpture, music, elegance") outweighed its "sufferings, cares and crimes" and "the daily anxieties and battles for its miscalled prizes." Street declared he was "sick of the griefs and strifes and follies of the world," and that he would rather live "here, in this wilderness . . . where honor is not measured by success, where pretention does not trample upon merit, where genius is not a jest, goodness not a seeming and devotion not a sham."[32]

Emerson, too, valued experiences in nature. Long before he ever set foot in the Adirondacks' primeval forest, he said, "In the wilderness, I find something more dear and connate than in streets or villages." Headley similarly believed that a tree waving in the summer wind was "fuller of meaning and instruction than the crowded mart or gorgeously built town." But Emerson believed nature should be experienced in moderation. Just three months before he ventured to Follensby in August of 1858, Emerson had told Thoreau, "A frog was made to live in a swamp, but a man was not made to live in a swamp." In 1872, Emerson delivered similar advice to the naturalist and preservation movement leader John Muir, who he hoped would bring his "ripe fruits so rare and precious into waiting Society [in Cambridge]" when his "sequestration in the solitudes & snows had reached their term."[33]

It is not clear when Stillman first read "The Adirondacs," but it ultimately met with his approval. Stillman called it "the most curiously truthful and interesting revelation of her [Nature's] aspect, seen for the first time with a mind trained for the finest shades of impression and reflection—the most

Homeric and Hellenic of all nature poems ever written."[34] Stillman did not see himself, however, as one of Emerson's "polished gentlemen." In his future writings about the Philosophers' Camp, Stillman distanced himself from the scholars of civilization and portrayed himself as belonging more to the guides of the wilderness. The fact of the matter is that he had wandered between both worlds: the wilderness and civilization. It was not until his tour at the consulate at Crete ended in 1868 that his life started heading irreversibly toward the latter.

Letting go of the wild, nevertheless, was not easy. Six years after *May Day*'s publication, Stillman was living at Clapham Common in London. "I must go back to America," he told his friend and former *Crayon* contributor Bayard Taylor. Stillman claimed that "no other land has all the other elements of life I need and I shall go [to America] the first good chance I get." He wanted to go shooting and fishing and "indulge for one instant in any of my savage propensities." He lamented that his overwhelming desire for "a healthy day in a savage state" depressed him, insisting, "I must go back."[35]

❧ Chapter 14

The Ravages of Modern Improvement

Not even twenty years had passed since William Martin had constructed the Adirondack Club's cabin at Ampersand Pond before it was reduced to ruins. The clubhouse's roof had caved in; raspberry bushes jutted from wide crevices between the logs forming its walls. A dense barricade of bushes surrounded the structure.[1]

One summer day in 1878, Henry Van Dyke, a twenty-six-year-old recent graduate of the Princeton Theological Seminary, found himself circling these ruins at Ampersand. At the front of the cabin's sunken doorsill he found a rusty, broken iron stove. To him it looked "like a dismantled altar on which the fire had gone out forever." Van Dyke had heard about this cabin. Here, he thought, was where Agassiz, Appleton, Norton, Emerson, Lowell, Hoar, Gray, John Holmes, and Stillman had established their "successor of 'the Philosophers' Camp' on Follensbee Pond." But by the summer of 1878, when Van Dyke spent three weeks at Ampersand, he said the "only philosophers to be seen were a family of what guides called 'quill pigs'" (porcupines).[2]

By September 1878, Van Dyke had reached a crossroads in his young life: he could either follow his father into the ministry or follow his dream of becoming a writer and a poet. Ampersand's renown for fishing and the views promised by its namesake mountain tempted Van Dyke to the area. Ampersand's association with the Adirondack Club, too, likely added to the pond's appeal. To him, Emerson was one of America's six greatest writers. Although

Van Dyke in January 1879 accepted a position at the United Congregational Church of Newport, Rhode Island, he later settled on a career path similar to the one taken by Emerson. After spending twenty-one years in the ministry, he left the pastorate to write and teach.[3] In July 1885, *Harper's New Monthly Magazine* published his essay "Ampersand," which recounted his hike up Ampersand Mountain and his discovery of the Adirondack Club's decrepit cabin. This essay was just one among many that identified the club's old haunts as places of pilgrimage for spiritually minded sportsmen.

Other spiritually minded sportsmen included the Harvard physiologists William James and Henry Pickering Bowditch, along with James Jackson Putnam and Charles Pickering Putnam, two brothers who were Harvard Medical School students. Following an 1874 trip to Keene Valley during which the four lodged at a farmhouse, this group over several years acquired property in the vicinity, which became known as the Putnam Camp. According to Richard Plunz, the "Putnam Camp was conceived very much in the spirit of the Philosophers' Camp." Emerson's poem "The Adirondacs" likely familiarized these Harvard men with the Philosophers' Camp. Their Putnam Camp "became the logical successor" to the idealism associated with the Philosophers' Camp, "tempered of course by the intervening decades of enormous change in both the cities and Adirondacks alike."[4]

Leading hikers and fishermen such as Van Dyke to Ampersand and other destinations in the wilderness were troves of Adirondack guidebooks and travelogues. Two years after the release of Emerson's *May Day and Other Pieces,* William H. H. Murray, a preacher at the Park Street Church of Boston, had published his *Adventures in the Wilderness, or Camp-Life in the Adirondacks.* This work quickly became the era's definitive Adirondack guidebook, and it spurred a rush of tourism in the region.[5]

Although *Adventures in the Wilderness* mentioned neither Follensby nor Ampersand, other guidebooks published after it did. The Philosophers' Camp was often invoked in these books as the main reason for visiting these secluded lakes. In the 1876 edition of his *Descriptive Guide to the Adirondacks,* Edwin R. Wallace described Ampersand as "one of the most sequestered as well as most lovely of all the Wilderness sheets." He noted that the cabin near the pond's shore had been built by William Martin "for Agassiz and his companions." Wallace called this site "the celebrated Philosopher's Camp,'" perpetuating what became a grand confusion between the camps at Follensby and Ampersand. In *The Middle States: A Guide for Travelers,* Moses F. Sweetser made the same mistake in a chapter on the Adirondacks. Sweetser directed tourists to Ampersand, where "Agassiz, Lowell, and Holmes dwelt in the 'Philosophers'

Camp." However, in a correction that ran in the 1875 edition, he noted that "the famous Philosopher's Camp" was not at Ampersand Pond but at "Folingsby's Pond."[6] The book's publisher, James R. Osgood and Company, was a successor to Ticknor & Fields, which had published Emerson's Adirondack poem in *May Day*.

Regarding "Folingsby," Wallace said, "Agassiz, Ralph Waldo Emerson, James Russell Lowell, Judge Hoar, and other eminent literary gentleman, who have camped near this charming water gem, will testify to its many attractions." Wallace's *Descriptive Guide to the Adirondacks* was first published in 1872 and went into multiple editions over more than twenty years. In the 1876 edition, he noted that there was a "comfortable shanty" at the foot of the pond and a larger one called Dunkett's near its head. Sweetser's *Middle States* called Follensby the "summer home" of Emerson, Agassiz, Lowell, and Hoar.[7]

Throughout the 1870s, guidebooks were not alone in keeping alive the story, or at least the spirit, of the Philosophers' Camp and Adirondack Club. In 1870, Ticknor & Fields published Emerson's *Society and Solitude*. It was a collection of twelve essays, many of which he had read at lectures in the months after his August 1858 camping trip and while the Adirondack Club was being organized.

In "Civilization," Emerson continued his opposition to the retreat to primitivism that he had expressed in "The Adirondacs." He instead advocated for social progress. A true civilization, he said, must grow morally stronger and not succumb to "suicidal mischiefs," such as the suppression of free speech, the diffusion of knowledge tainted by "mob-law or statute law," and the importation of art at the expense of the it not having an "indigenous life." Civilization needed adventurous men but not when their adventures deprived them of worldly views. "The most advanced nations are always those who navigate the most," Emerson said. "The power which the sea requires in the sailor makes a man of him very fast, and the change of shores and population clears his head of much nonsense of his wigwam." It is not clear if by "wigwam" Emerson literally meant any rustic dwelling, similar to those built by the Indians, or if he was speaking metaphorically in relation to a man's rustic lifestyle or practical habits. In an 1859 letter to Lowell about the Adirondack Club's then forthcoming inaugural meeting at Ampersand, Emerson had commented on "the present state of the tribe & the wigwam." In "Civilization," he echoed his advice from his 1841 essay, "Self-Reliance," to "look abroad" for religion and art, because men will always fail to improve their own society without insights into others.[8]

In "Eloquence," Emerson revealed one of the analogies he had likely gleaned from his studies of Camp Maple's guides. While commenting on orators and their art, he put the guide in the wilderness on the same level as a judge in the courthouse. Both of them, he said, are uniquely capable of bringing a man to a desired point, whether it is to a lake or to the truth. Emerson said, "In every company the man with the fact is like the guide you hire to lead your party up a mountain, or through a difficult country. He may not compare with any of the party in mind or breeding or courage or possessions, but he is much more important to the present need than any of them." Here Emerson touched upon another theme from "Self-Reliance," though his stance on it changed after his experience in the wilderness. In "Self-Reliance" he had lamented over the loss of civilized man's "aboriginal strength" and his inability to know the stars in the sky or to observe the solstices. It was the self-reliant man's responsibility to tap into his "inborn" power without looking for "good out of him and elsewhere," he said. "It is only as a man puts off all foreign support and stands alone that I see him to be strong and to prevail. He is weaker by every recruit to his banner."[9] In "Eloquence," contrarily, Emerson is much more comfortable leaving such matters of might and instinct to other men, namely, guides. It is important to note that Stillman was one of these guides, and he succeeded where Emerson failed in being truly self-reliant and tapping his aboriginal powers.

In the same year of *Society and Solitude*'s publication, Thomas Wentworth Higginson made more direct references to the successor of the Philosophers' Camp with his essay, "Footpaths," which was published in the *Atlantic Monthly* that November. The essay recounted his 1859 visit to Ampersand, where he had encountered an ill-tempered Stillman and was laughed at relentlessly by the pond's loons. In 1869, another edition of Joel Headley's *The Adirondack: or, Life in the Woods* was published. Headley included in this edition stories about his adventures in the wilderness since *The Adirondack* was first published in 1849. Among these stories added to the book was one about a "special pilgrimage" Headley and his ten-year-old son had made to Ampersand to see what they thought was the Philosophers' Camp. Of the "neglected mansion" they found at Ampersand, Headley said, "Untenanted, desolate, and alone, the 'philosopher's camp' has ever since stood in the heart of the forest, a monument of disappointed hopes, and a warning to all speculators in wild lands."[10]

The railroad company that owned much of Township Twenty-Seven, much like its predecessors, ran into financial troubles. In 1865, the New York Legislature had authorized the Adirondack Company to extend the reach of its railroad and to raise more capital. In response, the corporation changed the terminus of the railroad from Newcomb in Essex County to Oswegatchie,

St. Lawrence County, and it also doubled its total amount of capital to $10,000,000. In 1872, the Adirondack Company mortgaged to the New York State Loan and Trust Company, serving as trustee, all of its rights, franchises, privileges, and immunities along with the property it had purchased. But work on the railroad was not completed, and foreclosure proceedings commenced in 1881. William Sutphen and William W. Durant bought the entire railroad, including its mortgaged lands. They reorganized the Adirondack Company into the Adirondack Railway Company. Among the lands that Sutphen and Durant purchased were most of Township Twenty-Seven, excluding parts of the northwest quarter. The Adirondack Railway Company ended up acquiring 27,433 acres of the township.[11]

The proposed railroad did not directly endanger Ampersand's pristine character, and for the time being it was safe from the ravages of the ax. Elsewhere in the Adirondacks, though, lumbering and tourism transformed the wilderness. And while throngs of tourists and timber-hungry railroad and lumber magnates welcomed this transformation, others recognized this change was not sustainable or desirable, no matter how profitable it was. A year before the Civil War ended, the *New York Times* had related in an editorial the consequences of the railroad line that the Adirondack Company had started building in 1863 from Saratoga Springs to North Creek in Warren County. Although the sixty-mile line promised to turn the Adirondacks into "a Central Park for the world," the writer noted that thousands of men were cutting down, blasting, and bridging the wilderness. "The furnaces of our capitalists will line its valleys, and create new fortunes to swell the aggregate of our wealth; while the hunting-lodges of our citizens will adorn its more remote mountain-sides and wooded islands of its delightful lakes." The Adirondack historian Frank Graham Jr. has identified the author of this editorial as the philanthropist Charles L. Brace, who had been camping in the Adirondacks with his family at the same time the scholars had convened at Follensby in August 1858.[12]

In a December 1870 report to the secretary of New York State's Board of Regents, Verplanck Colvin warned about the rampant cutting and burning of vast tracts of wilderness. This activity, he said, threatened not only the Adirondacks' ecosystem but the rest of New York's as well. He said the destruction of the forest would lead to disastrous flooding as snow melted from the mountain peaks. Colvin's remedy to this problem was the creation of an Adirondack park or a timber preserve. Within two years of the submission of Colvin's report, this preservationist proposal slowly started to gain traction in Albany. In 1872, Colvin was appointed the superintendent of an Adirondack survey, which was tasked with producing the first accurate map of the region. Also in 1872, the New York Assembly established a state park commission, which was charged with exploring the feasibility of the state ownership of land in several Adirondack counties. The commission, on which Colvin served as secretary, recommended the creation of a 1,730,000-acre Adirondack preserve, primarily for the sake of watershed protection. At the time, the state owned approximately 40,000 acres in the region. However, plans for a forest preserve took a dozen years to materialize, and the establishment of the Adirondack Park took an additional eight years.[13]

Transformative change did not come to the Adirondacks alone. By the late 1870s, almost every aspect of American culture that was represented by the scholars at the Philosophers' Camp had become outdated. New England was experiencing the end of what the Spanish American historian George Santayana called the "Indian summer of the mind." While teaching at Harvard in 1923, Santayana attributed the downfall of the poets, historians, orators, and preachers who had prospered in mid-nineteenth-century New England to their efforts to impose a piousness on American culture. He was especially critical of Washington Irving's "Rip Van Winkle," and Longfellow's "Evangeline" and "Hiawatha." These works did not flow from the American experience, Santayana said, and it took writers such as Walt Whitman to bring to the forefront the long-suppressed feelings and visions of the nation.[14]

Among those who had participated in the Philosophers' Camp, Agassiz was the first to experience the end of this Indian summer. He died from a cerebral brain hemorrhage on December 14, 1873, at the age of sixty-six. With his death, the last major impediment to Darwinism's adoption in mainstream American science was removed. The debate that had raged in the 1860s between Agassiz's creationist beliefs and Darwin's theories on evolution had calmed by the end of the decade. Since Agassiz had received from Darwin a copy of *On the Origin of Species* in 1859, there had been very little communication between the two scientists. In 1868 the creationist told the evolutionist his views were "mischievous," though he claimed not to hold any animosity for the scientist who produced them. Agassiz nevertheless remained far from willing to reconcile his beliefs with those of Darwin. In the months before his death, he gave a series of lectures in which he assessed Darwin and evolution more than he attacked them. The last of these addresses were published in the *Atlantic Monthly*, which was then being edited by William Howells. Agassiz's "Evolution and Permanence of Type" amounted to his final opinion on evolution, being published in the magazine a month after his death. It marked his first published work primarily on Darwinism since 1860. In the end, unable to devise a consistent argument that could refute Darwinism once and for all, Agassiz in this essay refuted everything, even his own beliefs, to an extent. He said that the more he studied the animal world, the more it seemed "we have not yet reached its hidden meaning." Acknowledging Darwin's prevalence in the debate over the origin of species, Agassiz added that he had regretfully watched the next generation's brightest scientists "give themselves to speculation rather than to close and accurate investigation."[15]

Although many of Agassiz's companions at Camp Maple—such as Stillman and to an extent Wyman—eventually subscribed to the theory of evolution, they never stopped holding the highest esteem for him. Agassiz's friend in England, Richard Owen, had convinced Stillman of the soundness of the theory of evolution. The conversion was liberating for Stillman, who in it found "the new perception of a spiritual religion and life, which was more consoling and vivifying by far than the older belief." Some transcendentalist historians, such as Higginson, identified parallels between Emerson's beliefs, particularly those regarding fate, and those of Darwin. According to Lawrence Buell, "Transcendentalist philosophy anticipated Darwin by viewing nature as organic and transitional rather than fixed and mechanistic, but the Transcendentalists remained prescientific in that they were finally interested in treating nature not as objective matter but as a manifestation of the divine nature and teleology."[16]

When Lowell heard of Agassiz's death while touring Italy, he responded with a long ode to the scientist that ran in the May 1874 edition of the *Atlantic Monthly*. Lowell's "Agassiz" was the only significant poem he wrote during his time abroad. He harked back to the bouts of wit and laughter he may had enjoyed with Agassiz in the Adirondacks. Making reference to Agassiz's reaction to one of Hoar's sharp and amusing debates, Lowell recalled how Agassiz would be "Pricked with cider of the judge's wit / (Ripe-hearted homebrew, fresh and fresh again)," and how the scientist often tried to hold back "The merriment whose unruly moods / Pass not the dumb laugh learned in listening woods / Of silence-shedding pine."[17]

Darwinism's prevalence, coupled with the disillusionment that came in the wake of a bloody war, contributed to the decline of Emerson's transcendentalism. The movement did not spread far beyond the greater Boston area, and American culture did not change course to follow its lead. No longer invigorated by debates over slavery and religion, transcendentalism lost its relevance as the late nineteenth century's economic and industrial trends made the movement's virtues of self-reliance and harmony with nature increasingly impractical. In the latter half of the nineteenth century, transcendentalism lost not only its relevance but also its leaders. Even before the Civil War ended, many in transcendentalism's avant-garde, such as Thoreau, Margaret Fuller, and Theodore Parker, had died.[18]

In the post–Civil War years the art of landscape painting, which Stillman had sought to advance at the *Crayon,* also faded in prominence. The journal, too, during John Durand's tenure as editor, had ceased publishing during the first year of the war. The divine in nature that artists such as Cole, Durand, and Church had captured in their landscapes seemed increasingly absent to Americans. It became difficult for them to embrace these paintings with the same fervor they had experienced before Darwinism seemed to form a wedge between God and the wilderness. That rift widened even further as the nation's westward expansion neared its conclusion, obscuring the sense of manifest destiny conveyed in Hudson River School paintings.[19]

Amid these developments, a revolt erupted within the National Academy of Design between its old-guard landscape painters and its younger artists. The younger generation readily embraced European influences and was more apt to paint still lifes or figures than landscapes. In 1878, a group of young artists formed the Society of American Artists as an alternative to the National Academy, which for almost fifty years had served as home to the Hudson River School. Finding their works harder to sell, many landscape painters gave up the trade. Only a handful of them, such as Sanford Gifford, found continued fame as the Hudson River School's light faded, mainly because they focused on provoking emotion in their works instead of portraying an actual place. These were the artists who had managed to execute the type of poetic vision that Ruskin praised in Turner and with which Stillman had struggled since his Lowell-induced epiphany on subjectivism at Big Tupper Lake in 1857. As an indication of how Gifford's emotive and luminist works had weathered American art's transition from landscape painting to impressionistic painting, he became the first artist to be honored at the Metropolitan Museum's new Central Park location with an exhibition in the fall following his death in August 1880. He was fifty-seven years old. Asher Durand, the lone surviving leader of America's first generation of landscape painters, died in 1886. His last painting was of an Adirondack landscape. Stillman's heart remained with landscapes. In his review of an exhibition of American paintings at the Paris Exposition in 1878, he lamented over foreign influences in American art. In vain he looked in these works "for something of the veteran Durand, who is always American and individual," and for "something of Cole."[20]

No longer able to rely on his brush to capture a landscape, Stillman in the 1860s and 1870s increasingly turned to his camera. While serving as the consul at Crete, he made photography his hobby and trade. In 1869, after seeking a reprieve from the Cretan insurrection's violence, Stillman went to Syra, Greece, though he told Norton he longed for "a breath of the hills, of a sound of running streams—a day in the Adirondacks." He extensively photographed Greece's ruins. After a Greek doctor diagnosed Russie with rheumatism and prescribed exercise and walks, Stillman had his limping son accompany him on photography expeditions to Marathon and other sites. The pictures Stillman took in Greece were published in London a year later in *The Acropolis of Athens,* a collection of twenty-six photographs of the ruins.[21]

Stillman returned to America in late November 1869, two weeks after his mother had died. The following summer, he found that his painting life was not completely dead. In September 1870, he traveled to Jackson, New Hampshire, near Glen Ellis Falls. There he attempted to paint a landscape commissioned by Forbes, but he was so out of practice that he felt "half paralyzed." Agassiz visited Stillman at his tent in the "Glen of the White Mountains," where they discussed nature and art. It was their last encounter. Stillman also received a visit from Edward Emerson and James Bryce, a British writer whose books on American culture were in the vein of Tocqueville. Eleven years had elapsed since Stillman had hosted Edward at Ampersand Pond. The young Emerson had ventured to New Hampshire with his father, and they encountered Bryce at Gorham, roughly thirty miles north of Jackson. The painter prepared for the young men a lunch of hasty pudding (maize), coffee, and preserved meats and went hiking with them to the falls for a swim. Bryce also brought Stillman a letter from Lowell.[22] It is not clear whether Stillman reunited with Emerson.

Back in Washington, Hoar tried to find another type of official employment for Stillman, perhaps remorseful that he had not protected his Cretan appointment. However, Grant's secretary of state informed the attorney general that Stillman could not be sent to any place under Turkish rule, and there were no worthwhile offices he could offer. Coming up empty-handed, Hoar told Stillman in March 1870, "I doubt whether any respectable person can count on long continuance in the public service in this government." Later in July, Hoar resigned as attorney general. Despite his disillusionment with politics, he was not through with Washington. In November 1872, he was elected to Congress. The following August he was also offered the position of chief justice of the Supreme Judicial Court of Massachusetts, but he declined this post, probably to not stand in the way of his former law partner and fellow Amperzander, Horace Gray, from assuming that position. Hoar did, however, accept an offer to serve as the first president of the Concord Free Public Library Corporation. The library was dedicated on October 1, 1873.[23]

Unable to resurrect his political career, Stillman returned to journalism. He wrote a history of the Cretan uprising he had witnessed in his capacity as consul, and in 1874 Henry Holt & Company published his *The Cretan Insurrection: 1866–1868*. Stillman also regularly contributed to the *Nation* and the *Atlantic Monthly*. He briefly found employment at *Scribner's Monthly*, a New York magazine that changed its name to the *Century Magazine* in 1881. Stillman left his position at *Scribner's* and moved to Notting Hill in London. In the spring of 1871, he became more firmly rooted in Europe when he married Marie Spartali, the artistic daughter of a Greek consul general. Spartali later gave Stillman three children, beginning with his daughter, Euphrosnye, or Effie.[24]

He continued to work for *Scribner's* as its literary agent in England, responsible for securing contributions from English authors. Wanting to live closer to Marie's parents, the Stillmans around the spring of 1872 relocated to Clapham Commons, where they later received visits from an Egypt-bound Emerson and from Lowell, who was on his way to Madrid. These visits, just like the one Stillman had received from Agassiz in the White Mountains in 1870, highlight how the interconnections forged by the Adirondack Club remained intact throughout the years, at least in regard to Stillman. Stillman remained an outsider to the intellectual circle that continued to meet at Parker's on the last Saturday of the month, but now he had more in common with his fellow Amperzanders, such as fatherhood. Russie's condition had been deemed incurable, leaving him crippled and in constant pain. Stillman told Lowell he feared Russie would die. Lowell, whose first wife had died of tuberculosis, responded, "I should be afraid he would not die."[25]

Although foreigners such as Bryce in 1870 considered Boston the nation's "sole literary centre," the city was in the midst of economic transformation that would leave it, much like its writers, with far less influence.[26] Parker's Hotel became a refuge for many of Boston's aging intellectuals, who increasingly saw their influence outside its doors diminish.

As the Industrial Revolution transformed America's business landscape, Boston, a "consumer city," suffered from lack of a manufacturing base. Instead of concentrating in the city, manufacturers developed facilities outside Boston, namely, those areas with availability to waterpower. Many Bostonians followed the manufacturing jobs out of the city, resulting in a massive influx of middle-class workers into the suburbs and leaving the very rich and very poor to dwell in Boston. Exacerbating Boston's economic woes was the 1867 advent of the stock ticker that the New York Stock Exchange aggressively controlled, transforming it from an underdog in the equities market to its most dominant player. Once a leader in that emerging industrial stocks market through most of the nineteenth century, the Boston Stock Exchange failed to keep up with market changes and quickly became one of the nation's weakest regional exchanges.[27]

Emerson's Concord was not immune to the changes in Boston. The development of the Fitchburg Railroad more than two decades earlier had marginalized many of the town's most important workers, namely, farmers and teamsters. After the Civil War, Emerson saw the town's commercial and industrial resources as being wood and grass. Meanwhile, its education services sector thrived. As Hoar entered his later years, he too watched the beloved village of his youth double in size and the nationalities of its residents become vastly more diverse. At an event celebrating Concord's 250th anniversary in 1885, Hoar publicly expressed doubts that a new prison and a philosophy school built at opposite ends of town were best for its future.[28]

By July 1873, a homesick Stillman was plotting to return to New York. He considered reporting for the *Tribune* or launching a new international art journal based in Clapham Common. After spending most of the past two decades abroad, he was eager to see whether there was no place like home for a well-traveled and well-cultured man like him. Nevertheless, he had his doubts. "It is strange and painful to be so lost to my native land and fellow countrymen," Stillman told Bayard Taylor in September 1873. But he aborted plans for the trip home partly because of the Panic of 1873. America, to Stillman, no longer looked like "the land of promise."[29]

Although career opportunities did not bring him back to America, Russie's illness did in 1874. At the advice of a doctor, Stillman and his son embarked on a vacation in the woods, though it is not clear whether the doctor recommended a transatlantic voyage to get to those woods. Either way, the two traveled to Moosehead Lake in Maine, but Russie's illness made them retreat to a nearby hotel. The woodland air and "influence of pine-trees power" did not help the boy as well as it had helped the father in the 1850s, and their camping trip was cut short. Stillman nevertheless managed to work some fishing into this trip, and he deemed Moosehead the "queen of all our forest lakes."[30]

It was likely after this summer camping trip that Stillman took his camera to Cambridge, where he photographed local landmarks, such as the Washington Elm, the Churchyard, the Oaks at Waverley, Harvard, an old churchyard, and the homes of Oliver Wendell Holmes, Lowell, and Longfellow. While a tranquil quietude marked the photographs taken in the rural areas around Cambridge, an eerie silence fills those taken within the city. In the pictures, the effects of morning sunshine imbue houses of Stillman's friends with a dream-like quality. The photographs were all taken from afar, and their subjects seem distant. The "old Cambridge" felt that way to Stillman and his friends.

In October, Stillman and Lowell walked to the Oaks at Waverley, where their friendship had blossomed in the 1850s. The place had not lost its charm. Even if the old oaks had not changed, the men themselves had changed a great deal in the nearly twenty years since they had first gone there together. Stillman had long outgrown his artistic zeal, and Lowell was even more ill-tempered and less admirable. When Bayard Taylor earlier that year commented on the poet's strange behavior when they had last met, Stillman said he was not surprised. "Long ago I saw with much pain the unsound side of his [Lowell's] character which now appears so painfully," Stillman told Taylor. He blamed Lowell's problems on the fact that he had suffered from "a youthful success so much greater than the true match of the man." He expressed an unending love for Lowell, but he wished the poet "could have been always what I once believed him."[31]

The cultural and economic trends that reshaped postwar America—and especially Cambridge—were not lost on Stillman. In 1876, James E. Osgood and Company published Stillman's Cambridge photographs in *Poetic Localities of Cambridge*. The book featured two poems and a fragment from Longfellow, two poems and an essay excerpt from Holmes, and six poems from Lowell. Stillman used photographs he had taken in or around 1874 to illustrate the subjects of their works. Believing that the Cambridge he had come to love would disappear within a few years, Stillman hoped his book would preserve the classical views of the city for another generation. In the book's preface, he said, "The ravages of modern improvement bid fair to destroy within not many years the few things amongst us which our poets have made classical."[32]

It is not clear whether the three "Old Cambridge" writers volunteered their poems or prose for the book or whether they consented to a request from Stillman for republication. Either way, their involvement in the project marked a significant change in their relationship with Stillman, especially the participation of Longfellow, who two decades earlier had upset the photographer by failing to submit any poems to the *Crayon*. If the poets were more accepting of Stillman than they had been in the 1850s, it did not change his sense of being an outsider. In the preface to *Poetic Localities of Cambridge,* he identified himself as "only a vagabond guest" who was "not unknown in some of the homes which are her pride."[33] Ironically, as Cambridge and her prided intellectuals moved further from their prime, it was this vagabond who endeavored to preserve what they were losing.

Stillman and Russie returned to London in December 1874. Stillman relocated his family to the Isle of Wight, hoping the air there would help Russie recover. However, the boy died in March 1875. To help Stillman recover from the devastation over Russie's death, his father-in-law, Michael Spartali, encouraged the journalist to report on a revolution that was brewing that year in the Balkans. The Balkans had been under Ottoman rule for centuries. Stillman was keen on the idea of exposing to the world the Turkish government's injustices, as he had done in Crete. In July 1875, an insurrection broke out in Herzegovina, due partly to the previous year's failed crop and partly to additional taxes levied on remaining crops, which exacerbated the plight of Christian and Muslim peasants in Bosnia-Herzegovina. These oppressed peasants found inspiration in the Cretans' resistance to the Turks a decade earlier. That summer Stillman became a foreign correspondent for the *London Times* tasked with reporting on the insurrection, which within two years morphed into the Russo-Turkish war, with Russia declaring war on the Ottoman Empire. The war ended with a defeat for Turkey, which in March 1878 signed the Treaty of San Stefano. The conflict's official conclusion temporarily ended Stillman's work for the *Times,* and he attempted to revive his literary career.[34]

Before the war ended, the *Atlantic Monthly* in July 1877 published Stillman's essay "Recreation and Solitude," in which he recounted his experiences at Moosehead Lake three years earlier. He was especially critical of the Adirondacks in this essay. Although both regions had been subjected to heavy logging, the Maine woods repulsed him less because they were "so long ago ravaged that the scars have healed" and there was almost nothing "to show the passage of the lumberman." Contrarily, in the Adirondacks, "one sees the ax everywhere, the scars fresh and the vacancies yawning, the ravages of the fires that follow those of the wood-cutter and multiply them by infinity are widespread on the hill and lake side."[35] This essay suggests that Stillman might have seen or at least heard about the devastation lumbermen and tourists had unleashed in the Adirondacks while he lived in Europe. The essay at least indicates Stillman should not have been surprised by the destruction he would soon find at Follensby.

The news came as a shock to Lowell. Stillman was dead—beheaded by Albanian tribesmen. Around early February 1882, obituaries for Stillman began appearing in American and European newspapers after a telegraph report out of Cettinje, Montenegro, broke the news. In New York, the *Tribune* surmised that Stillman's murder had come as retribution for his support of Greece, the country to where the *Times* had dispatched him after tensions over the terms of the Treaty of Berlin erupted. Europe's leading powers in 1878 had replaced the Treaty of San Stefano with this treaty created by the Congress of Berlin. Since then, parts of Albania, which had seen part of its land ceded to Montenegro, were considered hostile territory.[36]

Almost a decade had passed since Lowell and Stillman walked amid the Oaks at Waverley. Over that time, their relationship had soured further. Shortly before or after news of his reported murder spread around the globe, Stillman had sent to Lowell the silver tip of an ancient Albanian yataghan (a long curved sword) and asked to exchange some of the poet's "golden silence" for "a little silver speech." Despite the rift between them, when he read about Stillman's murder, Lowell still hoped his old camping friend was safe and alive. From London, where he had been serving as U.S. consul since May 1880, Lowell sent a message to the *Times* asking if the report on the demise of its foreign correspondent was true. To his relief, on February 9, the newspaper informed him it was false. A day later, he wrote to Stillman's wife in Florence to express "how deeply I have sympathies with you & how I rejoice in the goodness."[37]

In Florence, several women had been attempting to console Marie when Stillman telegraphed her that he was alive. Upon arriving at Athens from Cattaro, Montenegro, he had found several peculiar messages from diplomats, family members, and the *Times* inquiring about his whereabouts and safety. The telegraphs puzzled Stillman, whose journey, he thought, had merited no cause for alarm. At Cettinje, the Montegreans had given Stillman a hero's welcome, and the only danger he encountered while traveling to Scutari was muddy roads. Unable to rely on a Turkish escort through northern Albania, Stillman had joined a consular postman on his way to San Giovanni di Budua, where he caught a steamer.[38]

Back in Athens, Stillman reflected on the international alarm the report of his death had sounded. His obituaries identified him as an artist, literary art critic, journalist, and diplomat. They made no mention of his Adirondack adventures. The *San Francisco Daily Evening Bulletin* highlighted his involvement in several popular uprisings and called him "an earnest friend of the Greek cause." Stillman later said, "There was a small compensation in the reading of my obituary notices, a satisfaction that can rarely be given a man."[39]

On March 7, Lowell responded to Stillman's package with the silver Albanian artifact and his request for silver speech. Quoting the gospel, Lowell said, "'Silver and gold I have none' for I am at my wit's end that I have neither speech nor silence, or feel so, at last." He expressed how upset he had gotten over the false murder report. He asked Stillman for an ancient statue if he came across any he could send. This letter was the last that Lowell sent to Stillman.[40]

Stillman eventually reunited with his family in Florence. He later said his time spent living in this city was "the most tranquil and the happiest of my mature life." But his residency there was cut short by the city's unsanitary water, which left Stillman and his daughter ill. Consequently, he relocated his family back to London while he and his eldest daughter, Eliza, went to America. In New York, he resumed work for the *Evening Post,* though Bryant was no longer at its helm, having had died five years earlier.[41] The fact that Stillman left most of his family behind and that he brought his daughter with him suggests he was not intending to make a full-time career out of reporting for the *Evening Post.* Instead, he probably wanted to introduce his daughter to his home country and show her what he had not been able to show Russie, namely, the Adirondacks.

By December 11, 1883, Stillman was in New York City. There he probably heard a great deal about disheartening developments in the state's northern wilderness. Ironically, the *New York Times* and *Evening Post* in 1883 both printed editorials that lamented over the destruction the Adirondacks had endured over the previous twenty-five years, making 1858 their benchmark year. An early September correspondence in the *Times* from "An Old Adirondacker" described how "twenty-five years ago the most exquisite bit of wild river scenery in the Eastern States was the lower Raquet River, near Big Tupper Lake." However, "now it is a Dismal Swamp. The landscape is made of dead trees, the banks are covered with stagnant water, and as far as the eye can reach, are the tall giant forms of dead and dying trees." A year earlier, Governor Alonzo B. Cornell had warned of "imminent danger" from failed springs and streams caused by the reckless clearing of Adirondack timber. Early in 1883, New York's legislature had voted to shield the Adirondacks from further devastation by prohibiting the sale of state-owned lands in the region, which then totaled around six hundred thousand acres. The state had acquired much of this property through foreclosures spurred by unpaid taxes. Although much of the state's northern lands had already been logged or burned, this act marked the beginning of the earnest legislative effort to create a vast protected public park in the region.[42]

At a time when Stillman was in New York, the *Evening Post* in December declared in an editorial that "the condition of the Adirondack forest is alarming." The newspaper considered the greatest threats to the Adirondacks to be overlogging and the fires that came in its wake. It attributed this rampant logging to the rise in the value of forest products from Michigan, Pennsylvania, and Maine, which made it more profitable to operate in what a few years earlier had been a remote region with little commercial value. With plans under way to extend the Adirondack railroad several miles deeper into the woods so more timber could be hauled out of it, the *Post* predicted the "entire extermination of the Adirondack forest" within a short period of time unless actions were taken to preserve it. The editorial added that "twenty-five years ago," the state could have purchased all of the Adirondacks for "a merely nominal price," but that opportunity had passed, and if steps were not immediately taken, then preserving them would soon become a financial impossibility.[43]

Initially, Stillman spent the summer of 1884 inspecting America's new major cultural museums in Boston and New York. His trips to the Metropolitan Museum of Art in New York, which opened its permanent location in Central Park in March 1880, inspired only skepticism. Many of Stillman's fellow landscape painters, such as Church, Kensett, and Gifford had helped found the museum. So did Stillman's fellow Amperzander, Ward, who had relocated with his business's headquarters to New York from Boston. Fortunately for Stillman, the Boston Museum of Fine Arts opened in 1876. He toured this museum in mid-July and found it to have a praiseworthy collection of French art.[44]

Much was different in the Boston area by the time Stillman arrived there in July 1884. Although the obituary newspapers had printed about him a year earlier proved to be false, the death notices for other members of the Philosophers' Camp were true. Wyman had died on September 4, 1874. He had been stricken with a pulmonary illness that came over him while in New Hampshire. At the time of his death, Wyman was sixty years old and serving as the first curator of Harvard's Peabody Museum of American Archeology and Ethnology.[45]

In January 1879, a financially ruined Woodman had died, an apparent suicide. He was fifty-eight years old. Nine years earlier he had filed for bankruptcy, citing $199,896 in liabilities and $93,641 in assets. His financial troubles largely stemmed from land speculation, and after a trip to New York City yielded no funds, he vanished from a Newport-bound steamer midvoyage. After Woodman's death, the task of managing the Saturday Club's affairs fell to John S. Dwight, a critic, journalist, and music group organizer. Binney died a year later in Newport. He was fifty years old. Although Binney had his own share of financial disasters, they did not overtake his life as they did with Woodman. During the war, Binney had served as the chief paymaster of the U.S. Army. After the war, he had moved his family from Boston to New York, where he and several other ex-army colleagues established themselves as bankers and brokers. However, after their business failed because of the mismanagement of funds, Binney moved his family back to Boston.[46]

On April 27, 1882, four weeks away from his seventy-ninth birthday, Emerson had died. Over the past seven years, his brilliant intellect had been slowly eclipsed by aphasia, which affected his memory and concentration. In 1875, James R. Osgood and Company published Emerson's *Letters and Social Aims*. This collection of essays underwent heavy editing by his daughter, Ellen, and John E. Cabot, his soon-to-be-named literary executor.[47] In the essay, "Greatness," Emerson reiterated the point made in "The Adirondacs," and "Civilization," saying that a man's development rested not in his retreat from society and return to a primitive way of being but in his engagement with other men and his pursuit of a more civilized state. He said, "Young men think that the manly character requires that they should go to California, or to India, or into the army. When they have learned that the parlor and the cottage and the counting-room demand as much courage as the sea or the camp, they will be willing to consult their own strength and education in their choice of place."[48]

On October 6, 1882, in Birmingham, Lowell had delivered a lecture called "Democracy," which contained a eulogy for Emerson. He spoke of a man "enveloped as with a halo, the least vulgar of men, the most austerely genial, and the most independent of opinion." Hope, he added, was not all lost for a democratic nation so long as its institutions could produce men like Lincoln and Emerson. Lowell noted that everywhere the philosopher went he encountered not only strangers but also friends and neighbors who admired him. However, that was not entirely the case in the Adirondacks in 1858, as far as Stillman was concerned. Stillman undoubtedly respected Emerson, but it would be a stretch to say he admired him, especially after observing the philosopher's impracticality in Follensby's woods and the way he treated the artist and the guides as objects of study. While "admiration" might not have been the best word to describe Stillman's feelings for Emerson, "gratitude" was. Late in life, he repeatedly commented on how indebted he was to Emerson, Lowell, Longfellow, and Norton, who had introduced him to "the broadest form of Christianity" and had helped him break free from the more rigid beliefs of his upbringing in the Seventh-Day Baptist Church, which had held him in "bondage," stifled his happiness, and caused "much distress."

Under these scholars' influences, particularly during the late 1850s, Stillman said, the "question of formal morality was finally made clear to me, and life made a relatively simple matter."[49]

Two years after Emerson's death, when Stillman arrived in Boston, four of the nine scholars that Stillman had led to Follensby were alive: Lowell—then still serving as a diplomat in London—Holmes, Hoar, and Howe. Soon after visiting Boston, Stillman learned that even less of the Philosophers' Camp could be found in the Adirondacks.

They looked like the lower White Mountain peaks, Stillman thought as he and his daughter, Eliza, journeyed to Saranac Lake in July 1884. Seeing how many of Adirondacks' mountains had been stripped of trees and left with rocky faces, he felt as though he were in New Hampshire. In fact, he barely recognized where he was. It was not until he reached his destination that he learned the identity of localities he had known while he was last in the area years earlier. Not even Martin's Hotel was immune to the great change its surrounding woods had undergone. In 1881, Martin had lost his hotel to foreclosure. It had been renamed the Miller House and had undergone a series of expansions, though the main hotel burned down in March 1888. Meanwhile, Martin had built a new hotel on a 160-acre tract on an elevated piece of property where the Ampersand and Algonquin roads met, near the easternmost tip of Lower Saranac Lake.[50]

At some point during his Adirondack tour, Stillman and Stephen Martin likely traveled together to Follensby. Eliza likely stayed behind at Martin's while the two returned to what was left of Camp Maple. The trip to Follensby was likely as disturbing to Stillman as his discovery of the lake's disfigurement. A dam built by "speculating manufacturers" along the Raquette River, Stillman later said, had "flooded all the bottom-land, killing the trees over a large tract." Stillman was appalled by what he discovered in the Adirondacks during the summer of 1884. From Martin's new hotel on July 20, Stillman wrote a letter to the *Nation* that declared, "The changes in this section of the Adirondack country side, since I last saw it many years ago, are great. . . . Where there was, when I last passed this way, unbroken forest, or forest broken only by the effect of fire, for miles, now there is a large portion of the land under cultivation." Earlier in 1884, the legislature had appointed a commission of experts tasked with exploring ways to establish a forest preservation system in the Adirondacks. But Stillman expressed little faith in this Forestry Commission, whose most prominent member was the Harvard arboriculture professor Charles S. Sargent. While acknowledging that lumbermen were doing all they could to destroy the commercial value of the forest, Stillman said they did not need to be stopped but should be regulated. If anyone should be stopped from entering the Adirondacks, he argued, it was the tourist and sportsman, whose recklessness caused fires that did far more damage than the ax or plough. He said, "The increase of this class of visitor, the consequent increase of hotels and summer residences, each one the nucleus of a new clearing, the centre from which new fire invasions start, make this restriction every day more important."[51]

Back at Martin's, Stillman told stories about the Philosophers' Camp at Follensby and how William Martin constructed the Adirondack Club's cabin at Ampersand. He concluded that "nobody but Bill Martin would ever have done it!" Before leaving the region, Stillman and Stephen Martin went out into the woods together to visit Ampersand. It was around this time that New York State was taking steps to take possession of land around Ampersand, particularly Lots One and Three in the 1,561-acre parcel at the northern end of Township Twenty-Seven's northwest quarter. The longtime owner of these lots by the 1880s had failed to pay taxes on the property. Consequently, the state purchased the property at tax sales in 1881 and 1885.[52] However, ownership of this property would remain a contested matter for years to come.

After Stillman ended his Adirondack vacation, he and Eliza boarded a steamer back to Europe. In London, he managed to see Lowell one last time before the diplomat sailed back to America. Lowell had enjoyed five years as a well-respected diplomat in England. He reluctantly returned to Elmwood after the newly inaugurated president, Grover Cleveland, a Democrat, officially recalled his appointment in March 1885. The recall only added to the poet's sense of devastation. Lowell's wife had died suddenly a month earlier, and he did not look favorably on trading his life among London's elite for "John Holmes & the Brattle Street horse car." When Stillman last saw Lowell, the poet was in a state not unlike the one he had been in when they first met, excluding his wrinkles, gray hair, and tremulous hand. Despite Lowell's sorrow, he appeared to Stillman as serene and spiritual as ever. "I could imagine that he labored under his dispensations as a good ship in a storm," Stillman said, "burying his head at times under the waves, but rising to it, shaking off the weight, and keeping on." Stillman, too, returned to his homeland, preceding Lowell. There are indications that he may have left Liverpool for the United States as soon as October 1884. In New York, he carried out a commission authorized by the American Numismatic Society to investigate the Metropolitan Museum's Cesnola collection. The trip resulted in "The Report of WJ Stillman on the Cesnola Collection," and Stillman returned to England in July 1885.[53]

When Lowell returned to New England, he found the society that had once enlivened him intellectually in rapid decline. Although Hoar continued to regularly attend the Saturday Club's monthly meetings at Parker's, Lowell's affinity for Boston society waned. Oliver Wendell Holmes had complained to Lowell in 1883 that the company at Parker's was "more of ghosts than of flesh and blood." By June 14, 1885, Lowell was at his daughter's house in Southborough, Massachusetts, and a week earlier he had traveled to Washington, D.C., "to look at my decapitators." Lowell's brother-in-law and Adirondack camp mate, Estes Howe, later died of cancer in January 1887. Like Hoar, Howe had dabbled in politics and had been elected to the Massachusetts Senate in 1859 and 1871. He died at the age of seventy-three.[54]

In 1886, Stillman caught the biggest break of his journalistic career. The *London Times'* Italian correspondent died, and the newspaper recruited Stillman to take his place covering affairs in Greece and Italy. About a year later, Stillman returned to America on a "secret service mission" to track down for the *Times* documentation that could support claims the newspaper made in a libelous April 1887 article linking Charles S. Parnell, a powerful Irish political leader, to the 1882 murders of Ireland's then-newly appointed chief secretary, Lord Frederick Cavendish, and his undersecretary, T. H. Burke, in Dublin's Phoenix Park. In July 1888, the House of Commons created a special commission, dubbed the Parnell Commission, to investigate the *Times'* allegations against the Irish members of Parliament. But before the so-called Parnell Affair escalated to this point, Stillman's secret service mission saw him travel to New York City. While waiting there for instructions from London, Stillman took a ten-day trip to the Adirondacks. Since his last visit to the region a few years earlier, Sargent's Forest Commission had delivered its report, which resulted in the Forest Preserve Law of 1885. This law had made the state-owned lands in the Adirondacks part of a Forest Preserve, in which they were to be kept "forever wild" and maintained by a newly formed Forest Commission. Stillman's Adirondack trip is not noteworthy except for the fact that an Irish spy associated with Parnell's Irish Independent (Fenian) movement followed the journalist to Martin's hotel, where Stillman got him drunk on whiskey. Stillman learned his shadow was charged with ensuring that no one tried to secretly give the reporter anything that would undermine the Fenian cause.[55] The trip also provided Stillman with his last impressions of the Adirondacks before he went on to write about his camping experiences there for the *Century Magazine*.

✺ CHAPTER 15

The Old America and the New

The Adirondacks' burgeoning tourism indus-
try had been bracing for a lackluster summer in 1893, mostly because of
the World's Columbian Exposition in Chicago. This event ran from May
1 through October 30. The exposition attracted record levels of visitors for
an event of its kind in the United States, so it was surprising when the same
trend played out in the Adirondacks. "There is not a resort in the mountains
that is not open and entertaining a fair number of guests," the *New York Times*
reported.[1]

By early July, the *Times* reported that Saranac Lake and Lake Placid had
record levels of visitors. "To say that crowds of people have come into the
mountains during the past week no longer expresses the fact," the *Times*
reported in mid-August. The weather that summer was mostly perfect, and
the Adirondacks were buzzing with activities, such as horse races at Lake
Placid and a tennis tournament at Hotel Ampersand on Lower Saranac Lake.
There were lectures on women's suffrage at Round Lake and a church fair in
Saranac Lake featuring a Boston soprano, Miss Mattie McDonald.[2]

This surge of tourism followed the May 1892 enactment of legislation
that had established the Adirondack Park. The park encompassed 2,800,000
acres, of which the state owned 550,000 acres. Legislators that year also
had adopted a policy of selling state lands outside the park and using the
proceeds to purchase land within the park. In September 1892, the Forestry

Commission issued a report that added a sense of urgency to the debate of Adirondack preservation. The report noted that 1,932,130 acres of the Adirondacks' total 3,588,803 acres remained primitive forests. However, 1,348,587 acres had been lumbered, 77,027 acres denuded, and 27,274 acres burned. Approximately 80,000 acres of merchantable timber in the primitive forest were being cut annually, meaning the region could be commercially exhausted within twenty-five years.[3]

Stillman was far removed from the Adirondacks when its popularity reached a new zenith in the summer of 1893. He was in Rome, and Italy was in the midst of a financial crisis. Not long before the 1893 tourism boom hit the Adirondacks, the subject of the Philosophers' Camp had been fresh in Stillman's thoughts. Nine months before "The Philosophers' Camp" appeared in the *Century Magazine,* the *Atlantic Monthly* in December 1892 printed an essay by him about Lowell, who had died in August 1891. The essay, "A Few of Lowell's Letters," featured selected letters by the poet. Stillman recalled how "riotous" Lowell had been before the Civil War, and especially so during their camping trips. In the Adirondacks, he "cast off all dignity," exhibited the best marksmanship with a rifle, and ran "over with fun and contrivances with merriment."[4]

The *Century Magazine*'s August edition, which featured Stillman's "The Philosophers' Camp. Emerson, Agassiz and Lowell in the Adirondacks," hit newsstands in late July. A *New York Times* critic said the essay recounted an Adirondack adventure with Agassiz, Lowell, Emerson, and "other lights of another time, before the war." The *Times* critic said readers would find this article interesting and surprising.[5] Stillman's story, however, would need a few more years before the American public could fully embrace his account of the ten scholars' adventure to Follensby. The new generation of Americans was still too close in time to the older generation to appreciate what they had lost. Lowell, for example, had been dead for only two years (he had died at Elmwood at the age of seventy-two), and three members of the Philosophers' Camp (i.e., Hoar, Holmes, and Stillman) were still alive.

Stillman's intent in writing "The Philosophers' Camp" was to show the new generation of Americans what of the older generation had been lost—irrevocably. As tourists flocked to the Adirondacks to go fishing or to watch a tennis match, he wanted to remind them that the wilderness they saw in the Adirondacks of 1893 was anything but pure or primeval. He was not the first to point out that the character of the Adirondacks was no longer what it once had been. In fact, the *Evening Post* correspondent who had provided one of the earliest public reports of events at Camp Maple had repeatedly pointed out such changes in his August 1858 article.[6]

When assessing how Stillman managed to write an Adirondack camping story that far outlived those of his contemporaries, it is important to remember that by 1893 he had spent most of the previous thirty-five years abroad. In fact, his fondness for the region had cooled significantly since the early 1870s, the result of a combination of age, changing interests, and an inability to reconcile his memory of the Adirondacks with its current realities. Because Stillman was so distanced from the Adirondacks in time and space and emotion, he managed to view the story of this adventure through a more objective lens than did earlier Adirondack essayists, such as Thomas Richards and Alfred Street, who had more enthusiastically told their wilderness tales. Stillman's colder narrative added a more timeless quality to the *Century Magazine* essay. As the poet Jane Hirshfield noted in her poem "In Praise of Coldness," "And so at the center of many great works / is found a preserving dispassion, / like . . . the tiny packets of desiccant enclosed / in a box of new shoes or seeds."[7]

By 1893, several aspects of the Philosophers' Camp had already been reported in the press, such as Longfellow's rejection of the invitation to the Adirondacks and Agassiz's marksmanship. The *Century Magazine* essay filled in the gaps in previously published narratives. For example, "The Philosophers' Camp" told how Stillman led the scholars to the Adirondacks, and it provided the painter's insightful observations of Emerson, Lowell, and Agassiz in the wilderness. Stillman sought to correct errors in this preexisting narrative of the camp, such as Emerson's misidentification in "The Adirondacs" of oak, linden, and poplar in the deep woods and his statement that each scholar had a guide and boat, when actually Stillman had no guide. Stillman also highlighted an error in a map of the state survey that misidentified Osprey Bay as Agassiz Bay. A map of Franklin County by Julius Bien & Co., published in the *Atlas of the State of New York,* features this error.[8]

Stillman excused Emerson's errors as being part of the philosopher's "poetic experience." Stillman, too, took liberty recounting the events in and around Camp Maple. He portrayed the Adirondacks as an "almost undisturbed primeval forest" visited only by a "few land-scape painters and sportsmen."[9] However, his letters to the *Crayon* about his tour of the Saranac region in 1855 indicate that lumbermen were also among the Adirondacks' visitors. In this correspondence, he had commented on the lumberers' ugly handwork seen along the shore of Lower Saranac Lake. Additionally, Stillman made no mention of the journalists who had visited Camp Maple. He also glossed over the Adirondack Club's inaugural meeting in August 1859 and neglected to mention Higginson's visit to Ampersand later that summer.

Stillman's story about Emerson and other majestic men struck a chord in the heart of nostalgic Americans. Opposites though they were, the frontier's wilderness and New England intellectualism for decades had shaped the American character, to varying extents. However, with the census of 1890 showing the frontier had closed and the cemeteries of Concord and Boston filling up with famed scholars, Americans fretted they were losing the very forces that defined them.[10] In "The Philosophers' Camp," Americans found proof that the traditions of the frontier and an intellectual society could coexist, even if only for a few days. And as Americans ventured deeper into the wilderness of the twentieth century, they increasingly pointed to the interconnection of these rugged and refined traditions at the Philosophers' Camp as a reason for furthering preservation efforts in the Adirondacks.

Edwin Wallace, the Adirondack guidebook writer, also took note of Stillman's camping story. In his 1894 edition of *The Descriptive Guide to the Adirondacks,* Wallace updated his entry on Follensby by referencing the *Century Magazine* essay and even quoting from it. Despite the carnage Stillman described at the end of "The Philosophers' Camp," Wallace said Follensby was "still regarded as excellent sporting ground." Wallace also included in this edition a brief biography of the mysterious Captain Folingsby and noted that Stillman and John Holmes were the last surviving members of the Adirondack Club. Wallace jumped the gun, however, in writing off Hoar in his 1894 edition of this guidebook. Hoar actually died on January 31, 1895. Up to 1894, he had managed to remain active with the Concord Free Public Library Corporation. Upon his death, Hoar bequeathed Stillman's painting of Camp Maple to the library, providing the public with a visual to the story Stillman had told in the *Century Magazine* in 1893. In his will, Hoar had identified the painting as "'A Camp in the Adirondacks,' by W. J. Stillman"—not as *Morning at Camp Maple* and, more important, not as *The Philosophers' Camp in the Adirondacks.*[11] The phrasing in Hoar's will suggests he rejected the notion of the 1858 gathering at Follensby as being a Philosophers' Camp along with the intellectual connotations of the name.

The scene of the destruction at Follensby that Stillman described at the end of "The Philosophers' Camp" highlighted that the legislature in Albany needed to take further actions to preserve of New York's northern wilderness. By 1893, northern New York's expanding tourism industry, changes in the timber market, and rampant corruption surrounding the state's stewardship of its Adirondack lands had made it imperative for lawmakers to act quickly and decisively. Granted, Stillman's visit to Follensby had preceded the establishment of the Adirondack Park by eight years, during which time other important conservation legislation was enacted. But by the time the *Century Magazine* published "The Philosophers' Camp," lawmakers in Albany were still struggling to develop legislative solutions to reverse the trends that were destroying the region.

Governor Roswell P. Flowers had said in his State of the State address to the legislature in January 1893 that the nearly seven-year effort to establish the park in New York's northern wilderness had yielded "disappointing" results. He introduced a forestry bill and warned the legislature that "each year's devastations of forest land is making more difficult the attainment of the State's object." In April 1893, legislators approved Flowers's bill, which created a new forestry commission charged with carrying out the new law's provisions. Those included stricter regulations related to the selling and purchasing of lands in or outside the park and the authorization to sell soft standing timber on state lands, with proceeds going toward financing the new commission.[12]

As this effort to create a public preserve in the Adirondacks progressed slowly in the early 1890s, so did the separate effort to establish private preserves within the region, though the public and private initiatives did not always share the same conservation goals. In 1892, two huge preserves totaling more than 110,000 acres had been established in Franklin County. One was the 62,000-acre Santa Clara Preserve, and the other was the 50,000-acre Ampersand Preserve. An 1894 Forest Commission report claimed both preserves were owned by Dodge, Meigs, and Company, which had a large mill in Santa Clara, but this report was not entirely accurate.[13]

In 1889, Dodge, Meigs, and Company, whose executives were also behind the recently formed Santa Clara Lumber Company, had participated in a syndicate of lumber investors who purchased 400,000 acres of Adirondack Railway Company lands in Franklin, Herkimer, Hamilton, and Warren counties. However, the Ithaca, New York-based Adirondack Timber and Mineral Company initially acquired title to a sizable portion of Township Twenty-Seven, previously owned by the Adirondack Company, and the Santa Clara Lumber Company had options to purchase the property and to remove timber from it in the interim. This agreement was dated December 16, 1889, acknowledged on January 6, 1890 and August 6, 1897, and recorded on August 13, 1897. Titus B. Meigs was a key player at all three companies. The Ampersand Preserve contained parts of Townships Twelve, Twenty-Six, and Twenty-Seven in Harrietstown and the Old Military Tract in Essex County.

It held both Follensby and Ampersand ponds and Mount Seward. The "main objective of the owners" was to protect their property from fire, according to the Forest Commission. Unlike the state, the owners of these preserves wanted to protect their forests not so they could be kept forever wild but so they could be timbered at a later date.[14]

New York's position on the preservation of the Adirondacks shifted dramatically in 1894, when a constitutional convention was held, the first such event since 1867. The new state constitution that the convention produced and that voters approved on November 6, 1894, featured a provision stating that all state lands currently in or later acquired in the Adirondack forest preserve "shall be forever kept wild forest lands." It also prohibited the state from selling, leasing, or exchanging those lands or selling, removing, or destroying their timber.[15] The constitution took effect on the first of January 1895. Despite its forever-wild provision, large swaths of the Adirondacks—including the wilderness around Ampersand—remained endangered in the mid-1890s.

By late 1897, Stillman was preparing to retire from the *Times* of London, which would provide him with a pension. He relocated from Rome to a village in the English county of Surrey. In December, Houghton, Mifflin published Stillman's *Old Rome and the New: and Other Studies,* which consisted of ten revised essays that had been previously published in journals such as the *Atlantic Monthly* and the *Century Magazine.* The essays covered a thirty-five-year period in Stillman's writing career, beginning with "The Subjective of It" in 1858 and ending with "The Philosophers' Camp" in 1893. Stillman dedicated the book to Norton, who was the "sole survivor of that luminous circle in which once shone Lowell, Longfellow, Emerson, Holmes, Agassiz, etc.—circle to whose intellectual hospitality I owe my imprimatur for American letters."[16]

For the first time, this book paired Stillman's two Adirondack essays that recounted his 1857 camping trip to Big Tupper Lake with Lowell, John Holmes, and Howe ("The Subjective of It") and its sequel at Follensby with a much larger and more eminent party a year later ("The Philosophers' Camp"). "A Few of Lowell's Letters" served as a supplement to these Adirondack essays. Unlike the 1858 *Atlantic Monthly* version of "The Subjective of It," *The Old Rome* version identified Lowell and Holmes by name, though Howe remained the anonymous "doctor." Stillman included in this version more details on the rise and fall of the Adirondack Club. The revised essay on the Philosophers' Camp featured a new introduction in which Stillman recounted Ruskin's opinion that "the character of the American landscape was such as not to favor invention, but that its largeness must give the art a high degree of grandeur, once excited."[17] He also omitted the account of the scholars' welcome at Keeseville, where Agassiz was praised and Lowell and Emerson were ignored.

Reviews of the book in *Harper's New Monthly Magazine,* the *Nation,* and *New Outlook* did not even mention Stillman's Adirondack essays. The *Nation,* which Norton had cofounded, gave the book a harsh review. But it received more favorable reviews from *Harper's* and *New Outlook,* with the former praising his writing style and the latter as impressed with the company the author had kept as with the places he had traveled. However, *New Outlook* said the book "impresses us as one of those pictures which an artist will not let go forth from his studio." *Harper's,* likewise, conceded that the book's attempt "to unite the charm and freshness of youth with the maturity and mellowness of age . . . robbed . . . much that it would have enjoyed and profited by if these essays had been attainable in book form twenty or thirty years ago."[18]

Stillman made a return trip to America in or around 1898, and he spent much of this year working on what was to become the most ambitious and important literary project of his life: his autobiography. His research brought him in contact with Agassiz's second wife, Elizabeth Carey Agassiz, who said she had read *Old Rome* and was especially delighted by the essay about one of her late husband's "famous picnics in the Adirondacks." Stillman also reconnected with Ward. "To have remembered after an interval of near forty years and to come back to the old place as if there had been no interval is one of the things that makes life worth living," Ward said in a September 1898 letter. At the time this letter was sent, thirty-nine years had elapsed since Stillman, Ward, his son, and Edward Emerson camped at Ampersand Pond. Ward also told Stillman that he had always believed his fellow Amperzander would reach a high level of distinction, whether he devoted himself to art or to literature. But, Ward added, "You chose wisely."[19]

As always, Stillman received encouragement from Norton. "You are one of the new products of the western world to which there is nothing quite correspondent in the other hemisphere. . . . Lowell might have described you, but I know no one else who could do it," Norton told Stillman in June 1898. Stillman was a unique American, indeed, but the America in which he had grown up was rapidly disappearing. It appears Norton had become disillusioned by the United States' declaration of war on Spain on April 25, 1898, following the destruction of the *Maine* battleship in Havana, Cuba. He said, "It seems to me as though I were witnessing the end of the America in which we have lived." He added, "A new America is beginning; she has renounced the ideals of the old and, turning her back upon them, falls to the past instead of the future and enters on the ways of ancient wrong." Norton told his friend he was better off staying in England, unless Stillman visited Ashfield, Massachusetts, where they could spend long days walking together in the woods, and, when tired, watch "the squirrels, the woodchucks and the birds."[20]

Norton was not alone in sensing an American era slipping away. It was a sentiment other Saturday Club members felt profoundly. Shortly before dying on October 7, 1894, Oliver Wendell Holmes had said, "I feel as if I belonged to the past." This awareness that the country was evolving into something far different from what Holmes and his friends had lived in became acute when John Holmes became gravely ill in 1897. John Holmes was still as much of a bachelor as he had been at Camp Maple. A devoted housekeeper cared for him. He lived in a plain wooden house on a short street in Cambridge, not far from the spot where the home in which he had been born had once stood. That house had been razed to make way for the new Harvard Law School. The headlines for obituaries and tributes about John Holmes printed after his death on January 27, 1899, identified him as the "Brother of the Autocrat." He was eighty-seven years old. The *New York Times* said John Holmes "is the last link connecting the Cambridge of to-day with the Cambridge of the past."[21]

It was around the time of *Old Rome*'s publication that Stillman became a vocal advocate for animal rights. In February 1897, the *Century Magazine* published his essay "Billy and Hans: A True Story," about his two pet squirrels from Germany. Two years later, in a *Living Age* article, Stillman publicly renounced the pleasures of hunting that he had enjoyed as a young man. Although he consoled himself in knowing he had killed only what he needed for food, he said he regretted having "inflicted deaths which at the intervals of an ordinary lifetime bring tears into my eyes to recall them." He also revealed how the memory of one of his nighttime hunting experiences in the Adirondacks had haunted him for decades. It is possible he had gone through this traumatic experience shortly before the party of scholars arrived at Follensby Pond in 1858 or Ampersand Pond a year later.[22]

Stillman said he remembered this one death "almost as a human tragedy." After having "built a camp in the Adirondacks" and finding he lacked food for the party, he had gone out on the lake at night with a rifle and lantern for some jack hunting. He found a deer feeding in the shallows, but his shot at it from the boat failed to kill the creature. The wounded deer galloped away, leaving a trail of blood behind it. The next day, during daylight, Stillman used a terrier to drive out the deer that had escaped the previous night. It was driven into the lake, where Stillman killed it with a shot through the heart. Upon closer examination, he found that three of its legs had been broken from the previous night's buckshot. Stillman agonized over the thought of how severely the deer had suffered through the night. "All the pleasures of memory drawn from my deer shooting do not weigh me with so much as the pain of that night's shot," he said.[23]

After making this public confession, Stillman began making many more. In its January 1900 issue, the *Atlantic Monthly* began serially publishing his *Autobiography of a Journalist*. The magazine's May edition featured the chapter titled "Journalism," in which Stillman lumped together accounts of his early experiences with journalism at the *Evening Post* and the *Crayon,* his introduction into Cambridge's literary circle, and his Adirondack camping trips at Big Tupper Lake, Follensby, and Ampersand. The last installment of the autobiography ran in the June edition of the *Atlantic Monthly;* thus about half of the two-volume work that Houghton, Mifflin was preparing to publish had already appeared in print. With each of these autobiographical works, Stillman slipped in a few new details about the camps at Follensby and Ampersand. Compared with *The Old Rome, The Autobiography of a Journalist* was far better received by critics, who valued the glimpses it provided into the Old Cambridge. The *New York Times* said Stillman's life story "opens vistas not seen in those of Dr. Hale, Colonel Higginson, Lowell, and Parkman." Ironically, it was Stillman—the outsider—who provided these insights into Old Cambridge's intellectual circles. As he had done with *Poetic Localities* two decades earlier, he again played an integral role in preserving the illustrious world to which he was no more than a "vagabond guest." The *Autobiography* was even more valuable, the *Times* reviewer said, "in estimating the average Yankee character and its possibilities under the happy influences of cosmopolitan experience."[24]

This comment is interesting because it exemplifies how Stillman, as a mature man, had adopted Emerson's philosophy that deemed social environments more beneficial to a man's development than primitive environments. It was Stillman's experiences in Cambridge, Rome, London, and Florence—more than his Adirondack camping trips—that made him a happy Yankee. Nevertheless, it was his youthful experiences in the wilderness that had shaped him into the person whom great men in these cities would later embrace.

Although the *Times'* reviewer described the chapters about the Philosophers' Camp, Adirondack Club, and Lowell as "charming," he found the subsequent chapters on Stillman's European adventures more interesting. However, a widely reprinted review of the book that appeared in newspapers

such as *Omaha World Herald* and the *Duluth News-Tribune* called the Adirondack chapters the book's "most attractive portions." The author of this
review noted that two years earlier he had camped at the site of the Philosophers' Camp at Follensby, which remained crowded with deer. Regarding
the Adirondack Club's purchase of the Township Twenty-Seven tract, the
reviewer noted that the land that Stillman and his friends had acquired for
$600 could not be bought in 1901 for $100,000. An *American Historical
Review* critic, John W. Chadwick, compared *The Autobiography of a Journalist*
to Rousseau's *Confessions* for its frankness. He too found the chapters on the
Adirondack Club "of striking interest." In this reviewer's eyes, Longfellow's
refusal to join the 1858 party because of Emerson's gun remained one of the
most amusing and noteworthy aspects of the Philosophers' Camp story.[25]

In June, Stillman became the subject of a *North American Review* essay by
William Howells. The essay, "An Earlier American," was more of a social
commentary than a book review, though *The Autobiography of a Journalist*
provided its foundation. In Stillman, Howells saw the vestige of an America
that was "rapidly and irrevocably passing." Stillman was of a New England
stock that was influenced by a "condensed and intensified" Puritanism.
When considering the period in which Stillman had come of age, Howells
noted that the America of 1850–60 was far more similar to the America of
1800 than to that of 1900. "Between 1850 and 1900," he said, "events have
fixed a gulf toward which the uninterrupted course of evolution in the earlier half century did not even seem tending." Like Norton, Howells believed
the epoch of the "old America" had ended with the war in Cuba. Although
Howells assumed America would become more powerful in the aftermath
of the Spanish-American War, he said it would no longer be "the sun of the
morning." The nation's venture into colonialism undermined the old Americans' belief in a "universal liberty" that had differentiated them from all the
monarchies, conquerors, and oppressors.[26]

Although *The Autobiography of a Journalist* stirred Howells's pessimism about
America's future, he did find it to be a story full of charm and romance. Most
delightful to him was the chapter on the Philosophers' Camp, misleadingly
titled "The Adirondack Club—Emerson and Agassiz," which is ironic, given
the poor review he had written for Emerson's "The Adirondacs" in 1867.
Howells was amused by the story of the Follensby-bound party's welcome
in Keeseville, where the poets and philosophers were ignored and Agassiz
was treated like a hero. Howells noted that Agassiz had been so popular in
Keeseville not because he was the world's greatest scientist but because he
had chosen to stay in America out of a love for freedom rather than accept
Napoleon III's offer for prestigious political and scientific posts in Paris.

Driving home the point that a schism existed between the Americans of the nineteenth and twentieth centuries, Howells surmised that it was possible a great patriot who ventured into the wilderness in 1900 could still receive the type of welcome bestowed upon Agassiz in Keeseville in 1858. But the "difficulty would be in finding any such idealizing backwoodsman to give it; and this may be the saddest part of it all."[27]

Stillman spent his final months enjoying the peace and quiet and beauty of the English countryside. He continued to regularly contribute to the *Nation*, providing full-page commentaries on everything from Venetian architecture to English foreign policy to his observations of the socioeconomic dynamics around his home in Deepdene, part of the village of Frimley Green in Surrey County. There he had a "modest cottage" and employed servants. He was enjoying the fruits of his success, but he kept at arm's length the wealthy Englishmen from London who traveled to their country homes over the weekend to go hunting or fishing. He acknowledged that Englishmen had the reputation of being cold and selfish, but he said the "hard workers . . . in this country population, especially among the women, make one love the people in proportion as one knows them."[28] To the end, Stillman was not one of Emerson's "polished gentlemen."

Sometime around March 1901, Stillman became gravely ill, and he knew his time was running short. In the preface the *Autobiography*, he had commented that out of all his friends from the mid-1850s, all but Norton and Samuel Rowse, were "gone [to] where I must soon follow." He also noted that the book featured a portrait of himself in his late twenties that Rowse had executed. Stillman recalled that when Lowell had seen the portrait of the young man with a sense of purpose in his eyes, he had told him, "You have nothing to do for the rest of your life but to try to look like it."[29] Stillman's inclusion of this anecdote suggests that for all its ups and downs, he continued to be thankful for Lowell's support.

On July 6, 1901, Stillman died at his home. While he had been pleased by the obituaries for him he read in newspapers after his reported murder in 1882, the notices that followed his actual death would have been even more comforting. They noted an extraordinary life. Throughout his seventy-three years, Stillman had been a Union College graduate, an artist, a journalist, an editor, a poet, an author, an art dealer, a photographer, an outdoorsman, a marksman, a hunter, a guide, a diplomat, an archeologist, a literary agent, a war correspondent, a secret agent, an animal rights activist, a husband, and a father.

Strangely, the obituaries failed to mention his involvement in the Philosophers' Camp or the Adirondack Club, even though his lasting fame would rest largely on his associations with them.[30] Nevertheless, with his autobiography published, Stillman left to the new America his most complete account of the time when the lights of the old America had never shone as brightly as when they were gathered in a wilderness that was quickly vanishing. Over the next century, their camp would become for future generations a beacon of harmony with nature and society.

Conclusion

The Story Reborn

> There are no fixtures in nature. The universe is fluid
> and volatile. Permanence is but a word of degrees.
> Our globe seen by God is a transparent law, not a mass
> of facts. The law dissolves the fact and holds it fluid.
> Our culture is the predominance of an idea which
> draws after it this train of cities and institutions. Let
> us rise into another idea; they will disappear.
>
> —Emerson, "Circles"

With the publication of Stillman's *Autobiography of a Journalist* in 1901, the story of the Philosophers' Camp was resurrected in popular American culture. The story, however, took on new meanings throughout the rest of the twentieth and early twenty-first centuries. After Stillman's death, the Philosophers' Camp entered a new public light. The surprise that many of Boston's leading intellectuals had roughed it together in the wilderness evolved into an acknowledgment that the camp was not only an unusual and unique gathering but a historic one as well. During the last quarter of the nineteenth century, writers such as Joel Headley and Henry Van Dyke, along with the authors of numerous Adirondack travelogues, had noted the significance of the camps at Follensby and Ampersand. It was during the twentieth century, however, that these two camps rose above the status of novel campfire stories and were recognized as being important to the environmental conservation movement, more in the Adirondacks than on a national level.

In the wake of Stillman's death, the influence of the Philosophers' Camp on Adirondack preservation efforts first appeared in 1907. Shortly after taking office early that year, New York's recently elected attorney general, William S. Jackson, received many complaints about lumbering crimes within the Adirondack Forest Preserve committed by various individuals and corporations. In response, he immediately launched an investigation into the complaints, even though the authority over the handling of legal matters regarding the Forest Preserve resided primarily with the New York State Forest, Fish and Game Commission, and the role of the office of the attorney general in the Adirondacks was disputed.[1]

After finding that a former legal representative with the Forest, Fish and Game Commission had unconstitutionally given the state's lands around Ampersand Pond to the Santa Clara Lumber Company, Jackson moved to recover the lands. His investigation discovered that a 1900 New York Court of Appeals ruling had not made the state's title to the Ampersand lands as secure as previously thought. This court decision had stemmed from the state's acquisition of Lots One and Three in the northwest quarter of Township Twenty-Seven at the 1881 and 1885 tax sales. In 1892, John H. Millard and George S. Ostrander had claimed title to portions of Lots One and Three from Thomas Frazier Jr., who since the mid-1850s had held title to the property. Ostrander and Millard, who together owned vast Adirondack land holdings, had applied for the cancellation of the 1881 and 1885 tax sales for 585 acres that adjoined Ampersand. In 1893, the controller had denied this request, and the New York State Appellate Division, Third Department, later affirmed that decision in 1896. The Court of Appeals had affirmed the Appellate Division's decision in 1897.[2]

Ostrander and Millard's bid for Lots One and Three had occurred around the same time that Dodge, Meigs, and Company had reportedly created the Ampersand Preserve in 1892. Around the time of the controller's denial decision in 1893, George E. Dodge, Titus B. Meigs, and Ferris J. Meigs had acquired interest in property in Lots Two and Four. A year later, Ferris Meigs, the lumber company's treasurer, had started acquiring interest in property in Lots One and Three from Ostrander, Millard, and other parties. Meigs had then filed a lawsuit in Franklin County Supreme Court, seeking to eject the state from Lots One and Three. The court had ruled against Meigs in 1898, but the Appellate Division reversed the trial court's judgment and ordered a new trial. This decision had threatened to upend conservation efforts in the Adirondacks because, as an attorney general report warned, "there are suits now pending involving substantially the same question and affecting some sixty-three thousand acres of land in the Forest Preserve." The Court of Appeals in 1900 had reversed the Appellate Division's decision. The state's title, the *New York Times* later said, had been "absolutely confirmed."[3]

However, by 1897, the year of the first Court of Appeals decision, Meigs had already invested heavily in the property and was not prepared to give it up. In 1897 the Santa Clara Lumber Company had constructed a logging camp on Ampersand's western shore. From there and until 1936 the lumber company cut down trees and sent logs down Ampersand Brook to its Tupper Lake mill. In June and July of 1903 his Santa Clara Lumber Company had cut and removed 835 cedar trees from the property.[4]

In response to this illegal cutting in 1903, the Forest, Fish and Game Commission had sued the lumber company for $8,350 in damages. The suit never went to trial and had ended in what Jackson described as the guise of a settlement under which the state's suit was dismissed and Meigs's claims to the state lands around Ampersand were confirmed. The Forest, Fish and Game commissioner had signed off on the deal. A judgment had been entered on the matter without any legal representation for the state at the time of this decision. Adding to the sensation of this political scandal was the historical significance of the property at stake in the land claim. The headline to the *New York Times* article announcing the findings of the Jackson investigation declared, "State Lands Given Away . . . Beautiful Ampersand Pond, Made Famous by Agassiz, is Controlled by a Lumber Company." The article went on to quote a state report that described Ampersand Pond: "Aside from beauty, this little lake has attained considerable fame by reason of the 'Philosophers' Camp' which Prof. Agassiz once established on its shore. He erected a roomy, substantial log building, and in company with Lowell, Emerson, Holmes, and others a club was formed with the intention of making this a summer home."[5]

This *Times* article linked the Philosophers' Camp (and Adirondack Club) to an effort to protect land in the Adirondacks. Jackson argued that the Court of Appeals ruling had eliminated the need to settle the land claim and the commissioner acted without authority and in violation of the constitution in doing so. Jackson filed a motion to vacate a judgment on the Ampersand settlement, but a court in 1907 ruled that the attorney general lacked the authority to take such action. The land claim remained dormant for several years thereafter, and in 1919 Santa Clara Lumber sold 17,920 acres of heavily logged forestlands in Township Twenty-Seven to the state for $508,081. The land dispute did not end there, however, because the lumber company retained ownership of Ampersand and approximately 4,000 acres around the pond. New York's claim to the Ampersand lands continued, but the case was litigated until 1926. Meigs eventually triumphed over the state. In 1938 he sold the 3,800-acre Ampersand tract for $157,700 to Griffith Mark, the brother-in-law and agent acting on behalf of Avery Rockefeller. New York State's efforts to add Ampersand to the Forest Preserve had largely ended by this time. Ampersand is presently an island of private ownership in a sea of Forest Preserve lands, but at least it has been free of logging since Avery Rockefeller bought it. It is presently owned by his descendants.[6]

Unlike that of Ampersand, ownership of Follensby changed several times during the early 1900s, all without attracting much public attention, even though Ferris Meigs, by then Santa Clara Lumber Company's president, was a key figure in some of these transactions. After the lumber company had cut down many of the softwood trees on the western half of Township Twenty-Six, it sold ten thousand acres of its property in the area to the Brooklyn Cooperage Company in 1902. Excluded from this transaction were lands around Meigs's summer camp, called Stag Head, and Follensby, to both of which Meigs retained title.[7]

In 1900, Brooklyn Cooperage, a barrel manufacturer, built a plant at Tupper Lake. It also constructed a seven-mile lumber railroad that extended from Tupper Lake to Wawbeek, near central Upper Saranac Lake. The primary purpose of this rail line was to transport logs cut at the school of forestry the legislature had authorized Cornell University to establish on thirty thousand acres in Harrietstown in 1898. The forestry school soon ran into financial problems because of the low rates Brooklyn Cooperage paid Cornell for cutting the logs and hauling them to the railroad. (This arrangement ceased in 1903 after the school lost its state funding and abruptly closed.) Not wanting a Brooklyn Cooperage lumber railroad to encroach on his paradise at Follensby, Meigs a year later had the Santa Clara Lumber Company repurchase the ten thousand acres in addition to another five thousand acres. In 1914, the Oval Wood Dish Corporation purchased most of Township Twenty-Six's lands, with the exception of Follensby and its shoreline, only to have the lumber company repurchase it. Shortly after these transactions, John E. Barbour, a Paterson, New Jersey, linen thread magnate, purchased the four thousand acres around Follensby—including the lake and its shoreline—for $75,000. In 1917, he built a resort at Follensby called White Birches. Barbour may have learned about Follensby from John L. Barbour, who served as the receiver of the Adirondack Company in the 1890s and handled transactions involving property in Township Twenty-Six.[8]

By 1950, the Barbour family's holdings around Follensby had grown to more than fourteen thousand acres, and White Birches consisted of a twenty-room main building, a nine-room lodge, three combination bathing pavilions and boathouses, and a cabin with maple syrup-making capabilities. The Barbours that year put the Follensby tract up for sale, and in 1952 it was purchased by John S. McCormick Jr., an army veteran who had served in the Philippines toward the end of World War II and who later settled in Pawlet, Vermont, with his wife. Despite having studied Thoreau while at Princeton University in the 1930s, McCormick was not aware of the Philosophers' Camp at Follensby until after he purchased the tract.[9] Similar to Ampersand's, Follensby's ownership did not change through the rest of the twentieth century, though beginning in the early 1990s public pressure mounted for this privately owned lake to be placed in the public domain.

In 1972, Dale Huyck, real property supervisor with the New York State Department of Environmental Conservation, reportedly first approached McCormick about purchasing Follensby. This inquiry came shortly after Governor Nelson Rockefeller's Temporary Study Commission on the Future of the Adirondacks had issued a report that recommended the acquisition of Follensby.[10] However, it was not until the early 1990s that preservation efforts linked to lands where Emerson and his fellow travelers camped began in earnest, at least publicly. Whereas the preservation efforts toward the beginning of the century had focused on Ampersand, those toward the century's end homed in on Follensby. In the decades between these two campaigns, the story of the Philosophers' Camp became deeply embedded in the Adirondack chronicle.

The story of the camp had played a prominent role in popular Adirondack history books, such as Alfred Donaldson's *A History of the Adirondacks* (1921), Paul F. Jamieson's *Adirondack Pilgrimage* (1986), and Frank Graham Jr.'s *The Adirondack Park: A Political History* (1978). In most instances, twentieth-century Adirondack historians embraced the story of the Philosophers' Camp and used it for what writers refer to as "color." It was a fantastic story, and these historians largely did not try to make it out to be more than that. But at the same time they turned it into a fixture of the Adirondack chronicle, perhaps more than they did with many of the region's other amusing camping stories.

This fixed place in the Adirondack chronicle, however, is not entirely merited. William C. White, a New York theatrical agent who retreated to the Adirondacks for health reasons, in 1954 challenged the Philosophers' Camp's place in Adirondack history. In his *Adirondack Country,* White noted that various stories about men who visited the region were a "distinctive part of the Adirondack chronicle," with some amounting to the status of legends or old wives' tales. "Others stood like one of the great white pines; when they went they left a place not easily filled." The party Emerson wrote about in "The Adirondacs," White said, was "not much of a camping trip and not much of a poem." In 1983, Philip Terrie similarly cautioned that "environmental and cultural historians may have overemphasized the importance of truly deep thinkers like Thoreau [and Emerson] at the expense of writers like Headley whose response to nature was less complex than Thoreau's but perhaps more representative of his day."[11]

Despite Terrie's warnings about these deep thinkers' responses to nature, the story of the Philosophers' Camp retained its status as representative of the region's popular romanticism. It continued to overshadow the writings of men such as Headley. Although Emerson's writings about his Adirondack experiences were more representative of what Terrie called a complex romanticism, the Philosophers' Camp retained its popular appeal because it was framed as an easily accessible story. It was, and remains, *The Canterbury Tales* of the Adirondacks. The travel writings of Headley and others lack the simple story line and identifiable characters of the Philosophers' Camp. Consequently, their narratives did not achieve its level of recognition as representative of the Adirondacks' early popular romanticism. The misconception of the camp as popular romanticism has not been entirely detrimental to the Adirondacks. Terrie noted that, regardless of confusion between popular and complex romanticism, Headley and Emerson made the wilderness tolerable and "helped lay the foundation for the later, more consistently positive response to the wilderness."[12]

By the early 1990s, this positive response to Emerson's story about the Philosophers' Camp was strongly felt among the Adirondack conservationists who frequently invoked the camp as they tried to convince the state to purchase Follensby from the McCormick family. Although the lake's ecological attributes drove the efforts to add Follensby to the Forest Preserve, it was the story of the Philosophers' Camp that "kept the initiative alive in the minds of conservationists for decades," according to Michael Carr, the executive director of the Adirondack chapter of the Nature Conservancy.[13]

When New York governor Mario Cuomo in his January 1990 annual address to the legislature proposed a nearly $2 billion bond act to support land acquisitions and recycling projects, he set in motion conservationists' efforts to have Follensby added to the Forest Preserve. In all, the act would have supported $800 million in land acquisitions and cost each New Yorker $7.00 in total throughout the life of the estimated thirty-year bonds. Emboldened environmental advocacy groups such as the Adirondack Council now set their sights on prized parcels in the Adirondacks such as Follensby. For example, in the second volume of its three-volume *2020 Vision,* the Adirondack Council identified Follensby as a necessary acquisition in the High Peaks Wilderness area.[14]

Conservationists, however, would have to achieve such ambitious goals without the support of the environmental bond act, which voters narrowly rejected in a November 1990 referendum. The act received 49 percent of the vote. According to the *New York Times,* upstate voters "trounced" the bond act because "they feared money from the act would be used to buy private land for conservation in areas like the Adirondacks." Some upstate voters feared the act would result in higher taxes and limit land development opportunities.[15]

The defeat of the environmental bond act delivered a blow to the Adirondack conservationist community. Governor Cuomo in January 1992 proposed creating a $277 million environmental assistance fund paid for by a new tire tax and unredeemed bottle deposit money. The New York State Department of Environmental Conservation that year also released a report titled "Conserving Open Space in New York State." It listed seventy-five sites targeted for acquisition, though no funding mechanism was in place at the time to fund such land purchases. The fourteen thousand-acre Follensby tract owned by the McCormick family was left out of a draft of the report issued in late 1991, angering many environmentalists. Around the same time, the McCormick family donated to the state an option to purchase Follensby. Follensby was included in the final draft of the report, but the state lacked the funds to buy the property. Helping Follensby land on the acquisition wish list, as a subsequent edition of the report noted, was its reputation for housing a "historic" bald eagle nesting site in the mid-1980s and the "historic" Philosophers' Camp in the 1850s.[16]

It was in this discouraging political environment that a group of nearly twenty conservationist leaders met at the Adirondack cabin of Paul Schaefer to strategize in 1992. The writer Paul Schneider later described this meeting as the beginning of "The Long Good Fight." David Gibson, the executive director of the Association for the Protection of the Adirondacks, which Schaefer had founded, organized this meeting. Others in attendance were representatives from the various Adirondack organizations. During the meeting, Schaefer, then eighty-two years old, tried to discourage his fellow conservationists from settling for minuscule land acquisitions and to "go for something big enough to be a banner to rally under." According to Schneider's account of the meeting in *The Adirondacks: A History of America's First Wilderness,* Schaefer told them to disregard small wetlands in the southern Adirondacks and "talk about the finest piece of private land in the whole park." This unifying "gem" that would reinvigorate the flagging conservation efforts in New York's northern wilderness was Follensby. Gibson, who attended the meeting, recalled that the story of the Philosophers' Camp later played into the strategizing for Schaefer's Follensby campaign.[17]

Sometime after Cuomo revealed his 1993–94 executive budget in January 1993, the Association for the Protection of the Adirondacks produced a pamphlet featuring on its cover an aerial photograph of Follensby beneath a headline that read "SAVE FOLLENSBY PARK!" and a subheadline that read "THE

HISTORICAL ADIRONDACK PHILOSOPHERS' CAMP." The pamphlet noted that the governor proposed allocating enough funds in the Environmental Assistance Fund to purchase Follensby. "Success now rests with the State Legislature." Later that year, in August, Cuomo signed legislation for New York's Environmental Protection Fund, a trust that over three years was supposed to fund $90 million in environmental projects, including the acquisition of wilderness lands such as the Follensby tract.[18]

At a June 1994 event marking the centennial of the addition of the "forever wild" clause in New York's constitution, Cuomo announced the state's plan to purchase three Adirondack parcels totaling seventeen thousand acres, including the Follensby tract. By this time, McCormick had repeatedly extended the state's option for Follensby, but there were indications he would not do so again, making it imperative for the legislature to perform what the *Albany Times Union* columnist Fred LeBrun called "a last-minute cavalry rescue."[19] But that legislative rescue did not come. Negotiations for the lake fell apart, and Follensby went from the top of conservationists' priority list to the back burner.

Little news about Follensby emerged over the following thirteen years after the state's failed bid to acquire the lake. Sometime in the early 2000s, Carr, at the Nature Conservancy, began privately and regularly communicating with McCormick but not specifically about purchasing Follensby. After getting strung along by the state, McCormick was in no rush to sell the Follensby tract. That changed in January 2007 when his wife, Bertha ("Bird") died. The following August he auctioned off items that had been housed at White Birches.[20]

In September 2008, just one month after the 150th anniversary of the Philosophers' Camp, the Nature Conservancy announced its purchase of the 14,600-acre Follensby tract for $16 million. The conservation organization planned to hold the property for an unspecified period until the state was able to purchase it and add it to the Adirondack Forest Preserve. Carr told the *New York Times* that ecological features, such as the property's hydrological systems and high-quality woodlands neighboring the Adirondack wilderness, drove the land deal. "But we cannot deny the romance and the mystique of Emerson and his colleagues, Stillman, Agassiz, at the Philosophers' Camp," Carr added.[21]

News about the sale of Follensby prompted a public accounting of the meaning of the Philosophers' Camp in the twenty-first century. Reports about the transaction reveal that many of the beliefs about the camp that had been evolving over the past century were all at once embraced. Carr's statement illustrates how the Philosophers' Camp continues to be viewed in the light of popular romanticism. Additionally, the event was seen as a nexus

FIGURE 20.   Carl Heilman II (1954–), *Boulder at Camp Maple Site,* 2008. Digital photograph. In his painting *Morning at Camp Maple: Adirondack Woods,* Stillman positioned a makeshift firing range near this boulder. When he returned to Follensby in 1884, the site of the Philosophers' Camp was recognizable only by this landmark boulder and a choked-up spring. Reproduced with permission of Carl Heilman II.

of the major social and cultural movements of the mid-nineteenth century. In an editorial, the *Albany Times Union* described the Philosophers' Camp as "a landmark in the 19th-century intellectual movement linking nature with art and literature, as well as a stimulus for early tourism in the Adirondacks." Further, the gathering was seen as a spark that helped set the preservation movement afire. LeBrun, the columnist, posited, "There are those who arguably point to that camp and the heavy thinking that went on that summer as the birthing of the American wilderness preservation movement. Maybe so." The unique and peculiar composition of the camp also earned it recognition as a gathering important not only to the history of the Adirondacks, as Donaldson suggested in 1921, but to the nation's history as well. In its press release announcing the Follensby acquisition, the Nature Conservancy quoted Bill McKibben, a well-known environmental activist and author: "The Philosophers' Camp at Follensby may have been as much intellectual firepower—in the humanities and sciences—as ever gathered together in the U.S., at least under the open air."[22]

As far as environmental conservationism goes, the movement and the Philosophers' Camp are at the same time perfect partners and strange bedfellows.

In the years running up to the Follensby purchase in 2008, writers increasingly emphasized the camp's influence on the conservation movement. For example, Schneider claimed that the "tradition of ecotourism" started with the camp. In its press release praising the purchase of Follensby, the Adirondack Council called the lake the "the birthplace of the American Wilderness Preservation movement," a claim that became widely repeated in news publications and travel literature. But the link between these movements and the 1858 camp at Follensby was weak in the nineteenth century, though it grew stronger in the twentieth century. Although Terrie noted that Emerson helped shape a "more consistently positive response to the wilderness," this feat was an indirect influence at most and fell short of sparking an entire movement. When asked to explain why Follensby was often seen as the wilderness preservation movement's birthplace, Carr said many people linked the camp to Emerson's transcendental philosophy, which hinged on the individual's harmony with and receptiveness to nature.[23]

However, not everyone who participated in the Philosophers' Camp in 1858 shared Emerson's views about nature; even the philosopher was not too keen on wilderness experiences when he camped at Follensby, and he became less so as time wore on. Additionally, in some respects the scholars acted quite unlike conservationists. At Follensby they engaged in hunting practices that were later outlawed. And at Ampersand, they developed one of the most pristine parcels in the Adirondacks by building a cabin there and roads through the wilderness. These practices have largely been overlooked by conservationists, but that may be due to a recognition that some compromises are necessary on both sides when civilization encounters the wilderness: the wilderness had to be tamed to an extent to accommodate the scholars; the scholars had to temporarily give up their refined modes to enjoy each other's company beneath the Adirondacks' white pines. Ultimately, neither the wilderness nor the scholars compromised so much of themselves that they could not both exist in the same story without one overshadowing the other.

Postscript

Several years have passed since the Nature Conservancy announced its acquisition of Follensby Pond in 2008. Despite having secured a U.S. Department of Agriculture Forest Legacy grant of $2.5 million for the Follensby tract in 2010, the New York State Department of Environmental Conservation in 2013 let the offer for this funding expire. The agency feared the lack of progress on the Follensby project would hurt its ability to secure two other Forest Legacy grant applications that were pending. The agency promised it would reapply for funds for Follensby "when the State has its portion of the purchase price available." Later in 2013, researchers from McGill University launched a two-year study on Follensby's lake trout population, continuing a tradition that began with Agassiz at the Philosophers' Camp.[1]

Meanwhile, the Nature Conservancy has concentrated on completing a five-year, $49.8 million deal it reached with the state in 2012 for eighty-nine thousand acres in the Adirondacks once owned by the Finch Pruyn paper company. In January 2013, Michael Carr of the Nature Conservancy told the *Adirondack Daily Enterprise* that New York's purchase of the Follensby Tract "was on the back burner for now." Under the 2012 deal, the state would buy the massive tract of wilderness over five years, with the final payment scheduled for the 2016–17 fiscal year.[2] Eden will have to wait a while longer to gain access to the Adirondack Forest Preserve.

❧ NOTES

Abbreviations

Abbreviations for frequently cited works and collections:

AALP	Amos A. Lawrence Papers, 1817–86
ABC	Albert Bierstadt Collection
AHA	*A History of the Adirondacks*
BTP	Bayard Taylor Papers
CENP	Charles Eliot Norton Papers
CSC	Charles Sumner Correspondence
DFP	Dana Family Papers
ERHM	*Ebenezer Rockwood Hoar: A Memoir*
HFP1	Hoar Family Papers
HFP2	Howells Family Papers
HWP	Horatio Woodman Papers
JDP	John Durand Papers
JRL	*James Russell Lowell*
LALS	*Louis Agassiz: A Life in Science*
LF1755	Letter File (1755–1995)
LHWL	Letters to Henry Wadsworth Longfellow
PSGW	Papers of Samuel Gray Ward and Anna Hazard Barker Ward
RRCSNL	Records Relating to Comptroller's Sale of Non-resident Lands for Unpaid Taxes, 1799–1928
RWEJN	Ralph Waldo Emerson Journals and Notebooks
RWELVC	Ralph Waldo Emerson Letters from Various Correspondents
"TA"	"The Adirondacs"
TAJ	*The Autobiography of a Journalist*
TC	The *Crayon*
TEYSC	*The Early Years of the Saturday Club*
TJMNRWE	*The Journals and Miscellaneous Notebooks of Ralph Waldo Emerson*
TLJRL	*The Letters of James Russell Lowell*
TLRWE	*The Letters of Ralph Waldo Emerson*
TORN	*The Old Rome and the New: and Other Studies*
"TPC"	"The Philosophers' Camp. Emerson, Agassiz, and Lowell in the Adirondacks"
WJSC	William James Stillman Collection

Introduction

1. Stillman, "TPC," 606. Even though Stillman in 1893 claimed, "Twenty-five years lapsed before I returned to Follansbee Water," ibid., he likely did not return to Follensby in 1883. A July 1884 correspondence to the *Nation* places Stillman in Saranac Lake that summer, suggesting he returned to Follensby not twenty-five but twenty-six years after the Philosophers' Camp in 1858. William James Stillman, "The Adirondacks To-day," *Nation,* August 14, 1884, 130–31.

2. Ralph Waldo Emerson, "TA," 150; Stillman, "TPC," 603, 606.

3. Stillman, "TPC," 606.

4. Ibid.

5. Ibid; see Stillman's painting *Morning at Camp Maple* (aka *The Philosophers' Camp in the Adirondacks*), figure 13 in chapter 9; see Charles E. Whitehead's engraving of the Philosopher's Camp in F. S. Stallknecht and C. E. Whitehead, "Sporting Tour in August, 1858," *Frank Leslie's Illustrated Newspaper,* November 13, 1858, 378 (figure 14 in chapter 10). Also see Don Carlos, "A Trip to the Saranac Lakes," *New York Evening Post,* August 30, 1858; Stillman, "TPC," 603.

6. [Don Carlos], "Agassiz, Emerson, Lowell, Holmes, and Stillman in the Woods," *The St. Paul Daily Minnesotian,* September 7, 1858; Don Carlos, "A Trip to the Saranac Lakes"; Jack Robinson, "Matters in Boston: Discoveries in Art—A Group of Statuary by Ball Hughes—The Cup and Ball—The Adirondack Club—Miscellaneous," *New York Times,* March 28, 1859.

7. Stillman, "TPC, 598, 605–6.

8. Nash, "American Cult of the Primitive," 518, 520–22; Stillman, "TPC," 606.

9. Stillman, "TPC," 606; Richard Plunz, "City, Culture, Nature: The New York Wilderness and the Urban Sublime," in Madsen and Plunz, *Urban Lifeworld,* 58.

10. Ralph Waldo Emerson, "Compensation," 169–70.

11. Ibid, 170; "The 'Century' for August," *New York Times,* August 4, 1893; Stillman, "TPC," 604.

12. Howells, "An Earlier American," 939.

13. Copplestone, *Hudson River School,* 14–15; Stillman, *TAJ,* 1:138–39.

14. C. M. Welsh, "These Glorious Mountains," *Antiques and the Arts,* June 27, 1997; N. Cikovsky Jr., "'The Ravages of the Ax': The Meaning of the Tree Stump in Nineteenth-Century American Art," *Art Bulletin* 61 (December 1979): 624; Stillman, "TPC," 598; T. Cole, "Essay on American Scenery," *American Monthly Magazine* (January 1836): 12.

15. Ralph Waldo Emerson, "Nature," 38–39, 43.

16. Kevin J. Avery, "Gifford and the Catskills," in Avery and Kelly, *Hudson River School Visions,* 25–28.

17. Ibid., 26, 36, 54; Stillman, *TAJ,* 1:199.

1. Path to the Adirondacks

1. Stillman, *TAJ,* 1:202.

2. Ibid., 1:200, 202.

3. Ibid., 1:202.

4. Ibid., 1:203.

5. Ibid., 1:203–5.

6. Ibid., 1:205–6; Stillman to Lowell, *Crayon* office, December 4, [18]54, WJSC (353); W. P. Garrison, "William James Stillman," *Century,* September 1893, 657.

7. Stillman, *TAJ,* 1:109–12, 170–72; Stillman, "Autobiography of W. J. Stillman: II. An American Education," 171–73.

8. Stillman, "Autobiography of W. J. Stillman: II. An American Education," 173–74; Stillman, *TAJ,* 1:83, 94–95.

9. Stillman, *TAJ,* 1:94–98, 112–13.

10. Kornhauser and Ellis with Miesmer, *Hudson River School,* 3–7, 69; Wall, Sutherland, and Hoffman, *National Academy of Design Exhibition Record,* 1:viii–xi.

11. Kornhauser and Ellis with Miesner, *Hudson River School,* 45, 65; Bryant, *Letters of William Cullen Bryant,* vol. 2, 532n3; Stillman, *TAJ,* 1:113–14; Kornhauser and Ellis with Miesner, *Hudson River School,* 45.

12. Kornhauser and Ellis with Miesner, *Hudson River School,* 45; Stillman, *TAJ,* 1:114–16.

13. Lane, *Pre-Raphaelites,* 12; Stillman, "Autobiography of W. J. Stillman: III. Art Study," 325; Stillman, *TAJ,* 1:116–36; Stillman, "Autobiography of W. J. Stillman: III. Art Study," 327–31.

14. Stillman, *TAJ,* 1:127–30; Stillman, "Autobiography of W. J. Stillman: III. Art Study," 325, 332–33; Stillman, *TAJ,* 1:167.

15. Stillman, *TAJ,* 1:136–39; Lane, *Pre-Raphaelites,* 78.

16. Stillman, "Autobiography of W. J. Stillman: III. Art Study," 334; Stillman, *TAJ,* 1:139; Wall, Sutherland, and Hoffman, *National Academy of Design Exhibition Record,* 2:141; Stillman, *TAJ,* 1:140, 142; Wall, Sutherland, and Hoffman, *National Academy of Design Exhibition Record,* 2:141.

17. Stillman to a brother, London, January 14, 1853, WJSC (380); Stillman, *TAJ,* 1:145–62; Stillman, "Autobiography of W. J. Stillman: IV. European Adventures and Life in the Wilderness," 466–71.

18. Bryant, *Letters of William Cullen Bryant,* vol. 3, 195–99, 348n2.

19. Stillman, *TAJ,* 1:175–78; unsigned review of the 1854 National Academy of Design Exhibition, *Putnam's Monthly,* May 1854, 566–68; Bullock, "William James Stillman: The Early Years" 126; Wall, Sutherland, and Hoffman, *National Academy of Design Exhibition Record,* 2:141; Stillman, *TAJ,* 1:177–78.

20. Review of the 1854 National Academy of Design Exhibition, *Putnam's Monthly,* 566–68.

21. Stillman, *TAJ,* 1:175–76; Stillman to a brother, Bellows Falls, Vermont, July 23, 1854, WJSC (381); Stillman, *TAJ,* 1:198–99.

22. Linda S. Ferber, "The Clearest Lens," in Ehrenkranz, *Poetic Localities,* 96; Stillman, *TAJ,* 1:199; Stillman to Norton, Raquette Lake, [September 1857], CENP (7081); Stillman, *TAJ,* 1:200–201.

23. Thoreau, *Henry David Thoreau: Collected Essays and Poems,* 652–53; Thoreau, *Walden,* 172.

24. Unsigned review of *Walden, Boston Evening Telegram,* September 9, 1854; Myerson, *Emerson and Thoreau,* 372; unsigned review of *Walden, Boston Daily Journal,* September 9, 1854; Myerson, *Emerson and Thoreau,* 389; R. W. Emerson to Emily M. Drury, Concord, June 12, 1853, *TLRWE,* 3:365.

25. R. W. Emerson to Emily M. Drury, Concord, November 23, 1853, *TLRWE,* 4:405; R. W. Emerson to Emily M. Drury, Concord, June 12, 1853,

TLRWE, 3:365; R. W. Emerson to Emily M. Drury, Concord, November 23, 1853, *TLRWE*, 4:405

26. Thoreau, *Writings of Henry David Thoreau,* vol. 8, 394; Thoreau, "Slavery in Massachusetts," 346.

2. Turning Points

1. Hoar, *Charge to the Grand Jury,* 3; Thomas Wentworth Higginson, *Cheerful Yesterdays,* 147–58; Stevens, *Anthony Burns,* 15; Schwartz, "Fugitive Slave Days in Boston," 207–8, 211.

2. "The Boston Fugitive Slave Case," *New York Times,* July 4, 1854; Hoar, *Charge to the Grand Jury,* 3–4; Stevens, *Anthony Burns,* 46–47.

3. Storey and Edward W. Emerson, *ERHM,* 26, 30, 36–62, 79.

4. M. Storey and E. W. Emerson, *ERHM,* 276–77, 296–97; "Judge Hoar on the Fugitive Slave Riot, and the Civil and Military Powers," *Boston Daily Atlas,* July 4, 1854; Schwartz, "Fugitive Slave Days in Boston," 201; M. Storey and E. W. Emerson, *ERHM,* 3.

5. Hoar, *Charge to the Grand Jury,* 7–8, 12–22.

6. "Judge Hoar on the Fugitive Slave Riot, and the Civil and Military Powers," *Boston Daily Atlas,* July 4, 1854; "The Boston Fugitive Slave Case," *New York Daily Times,* July 4, 1854; "Judge Hoar's Charge to the Grand Jury," *Fayetteville (North Carolina) Observer,* July 6, 1854; Ralph Waldo Emerson, *Ralph Waldo Emerson: Collected Poems and Translations,* 563; Pease and Pease, "Confrontation and Abolition in the 1850s," 926.

7. M. Storey and E. W. Emerson, *ERHM,* 107; Reynolds, *John Brown, Abolitionist,* 140–43; A. A. Lawrence, list of subscriptions for rifles for Kansas settlers, August 24, 1855, AALP; Sanborn, *Recollections of Seventy Years,* vol. 1:49.

8. Bishop, Freedley and Young, *History of American Manufacturers,* 2:590; "Death of Thomas B. Stillman," *New York Times,* January 3, 1866.

9. Stillman to Norton, New York, July 2, 1855, CENP (7068).

10. Lowell, *James Russell Lowell's Vision of Sir Launfal,* 2; Duberman, *JRL,* 47, 83, 92.

11. Duberman, *JRL,* 24, 26–29, 98–102.

12. Ibid., 87, 91, 134, 136–38, 140; Lowell, *James Russell Lowell's Vision of Sir Launfal,* 2.

13. Stillman, *TAJ,* 1:223; Stillman, "A Few of Lowell's Letters," 744; Duberman, *JRL,* 52; Stillman, *TORN,* 138; Stillman, "A Few of Lowell's Letters," 745.

14. Stillman, "A Few of Lowell's Letters," 745; Stillman to Lowell, *Crayon* office, December 4, 1854, WJSC (353); Lowell to Stillman, Cambridge, December 7, 1854; Lowell, *TLJRL,* 1:217–19.

15. Stillman, "Autobiography of W. J. Stillman: V. Journalism," 615; Stillman, *TAJ,* 1:224; Stillman, *TORN,* 133, 135.

16. Stillman to Lowell, *Crayon* office, December 4, 1854, WJSC (353); Stillman to Lowell, *Crayon* office, December 11, [1854], WJSC (351).

17. American Psychiatric Association, *Diagnostic and Statistical Manual,* 432–43; Stillman to Norton, Plainfield, [N.J.], October 15, [1861], CENP (7114); Stillman, *TAJ,* 2:469; Stillman to Norton, New York, March 21, [1856], CENP (7079).

18. Myerson, *Emerson and Thoreau,* xi–xv.

19. Stillman to Emerson, November 20, [1854], RWELVC (3074).

3. The *Crayon*

1. In an undated fragment of a letter, Stillman told Lowell that "an assembly of gentlemen [was] called together to see a picture which Leutze has just sent out." This letter was probably written sometime after *Washington at Monmouth* was placed at the National Academy in mid-October. The letter does not specifically identify the title of Leute's new painting. Stillman to Lowell, letter fragment, [New York], [late 1854 or early 1855], WJSC (332).

2. "Leutze's Picture, 'Washington at Monmouth,'" *New Orleans Times Picayune,* October 18, 1854. Stillman to Lowell, letter fragment, [New York], [late 1854 or early 1855], WJSC (332).

3. Stillman to Lowell, letter fragment, [New York], [late 1854 or early 1855], WJSC (332); Stillman, *TAJ,* 1:222.

4. Gerdts, "The Influence of Ruskin and Pre-Raphaelitism on American Still-Life Painting," 84; Wodehouse, "New Path and the American Pre-Raphaelite Brotherhood," 351; Avery and Kelly, *Hudson River School Visions,* 208; William James Stillman, "Pre-Raphaelitism," *TC,* April 4, 1855, 219–20; Sawyer, *Ruskin's Poetic Argument,* 265–69.

5. Baur, review of *The Daring Young Men,* 79; Ralph Waldo Emerson, "Nature," 59; J. D. Greenstone, "Dorothy Dix and Jane Adams: From Transcendentalism to Pragmatism in American Social Reform," *Social Service Review* 53 (December 1979): 547–48.

6. Kornhauser and Ellis with Miesmer, *Hudson River School,* 12; Heidi Applegate, "A Traveler by Instinct," in Avery and Kelly, *Hudson River School,* 54; Wall, Sutherland, and Hoffman, *National Academy of Design Exhibition Record,* 2:141.

7. Stillman, *TAJ,* 1:229; [Stillman], "Le[u]tze's Washington at the Battle on Monmouth," *TC,* January 10, 1855, 22; Stillman, *TAJ,* 1:226–27; Bullock, "William James Stillman: The Early Years," 141.

8. Stillman to Norton, New York, August 31, [1855], CENP (7061).

9. Stillman to Lowell, *Crayon* office, January 12, [1855], WJSC (335); Lowell to Stillman, Cambridge, [February 1855], *TLJRL,* 1:222–23; Stillman to Lowell, *Crayon* office, January 12, [1855], WJSC (335); Lowell to Stillman, Cambridge, May 10, 1855, *TLJRL,* 1:228–30.

10. [Stillman], editor's note on *The Wilderness and Its Waters, TC,* March 21, 1855, 188; W. Sylvester [Stillman], *The Wilderness and Its Waters,* chap. 1: "The Threshold," *TC,* March 14, 1855, 163.

11. Terrie, "Romantic Travelers in the Adirondack Wilderness," 59; William James Stillman, "Sketchings. Editorial Correspondence: Long Lake, 8 October 1855," *TC,* November 21, 1855, 328–29; Headley, *The Adirondack* (1849), 418.

12. Sylvester [Stillman], *The Wilderness and Its Waters,* chap. 1: "The Threshold," 163–65; Angus, *Extraordinary Journey of Clarence Petty,* 35.

13. William J. Miller, "The Adirondack Mountains," *New York State Museum Bulletin,* January 1, 1917, 75; Sylvester [Stillman], *The Wilderness* and *Its Waters,* chap. 3: "The Camp," *TC,* March 28, 1855, 194–95.

14. Sylvester [Stillman], *The Wilderness and Its Waters,* chap. 9: "The Hunter's Home," *TC,* May 16, 1855, 307–8; ibid., chap. 10: "The Hunt," *TC,* May 23, 1855, 324–25; Stillman, *TAJ,* 1:200; Sylvester [Stillman], *The Wilderness and Its Waters,* chap. 13: "Dolce Far Niente," *TC,* June 21, 1855, 187–88.

15. Ibid., chap. 1: "The Threshold," *TC,* March 14, 1855, 163–65; ibid., chap. 5: "The River," *TC,* April 18, 1855, 242; ibid., chap. 2: "A Forest Episode," *TC,* March 21, 1855, 181; ibid., chap. 1, 163; A. B. Durand, "Correspondence. North Conway, 29 August, 1855," *TC,* August 29, 1855, 133.

4. "Adieu to the World"

1. Duberman, *JRL,* 141–43; Lowell to Stillman, Elmwood, May 10, 1855, *TLJRL,* 1:228–30.

2. Duberman, *JRL,* 142; Lowell to Stillman, Elmwood, May 10, 1855, *TLJRL,* 1:228–30; Duberman, *JRL,* 143–44; Edward W. Emerson, *TEYSC,* 284.

3. Duberman, *JRL,* 163; Tucker, "James Russell Lowell and Robert Carter," 227, notes 2 and 3 to letter no. 33; Duberman, *JRL,* 144; Stillman to Norton, New York, June 14, [1855], CENP (7065).

4. Stillman, "A Few of Lowell's Letters," 748; Stillman to Lowell, Office of the *Crayon,* June 19, 1855, WJSC (356).

5. Stillman, *TAJ,* 1:216; Morison and Norton, "Reminiscences of Charles Eliot Norton," 364; DeWolfe Howe, "Charles Eliot Norton (1827–1908)," 405–6; Marsden, "Discriminating Sympathy," 464–65.

6. Stillman, *TAJ,* 1:106, 139; Stillman to Norton, [New York], May 15, [1855], CENP (7064).

7. Stillman to Norton, New York, July 2, 1855, CENP (7068); Wall, Sutherland, and Hoffman, *National Academy of Design Exhibition Record,* 2:141; Stillman to Norton, New York, July 2, 1855, CENP (7068); National Academy of Design, certificate naming Stillman an associate of the National Academy, May 10, 1855, WJSC (234); Wall, Sutherland, and Hoffman, *National Academy of Design Exhibition Record,* 2:141.

8. Stillman to Norton, New York, July 2, 1855, CENP (7068); Stillman, *TAJ,* 1:230; Stillman to Norton, New York, July 2, 1855, CENP (7068); Stillman to Norton, Plainfield, August 11, [1855], CENP (7072).

9. Norton to Lowell, September 23, [1855], *Letters of Charles Eliot Norton,* 1:132–33.

10. Stillman to Norton, New York, July 25, [1855], CENP (7069); Stillman to Norton, Plainfield, August 4 [or 9?], [1855], CENP (7071); Stillman to Norton, Plainfield, August 11, [1855], CENP (7072); Stillman to Norton, New York, August 24, [1855], CENP (7074).

11. Stillman to Norton, New York, September 13, [1855], CENP (7077); Turner, *Liberal Education of Charles Eliot Norton,* 125; Stillman to Norton, Plainfield, September 1, [1855], CENP (7075); Stillman to Norton, Plainfield, September 4, [1855], CENP (7076); Stillman to Norton, New York, August 31, [1855], CENP (7061).

12. Stillman to Norton, New York, August 31, [1855], CENP (7061).

13. Norton, *Letters of Charles Eliot Norton,* 1:136; Stillman to Norton, Plainfield, September 4, [1855], CENP (7076); Norton to Lowell, September 23, [1855], *Letters of Charles Eliot Norton,* 1:132–33.

14. William James Stillman, "Sketchings. Editorial Correspondence: Newburgh, September 25, 1855," *TC,* October 3, 1855, 216.

15. William James Stillman, "Sketchings. Editorial Correspondence: Saranac Lake, September 29, 1855," *TC,* October 10, 1855, 232.

16. H. P. Pushing, "Geological Survey of the Long Lake Quadrangle," New York State Museum, Bulletin 115 (September 1917): 451–52; William James Stillman, "Sketchings. Editorial Correspondence: Saranac Lake, September 30, 1855," *TC,* October 24, 1855, 264–65; Donaldson, *AHA,* 1:292, 298; Murray, *Adventures in the Wilderness,* 48; Headley, *The Adirondack* (1869), 303.

17. Donaldson, *AHA,* 1:294–95; Brumley, *Guides of the Adirondacks,* 1–20.

18. Stillman, "Sketchings," October 24, 1855, 264–65.

19. Ibid.; William James Stillman, "Sketchings. Editorial Correspondence: Raquette Pond, October 2, 1855," *TC,* October 31, 1855, 280–81.

20. Stillman, "Sketchings," October 31, 1855, 280–81; Donaldson, *AHA,* 1:311; William James Stillman, "Sketchings. Editorial Correspondence: Tupper Lake, October 3, 1855," *TC,* November 7, 1855, 296.

21. William James Stillman, "Sketchings. Editorial Correspondence: Tupper Lake, October 5, 1855," *TC,* November 14, 1855, 312–13; William James Stillman, "Sketchings. Editorial Correspondence: Long Lake, October 8, 1855," *TC,* November 21, 1855, 328–29.

22. William James Stillman, "Sketchings. Editorial Correspondence: Lower Saranac Lake, October 11, 1855," *TC,* November 28, 1855, 344–45; Stillman, *TAJ,* 1:205.

23. William James Stillman, "Sketchings. Editorial Correspondence: Lower Saranac Lake, October 13, 1855," *TC,* December 5, 1855, 360; Lowell to Stillman, Dresden, October 14, 1855, *TLJRL,* 1:243–47; Stillman to Lowell, office of the *Crayon,* December 17, 1855, WJSC (357); Lowell to Stillman, Dresden, October 14, 1855, *TLJRL,* 1:243–47.

5. The Artist Reborn

1. Stillman to Norton, North Conway, October 23, [1856], CENP (7089).

2. Stillman, *TAJ,* 1:230; editorial notice, *TC,* July 1856, 216; Stillman to Norton, New York, March 21, [1856], CENP (7079); editorial notice, *TC,* July 1856, 216; Stillman to Durand, North Conway, October 23, [1856], JDP.

3. Stillman, *TAJ,* 1:230–31; Stillman to Norton, North Conway, October 23, [1856], CENP (7089); William James Stillman, "Sketchings. Editorial Correspondence: Lower Saranac Lake, October 13, 1855," *TC,* December 5, 1855, 360.

4. Stillman, *TAJ,* 1:231; Stillman to Lowell, New York, February 28, 1857, WJSC (358).

5. Stillman to a brother, North Conway, October 11, [1856], WJSC (372); Stillman, *TAJ,* 1:231; Goldstein, "Women Enter Medicine in the Western Reserve," 66, 68; Binney, *Genealogy of the Binney Family in the United States,* 128–31, 171–72.

6. Stillman, *TAJ,* 1:231; Duberman, *JRL,* 152–53.

7. Stillman to Lowell, September 29, [1856], WJSC (343); Stillman to Norton, October 23, [1856], CENP (7089); Stillman to Lowell, October 23, [1856], WJSC (346).

8. Stillman to Lowell, New York, February 28, 1857, WJSC (358); Stillman to a brother, Boston, April 26, [1857], WJSC (369); Lowell to Stillman, Cambridge, May 14, 1857; Stillman, *TORN,* 155–56; Stillman to a brother, April 26, [1857], WJSC (369); Stillman, *TAJ,* 1:232; Dearinger, *Paintings and Sculptures in the Collection of the National Academy of Design,* 265.

9. Stillman to Lowell, South Manchester, Connecticut, June 2, 1857, WJSC (359); Wall, Sutherland, and Hoffman, *National Academy of Design Exhibition Record,* 2:141; Stillman to Lowell, South Manchester, Connecticut, June 2, 1857, WJSC (359); Stillman to a brother, June 1, 1857, South Manchester, Connecticut 1857, WJSC (382); Stillman to Lowell, South Manchester, Connecticut, June 2, 1857, WJSC (359).

10. Lurie, *LALS,* 202–203; Edward W. Emerson, *TEYSC,* 6–10, 96, 162–163.

11. Blumin, *Emergence of the Middle Class,* 207–9; Andrew Oliver, review of *A Social History of the Greater Boston Clubs* by Alexander W. Williams, *Pennsylvania Magazine of History and Biography* 95 (January 1971): 140–41; Keyes, Hoar, Harris, and Emerson, *Memoirs of Members of the Social Circle in Concord,* iii, xi.

12. Blumin, *Emergence of the Middle Class,* 207; Lamb, *History of the City of New York,* 2:707; Blumin, *Emergence of the Middle Class,* 207.

13. Emerson, *TEYSC,* 5–7; Wilkins, *History of Foreign Investment in the United States to 1914,* 57; Emerson, *TEYSC,* 7–10, 13, 19–21; Brandon G. Lovested, "Omni Parker House Hotel," http://www.iboston.org/mcp.php?pid=parkerHouse.

14. "The Saturday Club. Quaint Letter from Emerson and a Note from Longfellow," *New York Times,* December 26, 1890; Ralph Waldo Emerson, *TJMNRWE,* 14:143–44.

15. Emerson, *TEYSC,* 21, 124; Adams, *Richard Henry Dana,* 2:162–65.

16. Emerson, *TEYSC,* 131; Lurie, *LALS,* 179; Marcou, *Life, Letters, and Works of Louis Agassiz,* 2:217–18; Emerson, *TEYSC,* 30; Agassi, *Intelligence of Louis Agassiz,* 233; Lurie, *LALS,* 94–97.

17. Lurie, *LALS,* 116–26, 133–46, 256; C. Irmscher, *Louis Agassiz,* 239.

18. Lurie, *LALS,* 186–87, 195–96.

19. Emerson, *TJMNRWE,* 14:143–44; Adams, *Richard Henry Dana,* 2:167–68; Emerson, *TJMNRWE,* 14:143–44.

20. Stillman to Lowell, New York, July 13, [1857], WJSC (339); Duberman, *JRL,* 153–55; Stillman to Lowell, New York, July 13, [1857], WJSC (339).

21. Stillman, *TAJ,* 1:237; Duberman, *JRL,* 133, 196; Emerson, *TEYSC:* 284; "Brother of the Autocrat: Serious Illness of John Holmes at His Home in Cambridge," *New York Times,* November 3, 1897.

6. Trial Run

1. Stillman, *TORN,* 232–33.

2. Ibid., 233–34.

3. Ibid., 235–36.

4. Ibid., 237–39.

5. Ibid., 239; Comfort and Elwell, *Tyndale Bible Dictionary,* 441; Stillman, *TORN,* 239–40; May, *Love and Will,* 123n1, 123–25 .

6. Stillman, *TORN,* 240–43.

7. Ibid., 249.

8. Stillman, "The Subjective of It," 857–58; Stillman to Norton, Raquette Lake, August 22, 1857, CENP (7080); Stillman, *TORN,* 251; Norton to Clough, Lenox, August 27, 1857, *Letters of Charles Eliot Norton,* 182–84; Lowell to Stillman, Cambridge, October 28, 1857, *TLJRL,* 1:279–80; Stillman to Norton, Raquette Lake, August 22, 1857, CENP (7080).

9. Stillman to Norton, Raquette Lake, August 22, 1857, CENP (7080); Stillman to Norton, Raquette Lake, [September 1857], CENP (7081); Stillman to Norton, Raquette Lake, August 22, 1857, CENP (7080).

10. Stillman to Norton, Raquette Lake, [September 1857], CENP (7081).

11. Stillman to Norton, [Saranac], September 29, 1857, CENP (7082); Markham, *Financial History of the United States,* 201–2; Ralph Waldo Emerson, *TJMNRWE,* 14:138, 141.

12. Stillman to Norton, [Saranac], September 29, 1857, CENP (7082); Stillman to Norton, New York, October 10, [1857], CENP (7083).

13. Stillman to Lowell, studio building, November 1, [18]57, WJSC (360); Stillman to Norton, New York, October 10, [1857], CENP (7083); Stillman to Lowell, studio building, November 1, [18]57, WJSC (360).

14. Norton to Clough, Lenox, August 27, 1857, *Letters of Charles Eliot Norton,* 182–84; Lowell to Stillman, Cambridge, October 28, 1857, *TLJRL,* 1:279–80.

15. Edward W. Emerson, *TEYSC,* 130; Ralph Waldo Emerson to Margaret Fuller, Concord, August 29, 1847, *TLRWE,* 3:412–14; R. W. Emerson to S. G. Ward, Concord, August 23, 1847, *TLRWE,* 8:124–25; R. W. Emerson to Drury, Concord, March 31, 1855, *TLRWE,* 4:499–500n80.

16. Richard Henry Dana, "How We Met John Brown," *Atlantic Monthly,* July 1871, 1–7.

17. Reynolds, *John Brown, Abolitionist,* 111–13, 171–73, 199–201.

18. Sanborn, *Recollections of Seventy Years,* 1:84–85; Reynolds, *John Brown, Abolitionist,* 89.

19. R. W. Emerson to K. Field, Concord, October 28, 1869, *TLRWE,* 6:91–92; Sanborn, *Recollections of Seventy Years,* 1:102–5; Emerson, *TJMNRWE,* 14:125.

20. Duberman, *JRL,* 154–55; Stillman to Lowell, studio building, November 1, [18]57, WJSC (360); Duberman, *JRL,* 162–65.

21. Lurie, *LALS,* 181, 192, 222; "Letter of the Minister of Public Instruction and Religion," *Charlestown Mercury,* October 13, 1857; Lurie, *LALS,* 219–20.

22. Edward W. Emerson, *TEYSC,* 24, 131; Ralph Waldo Emerson to Lowell, Boston Athenaeum, June 22, 1858, *TLRWE,* 5:110–11.

7. The Procession to the Pines

1. Stillman to Lowell, New York, January 3, [1858], WJSC (361); Stillman to Norton, New York, February 6, [18]58, CENP (7084).

2. Perkins and Grant, *Boston Athenaeum Art Exhibition Index,* 262; David Dearinger, the Susan Morse Hilles Curator of Paintings and Sculptures, informed me that *The Procession of the Pines* "disappeared from the collection, evidently by 1870" (e-mail to author, November 16, 2009). However, Stillman biographer Richard D. Bullock claimed in his 1976 thesis that the painting was sold in 1924. Bullock, "William James Stillman," 122. Ralph Waldo Emerson, *Complete Works of Ralph Waldo Emerson,* vol. 9, 463.

3. Stillman, "TPC," 602; Higginson, "Footpaths," 518–19.

4. Stillman, *TAJ,* 1:281; Smith and Smith. *Genealogical Records of the Descendants of David Mack,* 30–31. Stillman, "A Few of Lowell's Letters," 755–56.

5. Stillman to Norton, New York, May 15, [1858], CENP (7078); Stillman, *TAJ,* 1:232–33.

6. Emerson to Lowell, Boston Athenaeum, June 22, 1858, *TLRWE,* 5:110–11; R. W. Emerson to W. Emerson, Concord, July 1, 1958, *TLRWE,* 5:111–12; Thoreau, *The Writings of Henry David Thoreau,* vol. 11, 3, 55.

7. Gassan, *Birth of American Tourism,* 2–3, 13.

8. Ibid., 3–5, 71–79; R. W. Emerson, journal entry for "Ethan Allen Crawford's, White Mountains, July 14, *The Heart of Emerson's Journals,* 57–58.

9. R. W. Emerson to W. Emerson, Concord, July 1, 1858, *TLRWE,* 5:111–12; Stillman, "TPC," 599; Lurie, *LALS,* 222–23.

10. R. W. Emerson to Clough, Concord, May 17, 1858, *Emerson-Clough Letters;* "Personal Intelligence," *New York Herald,* June 21, 1858; "Professor Agassiz," *Daily Ohio Statesman,* June 24, 1858; "Agassiz to Remain in America [from the *Boston Courier*]," *New York Times,* June 28, 1858.

11. R. W. Emerson to W. Emerson, Concord, July 1, 1858, *TLRWE,* 5:111–12; Holmes, "Professor Jeffries Wyman," 613–15, 621.

12. R. W. Emerson to G. Bancroft, July 2, 1858, *TLRWE,* 8:571; R. W. Emerson to H. G. O. Blake, Concord, July 27, 1858, *TLRWE,* 5:116; R. W. Emerson to J. M. Forbes, Concord, July 25, 1858, *TLRWE,* 5:115; Stillman to R. W. Emerson, Belmont, July 22, [1858], RWELVC (3075); R. W. Emerson, *Account Book 6 [1853–1859],* RWEJN (112e), pages not numbered, ordered chronologically, entry dated July 24, [1858]; Thoreau, journal entry, August 6, 1858, *The Heart of Thoreau's Journals,* 196.

13. Longfellow to Lowell, Nahant, July 23, 1858, Longfellow, *The Letters of Henry Wadsworth Longfellow,* vol. 4, 88–89n2; Stillman, "TPC," 599.

14. Hoar to Dana, Boston, July 29, 1858, DFP (MS. N-1088).

15. Stillman to Lowell, Belmont, July 29, [1858], WJSC (340); R. W. Emerson to Stillman, [July 20?, 1858], *TLRWE,* 8:573; Stillman to R. W. Emerson, Belmont, July 22, [1858], RWELVC (3075); Longfellow, journal entry, July 31, 1858, *Life of Henry Wadsworth Longfellow,* vol. 2, 361; Stillman, "TPC," 598.

16. Stillman, "TPC," 598–99; W. Sylvester [Stillman] and H. K. Brown, *The Wilderness and Its Waters,* chap. 3: "The Camp," *TC,* March 28, 1855, 195.

17. Collins, *Brighton Story,* 178–79; Street, *Woods and Waters,* 142–47.

18. Stillman, "TPC," 598–99; E. R. Hoar to C. D. Hoar, Saratoga, August 15, 1858, *ERHM,* 145.

19. E. R. Hoar to C. D. Hoar, Saratoga, August 15, 1858, *ERHM,* 145; Don Carlos, "A Trip to the Saranac Lakes," *New York Evening Post,* August 30, 1858; Hurd, *History of Clinton and Franklin Counties,* 212.

20. Stillman, "TPC," 598.

21. Thoreau, *Maine Woods,* 33; E. R. Hoar to C. D. Hoar, Saratoga, August 15, 1858, *ERHM,* 145; Ralph Waldo Emerson, *The Topical Notebooks of Ralph Waldo Emerson,* 1:276; Ralph Waldo Emerson, *TJMNRWE,* vol. 13, 56l; Jamieson, "Emerson in the Adirondacks," 235–36n17.

22. Ralph Waldo Emerson, "TA," 149; Stillman, "TPC," 599; Emerson, "TA," 149; Stillman, "TPC," 599; Emerson, *Topical Notebooks,* 1:277; Sam Dunning served as F. S. Stallknecht's guide early that August. F. S. Stallknecht and C. E. Whitehead, "Sporting Tour in August, 1858," *Frank Leslie's Illustrated Newspaper,* November 13, 1858, 378.

23. E. R. Hoar to C. D. Hoar, Saratoga, August 15, 1858, *ERHM,* 146; Stillman, "TPC," 599; E. R. Hoar to C. D. Hoar, Saratoga, August 15, 1858, *ERHM,* 146; Stillman, "TPC," 599.

24. Stillman, *TAJ*, 1:246; Stallknecht and Whitehead, "Sporting Tour in August, 1858," 379; Emerson, "TA," 149.

25. E. R. Hoar to C. D. Hoar, Saratoga, August 15, 1858, *ERHM*, 146. (Only passages from this letter are included in *ERHM*. Attempts to locate the original manuscript were unsuccessful.) Ellen Emerson to R. W. Emerson, Concord, August 3, 1858, *The Letters of Ellen Tucker Emerson*, 1:145–46; Stillman, "TPC," 599; Emerson, *TJMNRWE*, vol. 13, 34; Jamieson, "Emerson in the Adirondacks," 235n15.

26. E. R. Hoar to C. D. Hoar, Saratoga, August 15, 1858, *ERHM*, 146; Howells, "An Earlier American," 940.

8. Acclimating to the Wild

1. Stillman, "TPC," 602–3.

2. Ibid.; Ralph Waldo Emerson, "TA," 150–51; Stillman, "TPC," 604.

3. New York History Net, "William H. Seward: On the Irrepressible Conflict [speech transcript]," http://www.nyhistory.com/central/conflict.htm.

4. Emerson, "TA," 152.

5. Ralph Waldo Emerson, *TJMNRWE*, vol. 13, 34; Stillman, "TPC," 600; Ralph Waldo Emerson, *Journals of Ralph Waldo Emerson*, vol. 9, 159; Emerson, "TA," 150; Emerson, *TJMNRWE*, vol. 13, 56; Emerson, "TA," 153.

6. Emerson, *TJMNRWE*, vol. 13, 56; E. R. Hoar to C. D. Hoar, Saratoga, August 15, 1858, *ERHM*, 148.

7. Emerson, *TJMNRWE*, vol. 13, 34; Stillman, "TPC," 606; Emerson, *TJMNRWE*, vol. 13, 34, 55–56.

8. Stillman, "TPC," 603; Ralph Waldo Emerson, *Poetry Notebooks of Ralph Waldo Emerson*, 517; R. W. Emerson et al. to L. Mack, Camp Maple, August 16, 1858, *TLRWE*, vol. 8, 573.

9. F. S. Stallknecht and C. E. Whitehead, "Sporting Tour in August, 1858," *Frank Leslie's Illustrated Newspaper*, November 13, 1858, 379.

10. Ibid.

11. Stallknecht's account here, as told in *Frank Leslie's Illustrated Newspaper* in November 1858, of how the scholars learned about the laying of the Atlantic cable differs from Emerson's account recorded in his draft and final versions of "The Adirondacs."

12. Stallknecht and Whitehead, "Sporting Tour in August, 1858," 379; "The Atlantic Cable Laid. The Great Event of the Age," *New York Herald*, August 6, 1858.

13. Gordon, *Thread across the Ocean*, 42–46, 66, 96–97.

14. Ibid., 109–24.

15. "Prospects of the Atlantic Telegraph," *New York Herald*, August 1, 1858; Emerson, *Poetry Notebooks*, 519.

16. Gordon, *Thread across the Ocean*, 130; "The Atlantic Cable Laid. The Great Event of the Age"; Emerson, "TA," 155; Emerson, *Poetry Notebooks*, 519.

17. Stallknecht and Whitehead, "Sporting Tour in August, 1858," 379.

18. Ibid., 380; Stillman, "TPC," 604.

19. Emerson, "TA," 150; Edward W. Emerson, *TEYSC*, 61; Stillman, "TPC," 601; Marcou, *Life, Letters and Works of Louis Agassiz*, vol. 2, 130.

20. Stillman, "TPC," 600; Agassiz, *Intelligence of Louis Agassiz,* 15.

21. Emerson, "TA," 153; Don Carlos, "A Trip to the Saranac Lakes," *New York Evening Post,* August 30, 1858.

22. Stillman, "TPC," 603; Emerson, *TJMNRWE,* vol. 13, 56.

23. Agassiz, *Lake Superior,* 25; Longfellow to Sumner, Nahant, August 12, 1858, *Letters of Henry Wadsworth Longfellow,* vol. 4, 92.

24. Agassiz, *Intelligence of Louis Agassiz,* 18; Agassiz, *Essay on Classification,* 205.

25. Agassiz, *Lake Superior,* 328.

26. Emerson, "The Preacher," 223; Lizabeth Paravisini-Gerbert, "'American' Landscapes and Erasures," in Niblett and Oloff, *Perspectives on the 'Other America,'* 92–93.

27. Ibid., 329.

28. Lurie, *LALS,* 255, 262; Agassiz, *Lake Superior,* 329–30; Irmscher, *Louis Agassiz,* 6.

29. Agassiz to Baird, June 23, 1858, *Correspondence between Spencer Fullerton Baird and Louis Agassiz,* 142; Stillman, "TPC," 604.

30. Rusk, *Life of Ralph Waldo Emerson,* 114–15; Ralph Waldo Emerson, *Topical Notebooks of Ralph Waldo Emerson,* 1:275–77; E. R. Hoar to C. D. Hoar, Saratoga, August 15, 1858, *ERHM,* 146; Emerson, *Topical Notebooks,* 1:275.

31. Stillman to C. E. Norton, Belmont, October 6, 1858, CENP (7088); Emerson, *Topical Notebooks,* 1:276; Stillman, "TPC," 600–603.

32. Stillman, "TPC," 602; E. R. Hoar to C. D. Hoar, Saratoga, August 15, 1858, *ERHM,* 146–48; Stillman, "TPC," 601–2.

33. Emerson, *TJMNRWE,* vol. 13, 56; E. R. Hoar to C. D. Hoar, Saratoga, August 15, 1858, *ERHM,* 147–48.

34. Emerson, "TA," 152; Stillman, "TPC," 599.

35. Stillman, "TPC," 600–601.

36. Ibid.

9. The Worthy Crew Chaucer Never Had

1. Stillman, "TPC," 602.

2. Ibid. Ralph Waldo Emerson, *Topical Notebooks of Ralph Waldo Emerson,* 1:275.

3. Emerson, *Topical Notebooks,* 1:275. This version of the nighttime hunt is based on Stillman's account of it in his *Century* essay, "TPC," 602. Emerson recorded slightly different accounts in his notebook, *Topical Notebooks,* 1:275, and poem, "TA," 152. Stillman, "TPC," 602.

4. Stillman, "TPC," 602; Thoreau, journal entry for August 23, 1858, *The Heart of Thoreau's Journals,* 199.

5. Thoreau, journal entry for August 23, 1858; Marcou, *Life, Letters and Works of Louis Agassiz,* vol. 2, 130.

6. Edward W. Emerson, *TEYSC,* 424; M. Storey and E. W. Emerson, *ERHM,* 21; Hoar to Dana, July 29, 1858, DFP (Ms. 1088); Thoreau, journal entry for August 23, 1858.

7. Ralph Waldo Emerson, "TA," 151; Ellen Emerson, *The Letters of Ellen Tuck Emerson,* 1:146; E. R. Hoar to C. D. Hoar, Saratoga, August 15, 1858, *ERHM,* 148; Emerson, "TA," 151.

8. Emerson, "TA," 155, 157.

9. Thomas Wentworth Higginson, *Letters and Journals of Thomas Wentworth Higginson*, 262–63; Stillman, "TPC," 603; F .S. Stallknecht and C. E. Whitehead, "Sporting Tour in August, 1858," *Frank Leslie's Illustrated Newspaper*, November 13, 1858, 380.

10. Stillman, "TPC," 601, 603.

11. Ralph Waldo Emerson, "Man the Reformer," 146; Ralph Waldo Emerson, "American Scholar," 63.

12. Ralph Waldo Emerson, *English Traits*, 811, 822, 851; Stillman, "TPC," 601; Stillman, *TAJ*, 1:253.

13. Ralph Waldo Emerson, *Poetry Notebooks of Ralph Waldo Emerson*, 522.

14. Ibid., 724.

15. Ibid.

16. Ibid., 522; E. W. Emerson, *TEYSC*, 125, 283, 424.

17. Emerson, *Poetry Notebooks*, 523–24, 529–30.

18. Ibid, 527.

19. E. W. Emerson, *TEYSC*, 175–76.

20. Stillman, *TAJ*, 1:250, 278; R. W. Emerson, "TA," 153.

21. Ellen Emerson to R. W. Emerson, Concord, August 3, 1858, *Letters of Ellen Tucker Emerson*, 1:145–46.

22. R. W. Emerson, "TA," 158; *Hartford Daily Times*, [news brief on *Evening Post* report of Agassiz, Lowell, Dr. Holmes, and Emerson in the Adirondacks], August 10, 1858.

23. Digital Librarian, "Adirondack Mountains—New York State," http://www.digital-librarian.com/adirondacks.html; [Samuel] H. [Hammond], "Letters from Summer Resorts: Life in the Adirondacks," *New York Times*, August 5, 1858; Don Carlos, "A Trip to the Saranac Lakes," *New York Evening Post*, August 30, 1858.

24. Don Carlos, "A Trip to the Saranac Lakes," *New York Evening Post*, August 30, 1858.

25. H. W. Longfellow to C. Sumner, Nahant, August 12, 1858, *Letters of Henry Wadsworth Longfellow*, vol. 4, 91–92.

26. C. E. Norton to A. Clough, Newport, August 16, 1858; Norton, *Letters of Charles Eliot Norton*, vol. 1, 191–93; Stillman, "TPC," 603.

27. Stillman, "TPC," 600.

28. Emerson, "TA," 158; E. R. Hoar to C. D. Hoar, Saratoga, August 15, 1858, *ERHM*, 145; Stillman, *TORN*, 294; Stillman, "TPC," 603.

29. Stillman, "TPC," 599–601.

30. Ralph Waldo Emerson, *TLRWE*, 8:573.

31. Stillman to Norton, Belmont, October 6, 1858, CENP (7088); Stillman, *TAJ*, 1:280; Wall, Sutherland, and Hoffman, *National Academy of Design Exhibition Record*, 2:141.

32. R. W. Emerson to K. Field, Concord, 28 October 1869, *TLRWE*, 6:91–92.

33. Ralph Waldo Emerson, Account Book 6 [1853–59], RWEJN (112e) (pages not numbered, ordered chronologically); Eva Everson, "William J. Stillman: Emerson's 'Gallant Artist,'" 38n11; Thoreau, journal entry for August 23, 1858, *The Heart of Thoreau's Journals*, 199; "The Ocean Cable. The Metropolis in a Blaze of Glory. Ovation to Science and Civilization," *New York Herald*, August 18, 1858; Gordon, *Thread across the Ocean*, 137–41.

34. R. W. Emerson to J. M. Forbes, Concord, August 26, 1858, *TLRWE*, 5:117; Ellen Emerson to Edith Emerson, Naushon, September 1, 1858, *The Letters of Ellen Tucker Emerson*, 2:147–48.

35. Don Carlos, "A Trip to the Saranac Lakes," *New York Evening Post,* August 30, 1858; [Don Carlos], "Agassiz, Emerson, Lowell, Holmes, and Stillman in the Woods," *St. Paul Daily Minnesotian,* September 7, 1858.

36. Stillman to Norton, Belmont, October 6, 1858, CENP (7088); Stillman, *TAJ,* 1:280–81.

37. Stillman to J. Durand, Belmont, MA, October 22, [1858], JDP; Stillman, *TAJ,* 1:280.

38. Scudder, *James Russell Lowell,* 448.

39. Stillman to Lowell, Belmont October 13, [1858], WJSC (344).

40. Ibid.

10. Ampersand

1. Stillman, *TAJ,* 1:281–82.

2. Ibid, 1:281; Stillman to Norton, New York, August 31, [1855], CENP (7061).

3. William James Stillman, "Sketchings. Editorial Correspondence: Raquette Pond, 2 October 1855," *TC,* October 31, 1855, 280–81; Stillman, *TAJ,* 1:282; Donaldson, *AHA,* 1:62–71.

4. Stillman to Lowell, Plainfield, New Jersey, December 1, 1858, WJSC (362).

5. Ibid.; Ralph Waldo Emerson to S. G. Ward, [Concord?], December 6, 1859, *TLRWE,* 8:589; Stillman, *TAJ,* 1:282–83.

6. Stillman, *TAJ,* 1:282; Godfrey, "Enforcement of Delinquent Property Taxes in New York," pt. 1, 274, 292–93; Headley, *Adirondack, or Life in the Woods* (1869 ed.), 423.

7. Delaware and Hudson Company, *Corporate History,* 3:100; National American Society, "Rt. Rev. William Neilson McVickar, D.D.," *Americana (American Historical Magazine)* 13 (1919): 306; Supreme Court of the State of New York Appellate Division, Third Department, "The People of the State of New York—Plaintiff, Appellant—against Santa Clara Lumber Company et al.—Defendants, Respondent," 666. Although this lawsuit relates to litigation that occurred long after the demise of the Adirondack Club, evidence provided by the defendants and compiled in an exhibit book is of great interest, particularly the more than ninety abstracts for titles in Township Twenty-Seven (See "Defendants' Exhibit 15, Action No. 3"); Delaware and Hudson Company, *Corporate History,* 3:4; Supreme Court of the State of New York Appellate Division, Third Department, "The People of the State of New York," 667.

8. Supreme Court of the State of New York Appellate Division, Third Department, "The People of the State of New York," 667, 679–80, 682, 693–94.

9. Ralph Waldo Emerson, "TA," 153; Stillman, *TORN,* 267; Emerson to Ward, Concord, August 5, 1859, *TLRWE,* 8:624–25; ; S. G. Ward to R. W. Emerson, 52 Wall Street, March 28, 1876, LRWE (3361).

10. Donaldson, *History of the Adirondacks,* 1:188; Colvin, "Report of the Superintendent," 303.

11. Colvin, "Report of the Superintendent," 457; Colvin, "Ascent and Barometrical Measurement of Mount Seward," 9; Henry Van Dyke, "Ampersand," 217–18.

12. Raymond, *Story of Saranac,* 71; Hardie, *Where to Go in the Adirondacks,* 43; Donaldson, *AHA,* 1:28–29.

13. "A Poet Afraid of Philosophers," *Atchison (Kansas) Freedom's Champion,* October 30, 1858; "Anecdote of Professor Agassiz," *Macon (Georgia) Weekly Telegraph,* January 4, 1859; [J. Durand], "Sketchings," *TC,* November 1858, 328.

14. F. S. Stallknecht and C. E. Whitehead, "Sporting Tour in August, 1858," *Frank Leslie's Illustrated Newspaper,* November 13, 1858, 378.

15. Jack Robinson, "Matters in Boston: Discoveries in Art—A Group of Statuary by Ball Hughes—The Cup and Ball—The Adirondack Club—Miscellaneous," *New York Times,* March 28, 1859.

16. Lurie, *LALS,* 227–28.

17. Hoar to Stillman, Boston, January 8, 1859, WJSC (153).

18. Ibid.

19. Ibid.

20. Godfrey, "Enforcement of Delinquent Property Taxes," pt. 2, 44.

21. Robinson, "Matters in Boston"; New York State Comptroller, List of Lands to be Sold, title page; Robinson, "Matters in Boston."

22. [J. Durand], "Sketchings: National Academy of Design," *TC,* May 1859), 152–53; "Editor's Easy Chair," *Harper's New Monthly Magazine,* June 1859, 126; Robinson, "Matters in Boston."

23. Gerdts, "Influence of Ruskin and Pre-Raphaelitism," 80.

24. [Stillman], "Sketchings," *TC,* March 21, 1855, 186.

25. Stillman, *TAJ,* 1:283; Stillman to Norton, Savannah, March 25, [1859], CENP (7090); Stillman, *TAJ,* 1:283–84. As late as April 30, Stillman was in St. Augustine. Stillman to Norton, St. Augustine, April 30, [1859], CENP (7092. After that he joined a fishing party to the abandoned Spanish fort of Matanzas. Stillman, *TAJ,* 1:287.

26. Longfellow to C. Sumner, June 13, 1859, *Life of Henry Wadsworth Longfellow,* 2:386; Lurie, *LALS,* 237; Stillman to Longfellow, Cambridge, June 24, [1859], LHWL (5327); Stillman to Longfellow, Belmont, July 1, [1859], LHWL (5327); Storey and E. W. Emerson, *ERHM,* 107, 119.

27. Ralph Waldo Emerson, *TJMNRWE,* vol. 14, 311; R. W. Emerson, to S. G. Ward, Concord, July 9, 1859, *TLRWE,* 8:613.

28. Emerson to Forbes, Concord, July 4, 1859, *TLRWE,* 5:156; Ellen Tucker Emerson to A. [Manning], Concord, July 27, 1859, *Letters of Ellen Tucker Emerson,* 188; Emerson to Forbes, Concord, July 4, 1859, *TLRWE,* vol. 5:156.

29. Ward to Norton, Boston, July 13, 1859, CENP (7701); Hoar to Stillman, Boston, January 8, 1859, WJSC (153); Stillman to Longfellow, Cambridge, June 24, [1859], LHWL (5327); Emerson to Lowell, Concord, July 25, 1859, *TLRWE,* 5:166; Lowell to Emerson, Newport, July 18, 1859, *New Letters of James Russell Lowell,* 97; Edward W. Emerson, *TEYSC,* 124, 285; Longfellow to Ward, Nahant, August 9, 1859, *Letters of Henry Wadsworth Longfellow,* vol. 4, 160n1.

30. Longfellow, *Life of Henry Wadsworth Longfellow,* 2:387; Higginson, *Letters and Journals of Thomas Wentworth Higginson,* 107–10; T. W. Higginson to Louisa Higginson, Worcester, September 11, 1859, *Letters and Journals of Thomas Wentworth Higginson,* 123.

31. Lowell to Emerson, Newport, July 18, 1859, *New Letters of James Russell Lowell,* 97; Emerson to Lowell, Concord, July 25, 1859, *TLRWE,* 5:166; Emerson to Forbes, Concord, August 6, 1859, *TLRWE,* 5:168.

32. Lowell to Emerson, Newport, July 18, 1859, *New Letters of James Russell Lowell,* 97; T. W. Higginson to Louisa Higginson, Worcester, September 11, 1859, *Letters and Journals of Thomas Wentworth Higginson,* 123–24; Emerson to Lowell, Concord, July 25, 1859, *TLRWE,* 5:166.

33. Emerson to Abel Adams, Concord, July 20, 1859, *TLRWE,* 5:162–63; Stillman to Longfellow, Belmont, July 21, [1859], LHWL (5327); Stillman, *TAJ,* 1:289.

11. The Inaugural Meeting

1. Stillman, *TAJ,* 1:289–90.

2. Wallace, *Descriptive Guide to the Adirondacks* (1894), 256; Stillman, *TAJ,* 1:289; Wallace, *Descriptive Guide to the Adirondacks* (1894), 256; Stillman, *TAJ,* 1:289; D. M. Arnold to Silas Arnold, Esq., Port Henry [map of Ampersand Pond], August 15, 1859, HFP1; Donaldson, *AHA,* 1:303; D. M. Arnold to Silas Arnold, Esq., Port Henry; Bien, "Franklin County," in *Atlas of the State of New York,* 18.

3. Stillman, *TAJ,* 1:289; Stillman to C. E. Norton, in camp, Ampersand Pond, August ?, [1859], CENP (7093).

4. Edward W. Emerson to M. Spartali Stillman, February 21 [190?], *AHA,* 1:187; Ralph Waldo Emerson to S. G. Ward, Concord, August 5, 1859, *TLRWE,* 8:624–25; Ellen Tucker Emerson to Edith Emerson, Concord, August 13, 1859, *Letters of Ellen Tucker Emerson,* 1:190–93.

5. Stillman to Norton, in camp, Ampersand Pond, August ? [1859], CENP (7093); R. W. Emerson to J. M. Forbes, Concord, July 25, 1859, *TLRWE,* 5:165; S. G. Ward to C. E. Norton, Boston, July 13, 1859, CENP (7701); C. E. Norton to Wendell P. Garrison, Shady Hill, Cambridge, April 4, 1893, LF1755.

6. Thomas Wentworth Higginson to Louisa Higginson, Worcester, September 11, 1859, *Letters and Journals of Thomas Wentworth Higginson,* 124; Stillman to Norton, in camp, Ampersand Pond, August ?, [1859], CENP (7093); T. W. Higginson to Louisa Higginson, Worcester, September 11, 1859, *Letters and Journals of Thomas Wentworth Higginson,* 123–24; C. E. Norton to A. H. Clough, Newport, August 27, 1859, *Letters of Charles Eliot Norton,* 195.

7. Stillman to Norton, in camp, Ampersand Pond, August ?, [1859], CENP (7093).

8. Ibid.; Stillman to Norton, in camp, Ampersand Pond, September 30, [1859], CENP (7094).

9. Stillman to Lowell, Ampersand Pond, September 18, [1859], WJSC (342); Stillman to Norton, in camp, Ampersand Pond, August ?, [1859], CENP (7093); Stillman to Norton, in camp, Ampersand Pond, September 30, [1859], CENP (7094).

10. Thomas Wentworth Higginson, "Footpaths," 518.

11. T. W. Higginson to Louisa Higginson, Worcester, September 11, 1859, *Letters and Journals of Thomas Wentworth Higginson,* 121–23.

12. Higginson, "Footpaths," 518–19; T. W. Higginson to Louisa Higginson, Worcester, September 11, 1859, *Letters and Journals of Thomas Wentworth Higginson,* 124; Higginson, "Footpaths," 519.

13. Higginson, "Footpaths," 519.

14. Stillman to Lowell, Ampersand Pond, September 18, [1859], WJSC (342); Ward to Norton, Boston, July 13, 1859, CENP (7701); T. W. Higginson to Louisa Higginson, Worcester, September 11, 1859, *Letters and Journals of Thomas Wentworth Higginson,* 124.

15. Ralph Waldo Emerson, *TJMNRWE*, vol. 14, 312; Longfellow to Ward, Nahant, August 9, 1859, *Letters of Henry Wadsworth Longfellow*, vol. 4, 142–43.

16. Stillman to Norton, Ampersand Pond, September 30, [1859], CENP (7094); Stillman, *TAJ*, 1:290–91; Stillman to Norton, Ampersand Pond, September 30, [1859], CENP (7094).

17. Stillman, *TAJ*, 1:291; Stillman to Norton, London, April 1, [1860], CENP (7101).

18. T. W. Higginson to Louisa Higginson, Worcester, September 11, 1859, *Letters and Journals of Thomas Wentworth Higginson,* 124; Stillman to Lowell, Ampersand Pond, September 18, [1859], WJSC (342).

19. Stillman to Ward, Ampersand Pond, September 29, [1859], PSGW (1195).

20. New York State Comptroller, *List of Lands to Be Sold*, 178; Supreme Court of the State of New York Appellate Division, Third Department, "The People of the State of New York—Plaintiff, Appellant—against Santa Clara Lumber Company et al.—Defendants, Respondent," 751; Stillman to Ward, Ampersand Pond, September 29, [1859], PSGW (1195).

21. Higginson, "Footpaths,"518; Headley, *Adirondack, or Life in the Woods* (1869), 423; "A Week Later from Europe: The Arabia at Halifax, the Nova Scotia at Quebec, and the New York at This Port," *New York Times,* September 22, 1860; Longfellow to James McClelland, Cambridge, 22 September 1859, *Letters of Henry Wadsworth Longfellow,* vol. 4, 148.

22. Lurie, *LALS,* 238–39, 253–55.

23. New York State Comptroller, Register of Bids and Payments for Non-Resident Lands Sold for Unpaid Taxes, 1830–1928, book for tax sale of 1859, RRCSNL (B0845), entry under "Ward & Hoar"; Stillman, *TAJ*, 1:282; New York State Comptroller, Payment receipts for lands purchased at tax sales, 1859–1926, received from Samuel G. Ward and E. R. Hoar, Trustees, December 1, 1859, RRCSNL (B0930); Ward to Hoar, envelope, November [28?], [1859], HFP1.

24. Stillman, *TAJ*, 1:282; Supreme Court, Hamilton Trial Term, "People of the State of New York, plaintiff, v. Joseph H. Ladew and Jenne H. Ladew, defendants," in *The Miscellaneous Reports: Cases Decided in the Courts of Record of the State of New York Other Than the Court of Appeals and the Appellate Division of the Supreme Court,* volume 102 (Albany, J.B. Lyon, 1918), 605–6.

25. Stillman to Lowell, Ampersand Pond, October 13 [or 15], [1859], WJSC (345); Stillman, "Autobiography of William James Stillman. VI. England Again," 822.

26. Stillman to Lowell, Ampersand Pond, October 13 [or 15], [1859], WJSC (345); Stillman, *TAJ*, 1:292.

27. National Park Service, pamphlet, "Harpers Ferry: John Brown's Raid," http://www.nps.gov/hafe/historyculture/upload/John%20Brown%27s%20Raid.pdf; Sanborn, *Recollections of Seventy Years,* 1:163–64; Forbes and Hughes, *Letters and Recollections of John Murray Forbes,* 1:179–82.

28. Hoar to A. A. Lawrence, October 31, 1859, Amos A. Lawrence Papers; National Park Service, pamphlet, "Harpers Ferry: John Brown's Raid"; Thomas Wentworth Higginson, *Cheerful Yesterdays,* 226–28; Ralph Waldo Emerson, "Courage," 242–43; Longfellow, *Life of Henry Wadsworth Longfellow,* vol. 2, 396.

29. Stillman to Norton, mid-Atlantic, January 1, 5, 12, 1860, CENP (7096); Stillman, *TAJ*, 1:292; Stillman to Norton, London, February 17, [1860], CENP (7098).

30. Stillman to Norton, London, February 2, 1860, CENP (7097); Stillman to Norton, London, April 1, 1860, CENP (7101); Stillman to Norton, London, May 4, 1860, CENP (7102).

31. Stillman to Norton, London, February 2, 1860, CENP (7097); Stillman to Norton, London, February 17, [1860], CENP (7098).

32. Smithsonian American Art Museum, "Nineteenth Century American Views: William Stillman: The Forest: Adirondack Woods," http://www.americanart.si.edu/exhibitions/online/photographs/collection/views/stillman; James Schlett, "Stillman's Life, Work Still Gaining Value 100 Years after Death," *The Daily Gazette*, June 22, 2008; "Forest Photographs," *Atlantic Monthly*, January 1860, 109.

33. Longfellow to Ward, Nahant, August 9, 1859, *Letters of Henry Wadsworth Longfellow*, vol. 4, 160n1; Ellen Tucker Emerson to Ralph Waldo Emerson, Concord, February 11, 1860, *Letters of Ellen Tucker Emerson*, 1:209–10.

12. War

1. Stillman, *TAJ*, 1:299–300; Stillman to Lowell, Middlesex Hospital, London, February 21, [18]60, WJSC (363).

2. Stillman, *TAJ*, 1:297–98; Bullock, "William James Stillman," 264–70; Stillman, "Autobiography of William James Stillman. VI. England Again," 812–13.

3. Stillman, "Autobiography, England Again," 816–19; Stillman to H. Woodman, Paris, August 23, [1860], HWP (492); Stillman, *TAJ*, 1:317–18; Stillman, "Autobiography, England Again," 816–19; Ruskin to Norton, Neuchâtel, July 12, 1860, *Letters of John Ruskin to Charles Eliot Norton*, 1:97–99.

4. Stillman, *TAJ*, 1:320; Ruskin to Norton, June 2, 1861, *Letters of John Ruskin to Charles Eliot Norton*, vol. 1, 109–12.

5. Stillman, "Autobiography, England Again," 822–23; Stillman to Sumner, Belmont, Mass., November 20, [1860], WJSC (536).

6. Stillman, *TAJ*, 1:331; Stillman to Sumner, Paris, April 20, 1861, CSC.

7. Howells, *Literary Friends*, 89; Stillman to Lowell, New York, March 11, [1856], WJSC (372).

8. Citizens of Massachusetts, [1860 or 1861], WJSC (76); Stillman, *TAJ*, 1:97; Citizens of Massachusetts, [1860 or 1861], WJSC (76); letter by W. C. Bryant, J. Bigelow, P. Godwin and J. Henderson, [1860 or 1861], WJSC (44); Charles Baldwin Sedgwick to W. H. Seward, Syracuse, March 28, 1861, WJSC (300).

9. Howells, *Literary Friends*, 37; Lowell to Hawthorne, Cambridge, August 5, 1860, *Letters of James Russell Lowell*, 2:52; Duberman, *JRL*, 180–81.

10. Howells, *Literary Friends*, 80–81; Howells, *Interviews with William Dean Howells*, 306; Stillman to Sumner, Paris, April 20, 1861, CSC.

11. Stillman, *TAJ*, 1:331; Bowen, *Massachusetts in the War*, 249–50; Stillman, *TAJ*, 1:332; Stillman to Norton, Chevreuse, near Paris, July 12, 1861, CENP (7109).

12. Bowen, *Massachusetts in the War*, 249.

13. Stillman to Norton, Plainfield, N.J., August 14, 1861, CENP (7111); Stillman to Norton, off Sandy Hook, [July 1861], CENP (7110).

14. Stillman to Norton, Plainfield, N.J., August 14, 1861, CENP (7111); Stillman, *TAJ*, 1:332; Bowen, *Massachusetts in the War*, 250; Stillman to Norton, Plainfield, N.J., August 19, [1861], CENP (7112).

15. Stillman, *TAJ*, 1:332; Eliphalet Nott to W. H. Seward, August 29, [18]61, WJSC (242); Eurania E. Nott to F. Seward, Union College, August 29, 1861, WJSC (243).

16. Stillman to Norton, Saranac Lake, October 3, [1861], CENP (7113); Stillman to Bierstadt, Saranac Lake, Franklin County, September 16, [1861], ABC (64x39.138); Nancy Siegel, "'I Never Had So Difficult a Picture to Paint': Albert Bierstadt's White Mountain Scenery and *The Emerald Pool,*" *Nineteenth-Century Art Worldwide* 4 (Autumn 2005); Stillman to Bierstadt, Saranac Lake, Franklin County, September 16, [1861], ABC (64x39.138). Some scholars have suggested the year of Stillman's letter to Bierstadt is 1859. Although Stillman was in the Adirondacks in September 1859, it is unlikely that he wrote it that year for the following reasons. His letters to Lowell and Norton from August through October 1859 featured the dateline "Ampersand Pond." Stillman to Lowell, Ampersand Pond, September 18, [1859], WJSC (342); Stillman to Lowell, Ampersand Pond, October 13 [or 15], [1859], WJSC (345); Stillman to Norton, in camp, Ampersand Pond, August ?, [1859], CENP (7093); Stillman to Norton, in camp, Ampersand Pond, September 30, [1859], CENP (7094). One exception is a letter he sent to the *Crayon* that September from the "Adirondac Woods." Stillman, country correspondence from Adirondac Woods, September 18, *TC,* October 1859, 321. In contrast, the dateline of a letter Stillman sent to Norton on October 3, [1861], similar to the Bierstadt letter's dateline, is "Saranac Lake." Stillman to Norton, Saranac Lake, October 3, [1861], CENP (7113). Stillman in 1861 was a guide for hire, as evidenced by the services he provided to Edwin James, and that was not the case in 1959, when he was exclusively committed to the Adirondack Club. Finally, he was too busy in September 1859 making preparations for the Adirondack Club's permanent camp and for its acquisition of the Township Twenty-Seven tract to be offering his services as a guide to Bierstadt. Hence the year is 1861.

17. Stillman, *TAJ*, 1:332.

18. Stillman to Norton, Saranac Lake, October 3, [1861], CENP (7113); Wallace, *Descriptive Guide to the Adirondacks (1876),* 118.

19. Headley, *Adirondack, or Life in the Woods* (1869), 424–25; H. Van Dyke, "Ampersand," *Harper's New Monthly Magazine,* July 1885, 226.

20. Stillman to Norton, Saranac Lake, October 3, [1861], CENP (7113). In his 1958 essay "Emerson in the Adirondacks," Paul Jamieson claimed the cabin at Ampersand "served the club members in the summers of 1859 and 1860." This claim, according to Jamieson's citation, appears to have been based on Henry Van Dyke's brief history of the club included in his 1885 essay, "Ampersand," in *Harper's New Monthly Magazine.* Jamieson, "Emerson in the Adirondacks," 233–34n 49. But the clubhouse had not even been constructed by the summer of 1859, and Van Dyke did not say it was used that year or in 1860. Instead, he described the club's downfall, saying, it "existed but for two years, and the little house in the wilderness was abandoned." Van Dyke, "Ampersand," 225–67.

21. Ralph Waldo Emerson, *Later Lectures of Ralph Waldo Emerson,* vol. 2, 199–200; R. W. Emerson, "Genius and Temperament," 200–203.

22. Emerson, "Genius and Temperament," 204.

23. Stillman, "TPC," 604; Thomas Wentworth Higginson, "Barbarism and Civilization," *Atlantic Monthly,* January 1861, 59–60.

24. Stillman to Norton, Saranac Lake, October 3, [1861], CENP (7113).

25. Stillman to Norton, Plainfield, N.J., October 15, [1861], CENP (7114); Stillman to Norton, Plainfield, N.J., November 3, [1861], CENP (7115); Stillman, *TAJ,* 1:84, 97–98.

26. Stillman to Lowell, Plainfield, N.J., November 7, [1861], WJSC (347); Bowen, *Massachusetts in the War,* 250; Stillman to Lowell, Plainfield, N.J., November 7, [1861], WJSC (347).

27. Stillman, *TAJ,* 1:336; Howells, *Literary Friends,* 88–89.

28. Stillman to Norton, London, March 27 [1860], CENP (7100).

29. Goodman and Dawson, *William Dean Howells,* 71–74, 77; Stillman, *TAJ,* 1:336, 340.

13. Peace

1. Stillman, "TPC," 605; Stillman, *TORN,* 266; Headley, *The Adirondack, or Life in the Woods* (1869), 425.

2. Headley, *The Adirondack,* 425–26; R. W. Emerson to S. G. Ward, Concord, March 31, 1876, *TLRWE,* 10:184n 2; Ward to Emerson, 52 Wall Street, March 28, 1876, RWELVC (3361); Ward to Norton, Boston, July 13, 1859, CENP (7701); Emerson to Ward, Concord, August 5, 1859, *TLRWE,* 8:624–25; Rusk, *Life of Ralph Waldo Emerson,* 541.

3. Delaware and Hudson Company, "Referee's Deed, Edward A. Brown, Referee, to Alrick Hubell, June 23, 1860," *Corporate History,* 3:98–100.

4. Delaware and Hudson Company, "Quit-Claim Deed, Alrick Hubell, and Wife to the Adirondac Estate Railroad Co., Aug. 13, 1860," *Corporate History,* 3:128–30; Donaldson, *AHA,* 1:134–35; Supreme Court of the State of New York Appellate Division, Third Department, "The People of the State of New York—Plaintiff, Appellant—against Santa Clara Lumber Company et al.—Defendants, Respondent," 669–81.

5. Bowditch, *Life and Correspondence of Henry Ingersoll Bowditch,* 2:69–70; Packard, "Memoir of Jeffries Wyman," 91.

6. Donaldson, *AHA,* 1:215, 317–18, 322–25, 365.

7. Perkins and Grant, *Boston Athenaeum Art Exhibition Index,* 118; Richards, "A Forest Story [Part] I, 321.

8. Street, *Woods and Waters,* 13–25, 64, 142–47.

9. Lurie, *LALS,* 305–7, 312, 333, 336, 345, 350.

10. Duberman, *JRL,* 214–15, 220–21.

11. Stillman, *TAJ,* 1:341–60, 371–72; Stillman to Norton, [New York], September 29, 1863, CENP (7119); Dyson, *Last Amateur,* 110; Stillman, *TAJ,* 1:371–72; Dyson, *Last Amateur,* 120–23.

12. Stillman, *TAJ,* 1:373–74; Bryon Andreasen, research historian at the Abraham Lincoln Presidential Library and Museum in Springfield, Illinois, e-mail to author, December 16, 2011. According to Andreasen, Stillman's commission is located at the National Archives in College Park, Maryland. It is recorded in the Records of the Department of State, Group 59, Application Records, Commissions, Permanent Commissions, 1803–1910, vol. 5, p. 148. The Senate records contain Stillman's nomination for the appointment.

13. Stillman, *TAJ*, 2:388; Stillman Family Genealogy Home Page, "Children of Joseph Stillman II and Elizabeth Ward Mason," http://www.stillman.org/e44.htm; Dyson, *Last Amateur*, 126; Stillman, *TAJ*, 2:387–88; Stillman Family Genealogy Home Page, "Children of William James Stillman and 1st Wife—Laura Mack," http://www.stillman.org/f267.htm, December 4, 2011; Stillman, *TAJ*, 1:373–74; Reid, *Crisis of the Ottoman Empire*, 212–13.

14. Stillman to Lowell, U.S. Consulate, Rome, January 28, [18]65, WJSC (367).

15. Domestic Items, *New York Times*, March 21, 1867; Edward W. Emerson, *TEYSC*, 274, 411.

16. Stillman Family Genealogy Homepage, "Children of William James Stillman and 1st Wife—Laura Mack"; Stillman, *TAJ*, 2:400, 404, 436, 455–56, 461.

17. Storey and Emerson, *ERHM*, 162–63, 180–93; Stillman, *TAJ*, 2:455; Hugo Hillebrandt obituary, *New York Times*, April 7, 1896; Stillman, *TAJ*, 2:455; Hoar to Stillman, Washington, March 4, 1870, WJSC (154).

18. Ralph Waldo Emerson, *TLRWE*, 5:411; R. W. Emerson to Ellen Emerson, Williamstown, Mass., November 11, 1865, *TLRWE*, 5:434.

19. Gordon, *Thread across the Ocean*, 170–73.

20. Ibid., 177–83, 188, 198–202; "The Atlantic Cable: Successful Completion of the Great Work: The Old and New Worlds Joined Together," *New York Times*, July 30, 1866; "News of the Morning," *Sacramento Daily Union*, September 13, 1866; Ralph Waldo Emerson, *Journals of Ralph Waldo Emerson*, vol. 10, 155.

21. "What the Boston Writers Are Doing," *Flake's Bulletin*, November 7, 1866.

22. Ralph Waldo Emerson, *The Poetry Notebooks of Ralph Waldo Emerson*, 744.

23. Ralph Waldo Emerson, "TA," 158.

24. Stowe, "Transcendental Vacations," 502–05; Ralph Waldo Emerson, "Nature," 54.

25. Edward W. Emerson, *TEYSC*, 188; Whittier, "Questions of Life," in *Poetical Works of John Greenleaf Whittier*, 157–59.

26. Terrie, "Romantic Travelers," 68–74; Terrie, *Forever Wild*, 59–65; Terrie, "Romantic Travelers," 72.

27. David A. Wasson, review of *May Day and Other Pieces*, in Myerson, *Emerson and Thoreau: The Contemporary Reviews*, 313; C. E. Norton, "Mr. Emerson's Poems," in Myerson, *Emerson and Thoreau*, 308–10; C. E. Norton, review of *May Day and Other Pieces*, in Myerson, *Emerson and Thoreau*, 312; William Dean Howells, review of *May Day and Other Pieces*, in Myerson, *Emerson and Thoreau*, 317; "Emerson's New Poems," Christian Recorder, June 1, 1867.

28. Joseph Jones, "Thought's New-Found Path and the Wilderness," in Porte, *Emerson: Prospect and Retrospect*, 105–19.

29. Emerson, "TA," 150; Nash, "American Cult of the Primitive," 518, 520–22.

30. Nash, "American Cult of the Primitive," 523, 526; Jackson Lears, *No Place of Grace*, 4–10.

31. Emerson, "TA," 150–51, 157.

32. Street, *Woods and Waters*, 80–81.

33. Emerson, "Nature," 39; Headley, *The Adirondack* (1869), 167–68; Emerson to Thoreau, Concord, May 11, 1858, *TLRWE*, 8:56; Emerson to Muir, Concord, February 5, 1872, *TLRWE*, 10:67–68.

34. Stillman, "TPC," 599.

35. Stillman to Taylor, Clapham Common, July 6, 1873, BTP.

14. The Ravages of Modern Improvement

1. Henry Van Dyke, "Ampersand," in *Little Rivers*, 77–78.

2. Ibid. In the 1885 *Harper's* version of "Ampersand," Van Dyke claimed he went to the pond "ten years ago," probably prompting Paul Jamieson to date the year of this visit as 1875. Van Dyke, "Ampersand," *Harper's New Monthly Magazine*, 225; Jamieson, "Emerson in the Adirondacs," 234. But in a later version of the essay in *Little Rivers*, Van Dyke states, "In 1878, when I spent three weeks at Ampersand, the cabin was in ruins, and surrounded by an almost impenetrable growth of bushes." "Ampersand," in *Little Rivers*, 77.

3. Tetrius Van Dyke, *Henry Van Dyke: A Biography*, 76–79, 416.

4. Richard Plunz, "City, Culture, Nature: The New York Wilderness and the Urban Sublime," in Madsen and Plunz, *Urban Lifeworld*, 58.

5. Donaldson, *AHA*, 1:193–94.

6. Wallace, *Descriptive Guide to the Adirondacks* (1876), 118; Sweetser, *Middle States*, 3, 146.

7. Wallace, *Descriptive Guide to the Adirondacks* (1876.), 218; Sweetser, *Middle States*, 150.

8. Ralph Waldo Emerson, "Civilization," 18–19, 30; R. W. Emerson to J. R. Lowell, Concord, July 25, 1859, *TLRWE*, 5:166; R. W. Emerson, "Self-Reliance," 198.

9. R. W. Emerson, "Eloquence," 77; Emerson, "Self-Reliance," 200–202.

10. Headley, *The Adirondack, or, Life in the Woods* (1869), 426–29.

11. Delaware and Hudson Company, "Articles of Association of the Adirondack Railway company, Filed July 7, 1882," *Corporate History*, 3:256–62; Delaware and Hudson Company, "Deed, WM. Sutphen and WM. W. Durant to the Adirondack Railroad Co., Nov. 24, 1882," *Corporate History*, 3:265–77.

12. [C. L. Brace], "Adirondack," *New York Times*, August 9, 1864; Graham, *Adirondack Park*, 68.

13. Colvin, "Ascent and Barometrical Measurement of Mount Seward," 8–12; Terrie, *Forever Wild*, 78, 95–96, 102.

14. Santayana, *Character and Opinion in the United States*, 1–2.

15. Lurie, *LALS*, 381–85; Louis Agassiz, "Evolution and Permanence of Type," *Atlantic Monthly*, January 1874, 94–96, 101.

16. Stillman, *TAJ*, 1:306; Lawrence Buell, "The Transcendentalist Movement," in Myerson, *The Transcendentalists*, 152–53.

17. Duberman, *JRL*, 268, 287; James Russell Lowell, "Agassiz," *Atlantic Monthly*, May 1874, 587, 591.

18. Geldard, *Essential Transcendentalist*, 233–34; Miller, *Transcendentalists*, 13–14; Capper, "'A Little Beyond,'" 505–7.

19. Babcock Millhouse, *American Wilderness*, 171, 173; Eleanor Jones Harvey, "Tastes in Transition: Gifford's Patrons," in Avery and Kelly, *Hudson River School Visions*, 86.

20. Babcock Millhouse, *American Wilderness*, 168, 171, 173, 179; Harvey, "Tastes in Transition," 86, 75; Kevin J. Avery and Franklin Kelly, "Catalogue," in Avery and Kelly, *Hudson River School Visions*, 230; Philippe de Montebello, director's foreword to

Avery and Kelly, *Hudson River School Visions,* vii; Babcock Millhouse, *American Wilderness,* 178; William James Stillman, "The Paris Exposition.—IX: American Painting," *Nation,* October 3, 1878, 210.

21. Stillman, *TAJ,* 2:454; Stillman to Norton, Syra, Greece, September 8, 1869, CENP (7174); Stillman, *TAJ,* 2:462; Colin Eisler, "Stillman—Apostle of Art," in Ehrenkranz, *Poetic Localities* 111–12.

22. Stillman, *TAJ,* 2:465–66; Ralph Waldo Emerson, *Journals of Ralph Waldo Emerson,* vol. 10, 328; Lefcowitz, Lefcowitz, and Bryce, "James Byrce's First Visit to America," 322.

23. Hoar to Stillman, Washington, D.C., March 10, [1870], WJSC (155); Storey and Emerson, *ERHM,* 220–21, 229, 234.

24. Stillman, *TAJ,* 2:466, 485–86; Stillman Family Genealogy Home Page, "Children of William James Stillman and 2nd wife—Marie Spartali," http://www.stillman.org/f267.htm.

25. Stillman, *TAJ,* 2:466, 485–88.

26. Lefcowitz, Lefcowitz, and Bryce, "James Bryce's First Visit to America," 318.

27. Luria, "Wealth, Capital, and Power," 263–64; Angel, "Consolidation in the Global Equity Market," 10, 17–18.

28. Gross, "Transcendentalism and Urbanism," 377, 380; Storey and Emerson, *ERHM,* 312–13.

29. Stillman to Taylor, Clapham Common, July 6, 1873, BTP; Stillman to Taylor, Clapham Common, September 17, 1873, BTP; Stillman to Taylor, Clapham Common, September 8, 1873, BTP; Stillman to Taylor, Clapham Common, February 23, 1874, BTP; Stillman to Taylor, Clapham Common, March 20, 1874, BTP.

30. Stillman, *TAJ,* 2:500; Stillman, "Recreation and Solitude," 12.

31. Hosea Biglow [James Russell Lowell] to C. E. Norton, Elmwood, October 7, 1874, *Letters of James Russell Lowell,* 2:131–33; Stillman to Taylor, Clapham Commons, March 20, 1874, BTP.

32. Stillman, preface to *Poetic Localities of Cambridge,* n.p.

33. Ibid.

34. Stillman, *TAJ,* 2:500–501; Stillman Family Genealogy Home Page, "Children of William James Stillman and 1st wife Laura Mack," http://www.stillman.org/f267.htm; Stillman, *TAJ,* 2:505; Stillman, *Herzegovina and the Late Uprising,* 1; Reid, *Crisis of the Ottoman Empire,* 308–15; 506, 557; Stillman, *TAJ,* 2:622.

35. Stillman, "Recreation and Solitude," 13–14.

36. Lowell to Marie Spartali Stillman, 10 Lowndes Square, February 10, 1882, WJSC (189); Stillman, *TAJ,* 2:696; "Reported Murder of W. J. Stillman," *San Francisco Daily Evening Bulletin,* February 17, 1882.

37. Stillman, "A Few of Lowell's Letters," 757; Lowell to M. S. Stillman, 10 Lowndes Square, February 10, 1882, WJSC (189).

38. Stillman, *TAJ,* 2:692–95.

39. "Reported Murder of W. J. Stillman"; Stillman, *TAJ,* 2:696.

40. Stillman, "A Few of Lowell's Letters," 757.

41. Stillman, *TAJ,* 2:661–63.

42. Stillman to Howells, New York, December 11, 1883, HFP2 (457); "The Adirondack Forest: Seen Again after Twenty-Five Years," *New York Times,* September 2, 1883; Terrie, *Forever Wild,* 95–96.

43. "The Adirondack Forests," *New York Evening Post,* December 3, 1883.

44. William James Stillman, "The Curium Treasures," *New York Times,* June 14, 1884; "An Old Firm Retiring: S. G. & G. C. Ward to Give Up Business at the End of the Year," *New York Times,* December 1, 1885; William James Stillman, "Boston Museum of Fine Arts," *Nation,* July 24, 1884, 69.

45. Holmes, "Professor Jeffries Wyman," 614–15.

46. "Mr. Woodman's Disappearance: A Boston Lawyer's Supposed Suicide from a Fall River Steam-Boat," *New York Times,* January 12, 1879; Cooke, "Saturday Club," 29; Massachusetts Historical Society, Binney Family Papers, 1797–1878, Guide to the Collection, http://www.masshist.org/collection-guides/view/fa0338. Binney, *Genealogy of the Binney Family,* 172–73.

47. Rusk, *Life of Ralph Waldo Emerson,* 486, 507–08.

48. R. W. Emerson, "Greatness," 272.

49. Lowell, "Democracy," 481; Stillman, *TAJ,* 1:216, 2:716.

50. William James Stillman, "The Adirondacks To-day," *Nation,* August 14, 1884, 130–31; Donaldson, *History of the Adirondacks,* 303.

51. Stillman, "TPC," 606; Stillman, "The Adirondacks To-day," 130; Terrie, *Forever Wild,* 96; Stillman, "The Adirondacks To-day," 131.

52. Donaldson, *AHA,* 304n1. This footnote details Stillman's storytelling at Martin's and his return trip to Ampersand. Donaldson dated the Stillmans' visit to Martin's new hotel as 1886. However, Stillman's correspondence to the *Nation* places him in Europe in 1886. "State Lands Given Away: Attorney General Declares Company Got Title Despite Court of Appeals: Opens a Forest Scandal: Beautiful Ampersand Pond, Made Famous by Agassiz, Is Controlled by a Lumber Company," *New York Times,* May 13, 1907; New York State Commissioners of Fisheries, Game and Forests, *Third Annual Report,* 440.

53. William James Stillman, "Steamship Cuisine." *Nation,* September 4, 1884, 196; Stillman, "A Few of Lowell's Letters,"757; Duberman, *JRL,* 335–37; Stillman, "A Few of Lowell's Letters," 757; Elliot, *A Pre-Raphaelite Marriage,* 135–37.

54. Storey and Emerson, *ERHM,* 318–20, 325, Cooke, "Saturday Club," 32–34; Lowell to R. W. Gilder, Deerfoot Farm, Southborough, Mass., June 14, 1885, *Letters of James Russell Lowell,* 2:296; obituary for Estes Howe, M.D., *Boston Medical and Surgical Journal,* January 27, 1897, 100.

55. Stillman, *TAJ,* 2:682; Dyson, *Last Amateur,* 264–65; Lyons, *Charles Stewart Parnell,* 205–7, 370–75; "The Parnell Commission: Text of the Bill Offered by the Government," *New York Times,* July 19, 1888; Terrie, *Forever Wild,* 96–97; Stillman, *TAJ,* 2:685–86.

15. The Old America and the New

1. "Rush to the Adirondacks: More Guests at the Hotels Than Ever in the Month of June," *New York Times,* June 18, 1893.

2. "In the Heart of the Adirondacks: More Strangers at Saranac Lake and Lake Placid Than Ever Before," *New York Times,* July 9, 1893; "News from the Adirondacks: Fine Weather, Much Doing, and Throngs of Visitors," *New York Times,* August 13, 1893.

3. Terrie, *Forever Wild,* 102–3; "Gov. Flowers' Message: Many Suggestions Made to the Legislature," *New York Times,* January 4, 1893; "Adirondack Plateau: The Forest Commission Issues an Interesting Report," *New York Times,* September 4, 1892.

4. Stillman, "A Few of Lowell's Letters," 756.

5. "The 'Century' for August," *New York Times,* August 4, 1893.

6. Don Carlos, "A Trip to the Saranac Lakes," *New York Evening Post,* August 30, 1858.

7. Hirshfield, *Given Sugar, Given Salt,* 31.

8. Bien, "Franklin County," in *Atlas of the State of New York,* 18.

9. Stillman, "TPC," 598–600.

10. Nash, "American Cult of the Primitive," 522.

11. Wallace, *Descriptive Guide to the Adirondacks* (1894), 256, 448–49; Storey and Emerson, *ERHM,* 312; unidentified article quoting clauses of Hoar's will, [1895], Prichard Family Papers, William Munroe Special Collections, Concord Free Public Library.

12. "Gov. Flowers' Message"; "Gov. Flowers Is Satisfied: Much Pleased with the Legislative Session," *New York Times,* April 20, 1893.

13. New York State Forest Commission, *Annual Report of the Forest Commission for the Year 1893,* vol. 1, 198–99.

14. "Large Purchase of Timberland: A Syndicate to Control 400,000 acres—to Preserve the Forest," *New York Daily Tribune,* July 18, 1889; Supreme Court of the State of New York Appellate Division, Third Department, "The People of the State of New York—Plaintiff, Appellant—against Santa Clara Lumber Company et al.—Defendants, Respondent," 676–77; Syracuse University Library, "Adirondack Timber & Mineral Company Correspondence, Finding Aids, http://library.syr. edu/digital/guides/a/adirondack_timber.htm; New York State Forest Commission, *Annual Report,* vol. 1, 198–99.

15. Terrie, *Forever Wild,* 104–8.

16. Dyson, *Last Amateur,* 281; Stillman, *TORN,* b.

17. Stillman, *TORN,* 265–66.

18. "Stillman's Essays," *Nation,* January 13, 1898, 31; "Mr. Stillman's Essays," *New Outlook,* April 16, 1858, 977–79; "Editor's Study," *Harper's New Monthly Magazine,* March 1898, 640–44.

19. Elizabeth Carey Agassiz to Stillman, Cambridge, March 30, 1898, WJSC (1); Ward to Stillman, Seabright, September 30, [18]98, WJSC (574).

20. Norton to Stillman, Ashfield, Mass., June 26, 1898, WJSC (241). Norton in this letter did not specifically reference the Spanish-American War, but he explained that since February 1898, he had had "little disposition to write because of the condition of public affairs which made my heart heavy." The explosion of the USS *Maine* in Havana Harbor, Cuba—the impetus for the war—occurred on February 15, 1898.

21. Cooke, "The Saturday Club," 34; "Brother of the Autocrat: Serious Illness of John Holmes at His Home in Cambridge," *New York Times,* November 3, 1897.

22. Stillman, "Plea for Wild Animals," 841–42.

23. Ibid.

24. "William J. Stillman: His Autobiography as a Puritan Journalist," *New York Times,* March 30, 1901.

25. Ibid.; Books, *Omaha World Herald,* May 26, 1901; J. W. Chadwick, "The Autobiography of a Journalist by William James Stillman." *American Historical Review* 7 (October 1901): 171, 173.

26. Howells, "An Earlier American," 934–40, 942–43.

27. Ibid., 936, 944.

28. William James Stillman, "English Country Life," *Nation,* October 11, 1900, 286–87.

29. Notes, *Nation,* July 11, 1901, 35; Stillman, *TAJ,*1:vi.

30. "Death of W. J. Stillman: His Intimacy with Ruskin and Kossuth—His Work as a War Correspondent in Crete," *New York Times,* July 9, 1901.

Conclusion

1. Jackson, *Annual Report of the Attorney General,* 8.

2. "State Lands Given Away, Jackson Says," *New York Times,* May 13, 1907; Supreme Court of the State of New York Appellate Division, Third Department, "The People of the State of New York—Plaintiff, Appellant—against Santa Clara Lumber Company—Defendant, Respondent: Appellant's Brief," 6–8.

3. Supreme Court of the State of New York Appellate Division, Third Department, "The People of the State of New York—Plaintiff, Appellant—against Santa Clara Lumber Company et al.—Defendants, Respondent," 681–83; Davies, *Annual Report of the Attorney General,* 32–33; Edmund H. Smith, Reports of Cases Decided in the Court of Appeals, 372; "State Lands Given Away, Jackson Says," *New York Times,* May 13, 1907.

4. "State Lands Given Away, Jackson Says," *New York Times,* May 13, 1907; Supreme Court of the State of New York Appellate Division, Third Department, "The People of the State of New York—Plaintiff, Appellant—against Santa Clara Lumber Company et al.—Defendants, Respondent," 681–86; Jenkins, "Do Unharvested Adirondack Forests Contain Forest Interior Plants?," 14; "State Lands Given Away, Jackson Says."

5. "State Lands Given Away, Jackson Says," *New York Times,* May 13, 1907.

6. Jackson, "Annual Report of the Attorney General," 56–57; McMartin, *Privately Owned Adirondacks,* 111–12; Jenkins, "Do Unharvested Adirondack Forests Contain Forest Interior Plants?," 14.

7. Bill Frenette, "Transitions: Notes on a Proud Past with Attention to Future Annals," no. 128, *Tupper Lake Free Press,* October 20, 2004.

8. Seaver, *Historical Sketches of Franklin County,* 137–38; Bill Frenette, "Transitions: Notes on a Proud Past with Attention to Future Annals," no. 74, *Tupper Lake Free Press,* June 20, 2001; Frenette, "Transitions," no. 128; Supreme Court of the State of New York Appellate Division, Third Department, "The People of the State of New York," 717.

9. "To Sell 14,000 Acres: Agents Are Named for Resort near Tupper Lake," *New York Times,* August 6, 1950; obituary for John S. McCormick Jr. '35, *Princeton Alumni Weekly,* November 1, 2010; James Schlett, "Return to the Philosophers' Camp," *Schenectady Daily Gazette,* June 22, 2008.

10. Nathan Brown, "Nature Conservancy Buys Long-Sought Follensby Property," *Adirondack Daily Enterprise,* September 18, 2008; Christopher Shaw, "Back to the Source," *Adirondack Life,* August 2011.

11. White, *Adirondack Country,* 179; Terrie, "Romantic Travelers in the Adirondack Wilderness," 60.

12. Terrie, "Romantic Travelers in the Adirondack Wilderness," 73–74.

13. Michael Carr (executive director of the Adirondack chapter of the Nature Conservancy), in phone interview with author, October 23, 2012.

14. Allan R. Gold, "The 1990 Elections: New York—Bond Act: Voters Appear to Reject Environmental Measure," *New York Times,* November 7, 1990; Davis, *2020 Vision,* 22.

15. Allan R. Gold, "The 1990 Elections: New York—Bond Act: New Math on Both Sides of the Hudson; Defeat of the Environmental Bond Act May Mean Higher Taxes in New York," *New York Times,* November 8, 1990; "State Court Halts Bond Act Promotion," *Daily Gazette,* September 29, 1990.

16. "Environmental Critics Say Fund Is Doomed from the Start," *Albany Times Union,* January 22, 1992; Sam H. Verhovek, "A Plan to Conserve New York's Wilderness," *New York Times,* June 28, 1992; Peter Wehwrein, "Adirondack Sites Not Part of Report," *Albany Times Union,* December 6, 1991; Association for the Protection of the Adirondacks, "Save Follensby Park!" pamphlet, 1993; Verhovek, "Plan to Conserve New York's Wilderness"; New York State Department of Environmental Conservation and Office of Parks, Recreation and Historic Preservation, "Conserving Open Space in New York State," 183.

17. Schneider, *The Adirondacks,* 297–89; David Gibson (executive director of the Association for the Protection of the Adirondacks), in phone interview with author, October 19, 2012.

18. Association for the Protection of the Adirondacks, "Save Follensby Park!"; Peter Wehwrein, "Cuomo Signs Legislation to Create Environmental Protection Fund," *Albany Times Union,* August 18, 1993.

19. Associated Press, "State to Buy, Protect 3 Key Adirondack Parcels," *Albany Times Union,* June 10, 1994; Fred LeBrun, "Budgeting to Balance Soil and Sand," *Albany Times Union,* June 13, 1994.

20. Carr interview; Schlett, "Return to the Philosophers' Camp."

21. James Schlett, "Conservation Group Buys Site of Historic Gathering: Poet Emerson among Luminaries in 1858," *Schenectady Daily Gazette,* September 19, 2008; Martin Espinoza, "Preserving Adirondack Land Where Emerson Camped," *New York Times,* September 19, 2008.

22. "Emerson's Fabled Site Part of Sale," *Albany Times Union,* September 19, 2008; Fred LeBrun, "This Pond Is Golden to Us All," *Albany Times Union,* September 21, 2008; Nature Conservancy, "Nature Conservancy Purchases Follensby Pond in the Adirondacks," press release, September 19, 2008.

23. Schneider, *The Adirondacks,* 9; Adirondack Council, "Adirondack Council Praises Nature Conservancy's Purchase of Follensby Pond," press release, September 18, 2008, http://www.adirondackcouncil.org/follensby908pr.html; Carr interview.

Postscript

1. U.S. Department of Agriculture, "USDA Announces Grants to Protect Private Forest Land in 33 States," press release, April 14, 2010; Rick Karlin, "Historic Land Purchase Will Have to Wait," *Capital Confidential* (blog), *Albany Times Union,* February 4, 2013, http://blog.timesunion.com/capitol/archives/177669/historic-land-purchase-will-have-to-wait; Nature Conservancy (Adirondack Chapter),

"Field Notes: 2013 Annual Report," 7, http://www.nature.org/ourinitiatives/regions/northamerica/unitedstates/newyork/adirondacks-annual-report-2013-part-1.pdf.

2. Chris Knight, "State Loses Grant for Follensby Land Purchase," *Adirondack Daily Enterprise,* February 5, 2013; New York State Office of the Governor, "Governor Cuomo Announces Unprecedented Acquisition of 69,000 Acres of the Former Finch Pruyn Lands in the Adirondack Park," press release, August 5, 2012.

✨ SELECT BIBLIOGRAPHY

Original Manuscript Sources

Albert Bierstadt Collection. Collection 276, folder 17. Joseph Downs Collection of Manuscripts and Printed Ephemera. Winterthur Library, Winterthur, DE.

Amos A. Lawrence Papers, 1817–86. MS. N-1559. Massachusetts Historical Society, Boston.

Bayard Taylor Papers. Collection no. 14/18/1169. Division of Rare and Manuscript Collections. Cornell University Library, Ithaca, NY.

Charles Eliot Norton Papers. MS Am 1088. Houghton Library, Harvard University, Cambridge, MA.

Charles Sumner Correspondence. MS Am 1. Houghton Library, Harvard University, Cambridge, MA.

Dana Family Papers. MS. N-1088. Massachusetts Historical Society, Boston.

Hoar Family Papers. William Munroe Special Collections. Concord Free Public Library, Concord, MA.

Horatio Woodman Papers. MS. N-492. Massachusetts Historical Society, Boston.

Howells Family Papers. MS Am 1784. Houghton Library, Harvard University, Cambridge, MA.

John Durand Papers. Manuscripts and Archives Division, New York Public Library. Astor, Lenox, and Tilden Foundation.

Letter File (1755–1995). William Munroe Special Collections. Concord Free Public Library, Concord, MA.

Letters to Henry Wadsworth Longfellow. MS Am 1340.2. By permission of the Houghton Library, Harvard University, Cambridge, MA.

Papers of Samuel Gray Ward and Anna Hazard Barker Ward. MS Am 1465. Houghton Library, Harvard University, Cambridge, MA.

Ralph Waldo Emerson Journals and Notebooks. MS Am 1280H (112e). Ralph Waldo Emerson Memorial Association deposit. Houghton Library, Harvard University, Cambridge, MA.

Ralph Waldo Emerson Letters from Various Correspondents. MS Am 1280. Ralph Waldo Emerson Memorial Association deposit. Houghton Library, Harvard University, Cambridge, MA.

Records Relating to Comptroller's Sale of Non-resident Lands for Unpaid Taxes, 1799–1928. New York State Archives, Albany, NY.

William James Stillman Collection. Special Collections. Schaffer Library, Union College, Schenectady, NY.

Books and Articles

Adams, Charles F. *Richard Henry Dana: A Biography.* 2 vols. Boston: Houghton, Mifflin, 1890.

Agassiz, Jean Louis Rodolphe. *An Essay on Classification.* London: Longman, Brown, Green, Longmans, and Roberts, and Trubner, 1859.

——. *The Intelligence of Louis Agassiz: A Specimen Book of Scientific Writings.* Edited and with introduction by Guy Davenport. Boston: Beacon Press, 1963.

——. *Louis Agassiz: His Life and Correspondence.* Vol. 1. Edited by Elizabeth Cabot Cary Agassiz. Boston: Houghton Mifflin, 1886.

Agassiz, Jean Louis Rodolphe, and J. Elliot Cabot. *Lake Superior: Its Physical Character, Vegetable and Animals, Compared with Those of Other and Similar Regions.* Boston: Gould, Kendall and Lincoln, 1850.

American Psychiatric Association. *Diagnostic and Statistical Manual of Mental Disorders.* 4th ed. Washington, DC: American Psychiatric Association, 1994.

Angel, James. "Consolidation in the Global Equity Market: A Historical Perspective." Working paper, February 19, 1998.

Angus, Charles. *The Extraordinary Journey of Clarence Petty: Wilderness Guide, Pilot, and Conservationist.* Syracuse, NY: Syracuse University Press, 2002.

Avery, Kevin J., and Franklin Kelly, eds. *Hudson River School Visions: The Landscapes of Sanford R. Gifford.* New York: Metropolitan Museum of Art, 2003.

Babcock Millhouse, Barbara. *American Wilderness: The Story of the Hudson River School of Painting.* New York: Black Dome Press, 2007.

Baur, John I. H. Review of *The Daring Young Men: The Story of the American Pre-Raphaelites* by David H. Dickason. *Art Bulletin* 36 (March 1954): 79–81.

Bien, Joseph R. *Atlas of the State of New York.* New York: Julius Bien, 1895.

Binney, Charles James Fox. *Genealogy of the Binney Family in the United States.* Albany, NY: Joel Munsell's Sons, 1886.

Bishop, John Leander, Edwin Troxell Freedly, and Edward Young. *A History of American Manufacturers from 1608 to 1860.* 2 vols. London: Sampson, Low, Son & Co., 1864.

Blumin, Stuart M. *The Emergence of the Middle Class: Social Experience in the American City, 1760–1900.* Ithaca: Cornell University Press, 1989.

Bowditch, Henry I. *Life and Correspondence of Henry Ingersoll Bowditch.* Edited by Vincent Y. Bowditch. 2 vols. Boston: Houghton, Mifflin, 1902.

Bowen, James L. *Massachusetts in the War: 1861–1865.* Springfield, MA: Clark W. Bryan, 1889.

Brumley, Charles. *Guides of the Adirondacks: A Short Story of History: A Short Season, Hard Work, Low Pay.* Utica, NY: North Country Books, 1994.

Bryant, William Cullen. *The Letters of William Cullen Bryant.* Vol. 2, *1836–1849.* Edited by William Cullen Bryant II and Thomas G. Voss. New York: Fordham University Press, 1977.

——. *The Letters of William Cullen Bryant.* Vol. 3, *1848–1857.* Edited by William Cullen Bryant II and Thomas G. Voss. New York: Fordham University Press, 1981.

Bullock, Richard D. "William James Stillman: The Early Years." PhD dissertation, University of Michigan (Ann Arbor), 1976

Capper, Charles. "'A Little Beyond': The Problem of the Transcendentalist Movement in American History." *Journal of American History* 85 (September 1998): 502–39.

Collins, Geraldine. *The Brighton Story: Begin the History of Paul Smith, Gabriels and Rainbow Lake.* Lakemont, NY: North Country Books, 1977.

Colvin, Verplanck. "Ascent and Barometrical Measurement of Mount Seward." In *Twenty-Fourth Annual Report of the New York State Museum of Natural History, for the Year 1870.* Albany: Argus Company, 1872.

———. *Report of the Superintendent of the Land Survey of the State of New York* [for 1896], transmitted to the legislature March 9, 1897. New York: Wynkoop Hallenback Crawford, 1897.

Comfort, Philip W., and Walter A. Elell. *Tyndale Bible Dictionary.* Carol Stream, IL: Tyndale House, 2001.

Cooke, George W. "The Saturday Club." *New England Magazine,* September 1898, 23–34.

Copplestone, Trewin. *The Hudson River School.* New York: Gramercy Books, 1999.

Davies, John C. *Annual Report of the Attorney General of the State of New York for the Year Ending December 31, 1899.* Albany: J. B. Lyon, 1900.

Davis, George D. *2020 Vision: Fulfilling the Promise of the Adirondack Park.* Vol. 2. Elizabethtown, NY: Adirondack Council, 1990.

Dearinger, David B., ed. *Paintings and Sculptures in the Collection of the National Academy of Design.* Manchester, VT: Hudson Hills Press, 2004.

Delaware and Hudson Company. *Corporate History of the Delaware and Hudson Company and Subsidiary Companies.* 4 vols. No place or publisher, 1906.

DeWolfe Howe, M. A. "Charles Eliot Norton (1827–1908)." *Proceedings of the American Academy of Arts and Sciences* 56 (September 1921): 405–7.

Donaldson, Alfred L. *A History of the Adirondacks.* 2 vols. New York: The Century, 1921.

Duberman, Martin B. *James Russell Lowell: Poet, Critic, Editor, Teacher, Diplomat, Friend of Freedom—and a Man of Warmth, Wit and Integrity.* Boston: Houghton Mifflin, 1966.

Durand, John, and William James Stillman, eds. *The Crayon.* 8 vols. New York: W. Hollinger, 1955–61.

Dyson, Stephen L. *The Last Amateur: The Life of William James Stillman.* Albany: State University of New York Press, 2014.

Ehrenkranz, Anne, ed. *Poetic Localities: Photographs of Adirondacks, Cambridge, Crete, Italy, Athens.* New York: Aperture Books, 1988.

Elliot, David B. *A Pre-Raphaelite Marriage: The Lives and Works of Marie Spartali Stillman and William James Stillman.* London: Antique Collector's Club Limited, 2006.

Emerson, Edward W. *The Early Years of the Saturday Club: 1855–1870.* Vol. 1. Boston: Houghton Mifflin, 1918.

Emerson, Ellen Tucker. *The Letters of Ellen Tucker Emerson.* Edited by Edith E. W. Gregg. 2 vols. Kent, OH: Kent State University Press, 1982.

Emerson, Ralph Waldo. "The Adirondacs: A Journal." In *Ralph Waldo Emerson: Collected Poems and Selected Translations,* edited by Harold Bloom and Paul Kame, 149–58. New York: Library of America, 1994.

———. "The American Scholar." In *Ralph Waldo Emerson: Essays and Lectures,* edited by Joel Porter, 51–72. New York: Library of America, 1994.

———. "Civilization." In *Society and Solitude: Twelve Chapters,* 15–30. Boston: Fields, Osgood, 1870.

———. "Compensation." In *The Essential Writings of Ralph Waldo Emerson,* edited by Brooks Atkinson, 154–71. New York: Modern Library, 2000.

———. *The Complete Works of Ralph Waldo Emerson.* Edited by Edward W. Emerson. Vol. 7, *Society and Solitude: Twelve Chapters.* Centenary ed. Boston: Houghton, Mifflin, 1904.

———. *The Complete Works of Ralph Waldo Emerson.* Edited by Edward W. Emerson. Vol. 8, *Letters and Social Aims.* Boston: Houghton Mifflin, 1904.

———. *The Complete Works of Ralph Waldo Emerson.* Edited by Edward W. Emerson. Vol. 9, *Poems.* Concord ed. Boston: Houghton Mifflin, 1904.

———. *The Complete Works of Ralph Waldo Emerson.* Vol. 10, *Lectures and Biographical Sketches.* Concord ed. Boston: Houghton Mifflin, 1904.

———. "Courage." In *Society and Solitude: Twelve Chapters,* 225–50. Boston: Fields, Osgood, 1870.

———. "Eloquence." In *Society and Solitude: Twelve Chapters,* 53–90. Boston: Fields, Osgood, 1870.

———. *English Traits.* In Porter, *Ralph Waldo Emerson: Essays and Lectures,* 763–936. New York: Library of America, 1994.

———. "Genius and Temperament." In *The Later Lectures of Ralph Waldo Emerson.* Vol. 2, *1843–1871,* edited by Ronald A. Bosco and Joel Myerson, 200–211. Athens: University of Georgia Press, 2001.

———. "Greatness." In *Letters and Social Aims,* 267–86. Boston: James R. Osgood, 1876.

———. *The Heart of Emerson's Journals.* Edited by Bliss Perry. New York: Dover Publications, 1995.

———. *The Journals and Miscellaneous Notebooks of Ralph Waldo Emerson.* Vol. 13, *1825–1855.* Edited by Ralph H. Orth and Alfred R. Ferguson. Cambridge, MA: Belknap Press of Harvard University Press, 1977.

———. *The Journals and Miscellaneous Notebooks of Ralph Waldo Emerson.* Vol. 14, *1854–1861.* Edited by Susan Sutton Smith and Harrison Hayford. Cambridge, MA: Belknap Press of Harvard University Press, 1978.

———. *The Journals and Miscellaneous Notebooks of Ralph Waldo Emerson.* Vol. 15, *1860–1866.* Edited by Linda Allardt, Harrison Hayford, and Glen M. Johnson. Cambridge, MA: Belknp Press of Harvard University Press, 1982.

———. *Journals of Ralph Waldo Emerson: 1820–1876.* Edited by Edward W. Emerson and Waldo Emerson Forbes. Vol. 9, *1856–1863.* Boston: Houghton Mifflin, 1913.

———. *Journals of Ralph Waldo Emerson: 1820–1876.* Edited by Edward W. Emerson and Waldo Emerson Forbes. Vol. 10, *1864–1876.* Boston: Houghton Mifflin, 1914.

———. *The Later Lectures of Ralph Waldo Emerson.* Edited by Ronald A. Bosco and Joel Myerson. Vol. 2, *1843–1871.* Athens: University of Georgia Press, 2001.

———. *The Letters of Ralph Waldo Emerson.* Vols. 1–6. Edited by Ralph L. Rusk. New York: Columbia University Press, 1939.

——. *The Letters of Ralph Waldo Emerson*. Vols. 7–10. Edited by Eleanor M. Tilton. New York: Columbia University Press, 1991.

——. "Man the Reformer." In Porter, *Ralph Waldo Emerson: Essays and Lectures*, 133–50. New York: Library of America, 1994.

——. "Nature." In *Ralph Waldo Emerson: Selected Essays*, ed. Ziff, 35–81.

——. "The Poet." In *Ralph Waldo Emerson: Selected Essays*, ed. Ziff, 259–84.

——. *The Poetry Notebooks of Ralph Waldo Emerson*. Edited by Ralph H. Orth, Albert J. von Frank, Linda Allardt, and David W. Hill. Columbia: University of Missouri Press, 1986.

——. *"The Preacher."* In *The Complete Works of Ralph Waldo Emerson*, edited by Edward W. Emerson. Vol. 10, *Lectures and Biographical Sketches*, 215–38.

——. *Ralph Waldo Emerson: Collected Poems and Translations*. 2nd ed. Edited by Harold Bloom and Paul Kane. New York: Library of America, 1994.

——. *Ralph Waldo Emerson: Selected Essays*. Edited and with an introduction by Larzer Ziff. New York: Penguin Books, 1985.

——. "Self-Reliance." In *Ralph Waldo Emerson: Selected Essays*, ed. Ziff, 175–204.

——. *Topical Notebooks of Ralph Waldo Emerson*. Edited by Susan Sutton Smith and Ralph H. Orth. 3 vols. New York: Columbia University Press, 1949.

Everson, Eva. "William J. Stillman: Emerson's 'Gallant Artist.'" *New England Quarterly* 31 (March 1958): 32–46.

Forbes, John M. *Letters and Recollections of John Murray Forbes*. Edited by Sara Forbes Hughes. 2 vols. Boston: Houghton Mifflin, 1900.

Gassan, Richard H. *The Birth of American Tourism: New York, the Hudson Valley, and American Culture 1790–1830*. Amherst: University of Massachusetts Press, 2008.

Geldard, Richard G., ed. *The Essential Transcendentalists*. New York: Jeremy P. Tarcher / Penguin, 2005.

Gerdts, William H. "The Influence of Ruskin and Pre-Raphaelitism on American Still-Life Painting." *American Art Journal* 1 (Autumn 1969): 80–96.

Godfrey, Edward S. "Enforcement of Delinquent Property Taxes in New York." 2 parts. *Albany Law Review* 24 (1960): 272–316; 25 (1961): 39–66.

Goldstein, Linda L. "Women Enter Medicine in the Western Reserve: The Graduation of the First Six Women Doctors from Western Reserve College, 1852–1856." *Western Reserve Studies* 3 (1988): 66–73.

Goodman, Susan, and Carl Dawson. *William Dean Howells: A Writer's Life*. Los Angeles: University of California Press, 2005.

Gordon, John S. *A Thread across the Ocean: The Historic Story of the Transatlantic Cable*. New York: Walker, 2002.

Graham, Frank, Jr. *Adirondack Park: A Political History*. Syracuse, NY: Syracuse University Press, 1984.

Gross, Robert A. "Transcendentalism and Urbanism." *Journal of American Studies* 18 (December 1984): 361–81.

Hardie, George R. *Where to Go in the Adirondacks and on Lake George and Lake Champlain*. Canton, NY: J. H. Rushton, 1908.

Headley, Joel T. *The Adirondack, or, Life in the Woods*. New York: Baker & Scribner, 1849.

——. *The Adirondack, or, Life in the Woods*. New and enlarged ed. New York: Scribner's, 1869.

Herbert, Charles, ed. *Correspondence between Spencer Fullerton Baird and Louis Agassiz— Two Pioneer American Naturalists.* Washington DC: Smithsonian Institution, 1963.

Higginson, Mary Potter Thatcher. *Thomas Wentworth Higginson: The Story of His Life.* Boston: Houghton Mifflin, 1914.

Higginson, Thomas Wentworth. "Barbarism and Civilization." *Atlantic Monthly,* January 1861, 51–62.

———. *Cheerful Yesterdays.* Boston: Houghton Mifflin, 1898.

———. "Footpaths." *Atlantic Monthly,* November 1870, 513–21.

———. *Letters and Journals of Thomas Wentworth Higginson, 1846–1906.* Edited by Mary Potter Thatcher Higginson. Boston: Houghton Mifflin, 1921.

Hirshfield, Jane. *Given Sugar, Given Salt.* New York: HarperCollins, 2002.

Hoar, Ebenezer Rockwood. *Charge to the Grand Jury at the July Term of the Municipal Court in Boston* (reprint of the charge delivered on July 3, 1854). Boston: Little, Brown, 1854.

Holmes, Oliver Wendell. "Professor Jeffries Wyman: A Memorial Outline." *Atlantic Monthly,* November 1874, 611–24.

Howells, William Dean. "An Earlier American." *North American Review* 172 (June 1901): 934–44.

———. *Interviews with William Dean Howells.* Edited by Ulrich Halfmann. Arlington, TX: University of Texas at Arlington, 1973.

———. *Literary Friends and Acquaintances: A Personal Retrospect of American Authorship.* 2nd ed. New York: Harper & Brothers, 1911.

———. Review of *May Day, and Other Pieces.* In *Emerson and Thoreau: The Contemporary Reviews,* edited by Joel Myerson, 315–17. New York: Cambridge University Press, 1992.

Hurd, Hamilton D. *History of Clinton and Franklin Counties, New York: With Illustrations and Biographical Sketches of Its Prominent Men and Pioneers.* Philadelphia: J. W. Lewis, 1880.

Irmscher, Christoph. *Louis Agassiz: Creator of American Science.* Boston: Houghton Mifflin Harcourt, 2013.

Jackson, William S. *Annual Report of the Attorney General of the State of New York for the Year Ending December 31, 1907.* Albany: J. B. Lyon, 1908.

Jackson Lears, T. J. *No Place of Grace: Antimodernism and the Transformation of American Culture 1880–1920.* New York: Pantheon Books, 1981.

Jamieson, Paul. "Emerson in the Adirondacks." *New York History* 39 (July 1958): 215–37.

Jenkins, Jerry. "Do Unharvested Adirondack Forests Contain Forest Interior Plants? A Final Technical Report to the Northeastern States Research Consortium." Wildlife Conservation Society Adirondack Program, January 2010.

Keyes, John S., Ebenezer Rockwood Hoar, William T. Harris, and Edward W. Emerson. *Memoirs of Members of the Social Circle in Concord.* 2nd ser., *From 1795 to 1840.* Cambridge: Riverside Press, 1888.

Kornhauser, Elizabeth M., and Amy Ellis with Maureen Miesmer. *Hudson River School: Masterworks from the Wadsworth Atheneum Museum of Art.* New Haven: Yale University Press, 2003.

Lamb, Martha J. *History of the City of New York: Its Origin, Rise and Progress.* 2 vols. New York: A. S. Barnes & Co., 1880.

Lane, Allen. *The Pre-Raphaelites.* London: Tate Gallery Publications Department and Penguin Books, 1984.

Lefcowitz, Allan B., Barbara F. Lefcowitz, and James Bryce. "James Bryce's First Visit to America: The New England Sections of His 1870 Journal and Related Correspondence." *New England Quarterly* (June 1977): 314–31.

Longfellow, Henry Wadsworth. *The Letters of Henry Wadsworth Longfellow.* Edited by Andrew Hilen. Vol. 4, *1857–1865.* Cambridge, MA: Belknap Press of Harvard University Press, 1972.

———. *The Life of Henry Wadsworth Longfellow.* Edited by Samuel Longfellow. Vol. 2. Boston: Houghton Mifflin, 1891.

Lowell, James Russell. "Democracy." In *Essays, English and American: With Introductions and Notes,* edited by Charles W. Eliot, 464–85. Vol. 28 of Harvard Classics series. New York: P. F. Collier & Son, 1910.

———. *James Russell Lowell's Vision of Sir Launfal and Other Poems.* Edited and introduction by Mabel Caldwell Willard. Boston: Sibley & Ducker, 1896.

———. *The Letters of James Russell Lowell.* Edited by Charles E. Norton. 2 vols. New York: Harper & Brothers, 1894.

———. *New Letters of James Russell Lowell.* Edited by M. A. DeWolfe Howe. New York: Harper & Brothers, 1932.

Lowry, Howard, and Ralph L. Rusk, eds. *Emerson-Clough Letters.* Hamden, CT: Archon Books, 1968.

Luria, Daniel D. "Wealth, Capital, and Power: The Social Meaning of Home Homeownership." *Journal of Interdisciplinary History* 7 (Autumn 1976): 261–83.

Lurie, Edward. *Louis Agassiz: A Life in Science.* Chicago: University of Chicago Press, 1960.

Lyons, Francis S. L. *Charles Stewart Parnell.* New York: Oxford University Press, 1977.

Madsen, Peter, and Richard Plunz, eds. *The Urban Lifeworld: Formation Perception Representation.* New York: Routledge, 2002.

Marcou, Joules. *Life, Letters and Works of Louis Agassiz,* Vol. 2. New York: Macmillan, 1896.

Markham, Jerry W. *A Financial History of the United States: From Christopher Columbus to Robert Barons (1492–1900).* Vol. 1. Armonk, NY: M. E. Sharpe, 2002.

Marsden, Malcolm M. "Discriminating Sympathy: Charles Eliot Norton's Unique Gift." *New England Quarterly* 31 (December 1958): 463–83.

May, Rollo. *Love and Will.* New York: W. W. Norton, 1960.

McMartin, Barbara, *The Privately Owned Adirondacks: Sporting and Family Clubs/Private Parks and Preserves/Timberlands and Easements.* Canada Lake, NY: Lake View Press, 2004.

Miller, Perry, ed. *The Transcendentalists: An Anthology.* 14th ed. Cambridge, MA: Harvard University Press, 2001.

Morison, Samuel E., and Charles E. Norton. "Reminiscences of Charles Eliot Norton." *New England Quarterly* 33 (September 1960): 364–58.

Myerson, Joel, ed. *Emerson and Thoreau: The Contemporary Reviews.* New York: Cambridge University Press, 1992.

———, ed. *The Transcendentalists: A Review of Research and Criticism.* New York: Modern Language Association of America, 1984.

Murray, William H. H. *Adventures in the Wilderness, or Camp Life in the Adirondacks.* Boston: DeWolfe, Fiske, 1869.

Nash, Roderick. "The American Cult of the Primitive." *American Quarterly* 18 (Autumn 1966): 517–37.

New York State Attorney General. "Opinion of the Attorney-General in Response to a Resolution of the Senate of April 2, 1884, in Relation to the Adirondack Railway [April 15, 1884]." *Documents of the Senate of the State of New York. One Hundred and Seventh Session.* Vol. 3. Albany: Weed, Parsons, 1884.

New York State Commissioners of Fisheries, Game and Forests. *The Third Annual Report of the Commissioners of Fisheries, Game and Forests* [January 20, 1893]. Albany: Wynkoop Hellenback Crawford, 1893.

New York State Comptroller. *List of Lands to Be Sold or Arrears of Taxes for the Years 1852, 1853, 1854 & 1855.* Albany: Weed, Parsons, 1859.

New York State Conservation Department. *A Biological Survey of the Raquette Watershed: Supplement to the Thirty-Third Annual Report, 1933.* Albany: J. B. Lyon, 1934.

New York State Department of Environmental Conservation and Office of Parks, Recreation and Historic Preservation. "Conserving Open Space in New York State, 2002 Edition: State Open Space Conservation Plan & Generic Environment Impact Statement." Albany, N.p., June 2002.

New York State Forest Commission. *Annual Report of the Forest Commission for the Year 1893.* Vol. 1. Albany: James B. Lyon, 1894.

Niblett, Michel, and Kerstin Oloff, eds. *Perspectives on the 'Other America': Comparative Approaches to Caribbean and Latin American Culture.* Amsterdam: Rodopi, 2009.

Norton, Charles E. "Mr. Emerson's Poems." In Myerson, *Emerson and Thoreau,* 430–31.

——. *Letters of Charles Eliot Norton with Biographical Content.* Edited by Sara Norton and M. A. DeWolfe Howe. Vol. 1. Boston: Houghton Mifflin, 1913.

——. Review of *May Day, and Other Pieces.* In Myerson, *Emerson and Thoreau,* 325–27.

Packard, Alpheus Spring, "Memoir of Jeffries Wyman: 1814–1874." In *National Academy of the Sciences Biographical Memoirs.* Washington, DC: Judd and Detweiler Printers, 1886.

Pease, Jane H., and William H. Pease. "Confrontation and Abolition in the 1850s." *Journal of American History* 58 (March 1972): 923–37.

Perkins, Robert F. Jr., and William J. Grant III, eds. *The Boston Athenaeum Art Exhibition Index, 1827–1874.* Boston: Library of the Boston Athenaeum, 1980.

Porter, Joel, ed. *Emerson: Prospect and Retrospect.* Cambridge, MA: Harvard University Press, 1982.

Raymond, Henry W. *The Story of Saranac: A Chapter in Adirondack History.* New York: Grafton Press, 1909.

Reid, James J. *Crisis of the Ottoman Empire: Prelude to Collapse 1839–1878.* Stuttgart, Germany: Die Deutsche Bibliothek, 2000.

Reynolds, David S. *John Brown, Abolitionist: The Man Who Killed Slavery, Sparked the Civil War, and Seeded Civil Rights.* New York: Kopf, 2005.

Richards, Thomas Addison, "A Forest Story [Part] I: The Hunting Grounds of the Saranac." *Harper's New Monthly Magazine,* August 1859, 310–23.

Rusk, Ralph L. *The Life of Ralph Waldo Emerson.* New York: Scribner's, 1949.

Ruskin, John. *Letters of John Ruskin to Charles Eliot Norton.* 2 vols. Boston: Houghton, Mifflin, 1904.

Sanborn, Franklin B. *Recollections of Seventy Years.* 2 vols. Boston: Gorham Press, 1909.

Santayana, George. *Character and Opinion in the United States with Reminiscence of William James and Josiah Joyce and Academic Life in America.* New York: Scribner's, 1920.

Sawyer, Paul. *Ruskin's Poetic Argument: The Design of the Major Works.* Ithaca, NY: Cornell University Press, 1985.

Schneider, Paul. *The Adirondacks: A History of America's First Wilderness.* New York: Henry Holt, 1997.

Scudder, Horace E. *James Russell Lowell: A Biography.* 2 vols. Boston: Houghton, Mifflin, 1901.

Schwartz, Harold. "Fugitive Slave Days in Boston." *New England Quarterly* 27 (June 1954): 191–212.

Seaver, Frederick J. *Historical Sketches of Franklin County and Its Surrounding Towns; with Many Short Biographies.* Albany: J.B. Lyon, 1918.

Smith, Edmund H. *Reports of Cases Decided in the Court of Appeals for the State of New York from Decisions of February 16, to and Including Decisions of May 1, 1900.* Albany: James B. Lyon, 1900.

Smith, Sophia, and Charles Smith. *Genealogical Records of the Descendants of David Mack to 1879.* Rutland, VT: Tuttle, 1879.

Solomon, Eldra P., Linda R. Berg, and Diane W. Martin. *Biology.* 9th ed. Belmont, CA: Brooks/Cole, 2011.

Stevens, Charles E. *Anthony Burns: A History.* Boston: John P. Jewett, 1856.

Stillman, William James. *The Autobiography of a Journalist.* 2 vols. Boston: Houghton, Mifflin, 1901.

———. "Autobiography of W. J. Stillman." *Atlantic Monthly,* January 1900, 1–16.

———. "Autobiography of W. J. Stillman: II. An American Education." *Atlantic Monthly,* February 1900, 165–85.

———. "Autobiography of W. J. Stillman: III. Art Study." *Atlantic Monthly,* March 1900, 322–35.

———. "Autobiography of W. J. Stillman: IV. European Adventure and Life in the Wilderness." *Atlantic Monthly,* April 1900, 466–79.

———. "Autobiography of W. J. Stillman: V. Journalism." *Atlantic Monthly,* May 1900, 613–28.

———. "Autobiography of W. J. Stillman: VI. England Again." *Atlantic Monthly,* June 1900, 811–25.

———. "A Few of Lowell's Letters." *Atlantic Monthly,* December 1892, 744–57.

———. *Herzegovina and the Late Uprising: The Causes of the Latter and the Remedies.* London: Longmans, Green, 1877.

———. "A Mission for Kossuth." *Century Magazine,* June 1894, 270–76.

———. *The Old Rome and the New: and Other Studies.* 3rd ed. London: Grant Richards / Boston: Houghton, Mifflin, 1898.

———. "The Philosophers' Camp. Emerson, Agassiz, and Lowell in the Adirondacks." *Century Magazine,* August 1893, 598–606.

———. "A Plea for Wild Animals." *The Living Age* 221 (1899): 840–47.

———, ed. *Poetic Localities of Cambridge.* Boston: James R. Osgood, 1876.

———. "Recreation and Solitude." *Atlantic Monthly,* July 1877, 10–12.

———. "The Subjective of It." *Atlantic Monthly,* December 1858, 850–61.

Storey, Moorfield, and Edward W. Emerson. *Ebenezer Rockwood Hoar: A Memoir.* Boston: Houghton, 1911.

Stowe, William W. "Transcendental Vacations: Thoreau and Emerson in the Wilderness." *New England Quarterly* 83 (September 2010): 482–507.

Street, Alfred B. *Woods and Waters: or, The Saranac and the Racket.* New York: M. Doolady, 1860.

Supreme Court of the State of New York Appellate Division, Third Department. "The People of the State of New York—Plaintiff, Appellant—against Santa Clara Lumber Company—Defendant, Respondent." In *Appeal Book.* Albany: J.B. Lyons, 1907.

——. "The People of the State of New York—Plaintiff, Appellant—against Santa Clara Lumber Company et al.—Defendants, Respondent." In *Exhibit Book.* Vol. 2. Albany: J. B. Lyons, 1913.

Sweetser, Moses F. *The Middle States: A Handbook for Travelers: A Guide to the Middle States.* Boston: James R. Osgood, 1875.

Terrie, Philip G. *Contested Terrain: A New History of Nature and People in the Adirondacks.* Syracuse, NY: Syracuse University Press, 1997.

——. *Forever Wild: A Cultural History of Wilderness in the Adirondacks.* Syracuse, NY: Syracuse University Press, 1994.

——. "Romantic Travelers in the Adirondack Wilderness," *American Studies* 24 (Fall 1983): 59–75.

Thoreau, Henry David. *The Heart of Thoreau's Journals.* 2nd ed. Edited by Odell Shepard. New York: Dover Publications, 1961.

——. *Henry David Thoreau: Collected Essays and Poems.* Edited by Elizabeth Hall Witherell. New York: Library of America, 2001.

——. *Maine Woods.* 7th ed. James R. Osgood, 1873.

——. "Slavery in Massachusetts." In Witherell, *Henry David Thoreau: Collected Essays and Poems, 333–47.*

——. *Walden.* In *Walden and Other Writings by Henry David Thoreau.* 2nd ed. Edited and introduction by Joseph Wood Krutch. New York: Bantam Books, 1996.

——. *The Writings of Henry David Thoreau: Journal.* Vol. 11. Edited by Bradford Torrey. Boston: Houghton Mifflin, 1906.

——. *The Writings of Henry David Thoreau: Journal.* Vol. 8. Edited by Sandra Harbert Petrulionis. Princeton, NJ: Princeton University Press, 2002.

Tucker, Edward L. "James Russell Lowell and Robert Carter: The 'Pioneer' and Fifty Letters from Lowell to Carter." *Studies in American Renaissance,* edited by Joel Myerson, 187–246. Charlottesville: University of Virginia Press, 1987.

Turner, James. *The Liberal Education of Charles Eliot Norton.* Baltimore: Johns Hopkins University Press, 1999.

Van Dyke, Henry. "Ampersand." *Harper's New Monthly Magazine,* July 1885, 217–27.

——. *Little Rivers: A Book of Essays in Comfortable Idleness.* 6th ed. New York: Scribner's, 1896.

Van Dyke, Tetrius. *Henry Van Dyke: A Biography.* New York: Harper & Brothers, 1935.

Wall, Alexander J., Arthur Sutherland, and Eugene A. Hoffman. *National Academy of Design Exhibition Record: 1826–1860.* 2 vols. John Watts DePeyster Publication Fund Series. New York: J. J. Little & Ives, 1943.

Wallace, Edwin R. *Descriptive Guide to the Adirondacks, and Hand-Book of Travel to Saratoga Springs.* 5th ed. New York: Forest and Stream, 1876.

——. *Descriptive Guide to the Adirondacks, (Land of the Thousand Lakes) and to Saratoga Springs; Schroon Lake; Lakes Luzerne, George, and Champlain; the Ausable Chasm; Massena Springs; and Trenton Falls.* Syracuse, NY: W. Gill, 1894.

Wasson, David A. Review of *May Day, and Other Pieces.* In Myerson, *Emerson and Thoreau,* 313–14.

Weiss, Ila. "Sanford Robinson Gifford (1823–1880)." PhD diss., Columbia University, 1968. Published with a new preface, Outstanding Dissertations in the Fine Arts series. New York: Garland, 1977.

White, William Chapman. *Adirondack Country.* New York: Knopf, 1967.

Whittier, John Greenleaf. *The Poetical Works of John Greenleaf Whittier.* Household ed. Boston: Houghton, Mifflin, 1892.

Wilkins, Mira. *The History of Foreign Investment in the United States to 1914.* Cambridge, MA: Harvard University Press, 1989.

Wodehouse, Lawrence. "'New Path' and the American Pre-Raphaelite Brotherhood." *Art Journal* 25 (Summer 1966): 351–54.

INDEX

Adirondack Club, 4–6, 9–10, 42, 69,
  114, 119
  cabin, 147, 183, 206, 227n20;
    abandonment of, 151–53, 159 165–66,
    230n2; planning for, 112, 135, 138
  demise of, 3–4, 151–52, 159, 190
  Higginson's Ampersand visit, 130–31,
    168, 187
  inaugural meeting: at/around
    Ampersand, 127–30, 187; planning
    and preparations, 122–23, 125–27
  land acquisition efforts, 111–13, 115,
    119, 132–35, 151–52, 194
  membership, 111, 113, 123–25, 131–32 152
  post-1859 activities, 138, 145, 147,
    150–53, 174
Adirondack Company, 152, 168–69, 189, 200
Adirondack Council, 202, 206
Adirondack Estate and Railroad
  Company, 152
Adirondack Forest Preserve. *See*
  Adirondacks: conservation efforts
Adirondack Railway Company, 169, 189
Adirondacks
  conservation efforts, 5, 9–10, 169–70,
    180, 182–83, 185–86, 188–90, 197–99,
    201–7
  guide industry, 50
  lumber industry, 7, 50, 77, 169, 177,
    179–80, 182–83, 186–90, 197
  railroads. *See* Industrial Revolution: rail
    expansion
  surveys of, 2, 7, 115, 169, 187
  tourism. *See* tourism: in the Adirondacks
Agassiz, Elizabeth Carey, 191
Agassiz, Jean Louis Rodolphe, 58, 59*f*, 60,
  170–71
  Adirondack Club involvement, 123–24,
    138, 143, 165–66, 199; purchase of
    Ampersand, 113, 133, 151
  *Contributions to the Natural History of the
    United States*, 60, 69, 92
  creationist beliefs, 59–60, 91–93, 134,
    170–71

Darwinism, opposition to, 92–93, 134,
  154, 170
decline in influence, 5, 154, 170–71
European homecoming, 123, 133
ichthyological studies, 58, 60, 100; on
  trout, 91–93, 119, 207
Jardin des Plantes offers, 69, 74, 79, 194
Lake Superior, 60, 91–93
Museum of Comparative Zoology
  involvement, 59, 69, 117–18, 123
Philosophers' Camp involvement, 1–2,
  81, 167, 191, 204; at/around Follensby,
  3, 87–88, 90–91, 93–94, 98–100,
  105–7; in related works/news reports,
  101, 103, 104, 109–10, 116–17, 119,
  171, 186–87; journey to/from, 79–80,
  99, 108, 191, 194–95; planning and
  preparations, 73–74, 76
relationship with Stillman, 32, 99–100,
  173–74, 190
Saturday Club involvement, 45, 56–58,
  60–61
Albion Hotel, 57–58
American Art Union, 21
Ampersand Brook, 112, 115, 199
Ampersand Mountain, 49, 115, 166
Ampersand Pond
  features, 112, 115, 127, 147
  litigation over ownership, 197–99
  origins of name, 115
  sale. *See* Township Twenty-Seven: land
    transactions
Ampersand Preserve, 189–90, 198
Anakim, 63, 71. *See also* procession of
  the pines
Appleton, Thomas G., 32, 45, 57,
  123–24, 165
Arnold, Silas, 127
Arthur, Chester A., 16
Association for the Protection of the
  Adirondacks, 203–4
Atlantic Club, 124, 138
Atlantic Telegraph Company, 89, 157
Ausable Chasm, 79

249

INDEX

Baird, Spenser Fullerton, 93
Bancroft, George, 74
Bangs, Edward, 57, 123–24
Barbour, John E., 200
Barbour, John L., 200
Baring Brothers, 57, 180
Bartlett, Virgil C., 51
Bartlett's, 51–52, 80, 153
Berdan, Hiram, 146
Bierstadt, Albert, 146, 227n16
Big Tupper Lake, 49, 51, 88, 94–95, 130, 179
  as location of 1857 party, 62–64, 68, 71, 88,
    99, 116, 130, 149, 154, 172, 190, 193
Binney, Amos, 2, 180–81
  Philosophers' Camp involvement, 2, 76,
    80–81, 88, 94, 105, 107
  in related works/news reports, 101, 109,
    119, 121
  relationship with Stillman, 54–56, 76,
    136
  White Mountains honeymoon, 54–55
Bog River, 64, 95
Bog River Falls, 51
Boston Athenaeum, 70, 72, 85, 153, 217n2
Bowditch, Henry I., 153
Bowditch, Henry P., 166
Brace, Charles L., 105, 169
Briggs, Charles F., 30
Brooklyn Cooperage Company, 200
Brooklyn School, 37, 41
Brown, Henry K., 37, 40–41
Brown, John
  Harpers Ferry raid, 68, 135–36, 141
  North Elba homestead, 67, 108, 136
  Saturday Club members, connections to,
    67–68, 135–36, 141
Browning, Elizabeth Barrett, 143
Browning, Robert, 143
Bryant, William Cullen, 45, 57
  Evening Post editorship, 20–21, 179
  relationship with Stillman, 20–21, 36,
    39, 144
Bryce, James, 173–74
Burlington, Vermont, 21, 78, 88
Burns, Anthony, 24–25, 28, 32, 68

Camp Maple. See Philosophers' Camp:
  Camp Maple features
Carlos, Don, 3, 105, 108–9, 186
Carr, Michael, 202, 204, 206, 207
Carter, Robert, 40, 45
Century Club. See Sketch Club
Century Magazine, 5, 42, 174, 184,
  186–90, 192

Chaucer, Geoffrey, 100–101
  Canterbury Tales, The, 100–101, 122, 202
Cheney, Albert N., 152
Church, Frederic E.
  Cole's mentorship of, 8, 17
  Hudson River School, influences on, 7,
    92, 172, 180
  Niagara, 1857, 38
  Stillman: criticized by, 17, 65; mentorship
    of, 6, 8, 18, 30
  Twilight in the Wilderness, 92
Civil War, 2, 5, 145, 151, 169
  battles, 143, 145, 154–55
  malaise of, 86, 136, 141
  post-war disillusionment, 4, 171, 173
Clough, Arthur H., 65–66, 74, 105
Cold Brook, 127, 131, 147
Cole, Thomas, 8, 16–17, 172
  View of Schroon Mountain, Essex County,
    New York, After a Storm, 8
Colvin, Verplanck, 155, 169–70
Concord Free Public Library Corporation,
  135, 174, 188
Constable, William, 112–13
Cooper, James Fenimore, 73
Copley, John S., 38
Cornell University, 200
Crayon, 6, 37–40, 44–47, 49, 53, 143, 193
  Adirondack travel writing, 49–52, 85, 95,
    117, 187; Wilderness and Its Waters,
    The, 40–41, 43–44, 49, 77, 85, 117
  art commentary/criticism, 38, 116, 119,
    120–21
  contributors, 38–40, 45, 48, 52–53, 153,
    164, 176
  post-Stillman years, 53–54, 110, 116–17,
    119, 172
  pre-launch preparations, 29–30, 32–33,
    35–37
creationism. See Agassiz, Jean Louis
  Rodolphe: creationist beliefs
Cuomo, Mario, 202–4

daemon, 63–64, 129
Dana, Richard H., 32, 57–58, 67–69, 76, 98
Darwin, Charles, 134, 170–71
  Darwinism. See Agassiz, Jean Louis
    Rodolphe: Darwinism, opposition to
  On the Origin of Species, 134, 170
Davidson, Charles, 18
Delacroix, Eugene, 18
DeRuyter Academy, 16
Dickens, Charles, 19
Dodge, Meigs, and Company, 189, 198